The Next Five Years of CLArity

A compilation of articles from
issues of the CLA*rity* newsletter
published between
Spring 2017 and Holiday 2021

The Next Five Years of CLArity

All articles, artwork, poems, and cartoons in this book originally appeared in issues of CLArity, the Clutterers Anonymous newsletter, from the Spring 2017 issue through the Holiday 2021 issue.

CLArity Team

The CLArity Team makes all decisions regarding the CLArity newsletter, includdng when and where to print articles, need for and composition of Editor's Notes, and final proofreading of the newsletter. All edits are done with at least two people. The members of the CLArity Committee have changed through the years. This list comprises all those who were on the team between 2017 and 2022.

Alison B., New Jersey

Betsey K., New Jersey

Kathy H., California

Mariah W., New York

Ruthe S., Pennsylvania

Contributors

Contributors are those who helped edit articles or wrote a series of articles over many issues.

Carol N., California

Marcia R., Utah

Ted S., NY

Wendy L., Illinois

CLArity, 184 South Livingston Avenue, Suite 9-203, Livingston, New Jersey 07039

CLArity@ClutterersAnonymous.org

(866) 402-6685

Introduction

Welcome to CLA*rity*, the newsletter of Clutterers Anonymous. Whether you are a new reader or have been with us for some time, we hope that you will gain inspiration, knowledge, and solace from these pages.

Our first book, *Ten Years of CLArity,* consited of articles written during the first ten years of CLA*rity* production. It was so well received, the CLA*rity* Team decided to compile the next five years—from the Spring 2017 issue through the
Holiday 2021 issue—into a new book. We largely omitted "News Flash" articles and announcements, except for a couple of cases where we deemed the announcements were worthy of future notice.

For ease in finding certain subjects, we sorted the articles by topic, rather than publication order. Within each section (or subsection), the articles are laid out in chronological order.

CLA*rity* is produced entirely by CLA volunteers; all entries are written by members, and all editing, proofreading, typesetting, and layout is performed by members. If you are interested in writing an article, CLA*rity* would love to hear from you.

At CLA*rity*, we welcome feedback, so please let us know what you think. Also, we are interested in hearing about groups that use CLA*rity* in their meetings. How is that working out for you?

Happy reading!
The CLA*rity* Team

Notes

Several articles refer to CLA telephone meetings. Since the writing of these articles, meetings may have changed focus, meeting dates and times, phone numbers, and access codes. For current information, check the "CLA Meeting Directory" at ClutterersAnonymous.org; send a letter to CLA WSO, 184 South Livingston Ave., Suite 9-203, Livingston, NJ 07039, requesting the latest Meeting Directory; or call (866) 402-6685 and leave a message.

Some articles list duties and requirements of officers of the CLA World Service Organization (WSO). These requirements, duties, and positions may change from time to time. For an up-to-date listing of officers, along with the requirements for and the duties entailed in these positions, go to ClutterersAnonymous.org> Members>WSO Officers.

Be aware that other information may have changed since articles were written; check for up-to-date information using one of the contact methods listed above. This information includes, but is not limited to: price of literature and CLA*rity* and WSO committees (whether they are active, as well as meeting times and phone access information).

Interested in writing an article for CLA*rity?* Send it via email to CLArity@ClutterersAnonymous.org or via postal mail to CLA*rity*, 184 South Livingston Ave., Suite 9-203, Livingston, NJ 07039. For a listing of article columns and further information, see the section on "Guidelines for Submission of Articles" on page 257.

CLA*rity* is produced entirely by members for the CLA Fellowship, upholding all 12 Traditions. Names on articles submitted will be withheld upon request, and only first names and last initials or pseudonyms are ever used.

Table of Contents

Twelve Steps of Clutterers Anonymous

The Twelve Steps of Clutterers Anonymous are based upon the Steps of Alcoholics Anonymous. They are the basis for the spiritual program of recovery of Clutterers Anonymous. These articles are written from the personal experience of the author.

Step 1

I Think I am at Step 1

Spring 2018
Barbara

As I read the September 20 entry in A.A.'s "Daily Reflections[4]," the following sentence caught my attention: "It was when I admitted my powerlessness that a glimmer of light began to touch my soul, and then a willingness emerged to let God control my life."

I began to realize that I needed to admit how much of a deep impact that busyness, distraction, and clutter have had on my life and on the lives of others—here I named some others. I need to see their impact on my life. I need to face the fears of emptiness, abandonment, and victimhood that I am trying to escape. What are my fears about being in the moment?

I need to admit to myself how my busyness, distraction, and clutter have impacted my life and the lives of others around me and my powerlessness to do anything about them. Until then, I will not be willing to hand over my life.

Part of me thinks that reading good books on time management and household organization, coupled with a clutter buddy who's facing these same problems, would be enough. But another part of me is coming to understand that these things may not work if I am using busyness and clutter as a solution for unmet emotional and possibly spiritual needs. ◬

Step One

Summer 2020
Anonymous

Editor's Note: This was writing for a Step group and included a series of questions which were not CLA-approved, so the author has used only the answers.

I was going to a face-to-face meeting once a week, but it was not enough. We made commitments and reported the following week whether we had done them. Invariably, I found I had done only two-thirds of them or less. I was unwilling to go to phone meetings. I am becoming a bit more willing, but I am still very ashamed and shy.

I need to become willing to put away everything I take out. But things are already out. Not everything has a home. I would need to choose a 15-minute time slot every day for putting things away or decluttering surfaces.

From time to time, I receive postcards in the mail from places to donate to. They give a date when they will arrive with a truck to pick up goods. I used to donate often by putting my old clothes in big black plastic bags and books or pots in boxes. It is comforting to know that things I am attached to are going to be used by somebody who needs them. It takes a great deal of strength for me to donate, and I haven't done it in a long time, but I remember feeling much lighter and greatly relieved after I had done it. I am willing to try it again. Since I have written this, they are not currently picking up items.

I rinse a dish before I eat. I am becoming willing to wash a sink full of dishes more often—I have to force myself.

I have stopped bringing used items into my home. I actually got bedbugs from bringing in a piece of used furniture from the street, and it took me years to get rid of them. I will never make that mistake again. It was a horrible experience. And before that, I got a roach infestation from bringing in a kitchen cupboard from the street. That was horrible, too. The only things I bring in now are perishables. However, early this morning I found myself looking online to buy a housedress. Maybe that is because I need to do laundry!

Recently at a meeting, I realized not putting things away is adding new clutter. I don't put things away until I'm really fed up with looking at the cluttered surfaces. I really need to look at that. It really doesn't take much effort. Sometimes I leave things out because I'm afraid I will forget them…but I can always write them down in my trusty notebook. I'm sure there are many other kinds of clutter that I add to my life that I'm not really aware of or that I choose to hide my head in the sand about. Every time I indulge in a bad habit to excess, like watching TV or overeating, it is clutter. I need to look at what is clutter in my overall life. I am willing not to bring in any new clutter from the outside.

I discovered the other day when I thought my email inbox was messed up…I have about four to eight important emails daily, but I actually have about 14,000, including filed emails. And I wonder why over 70% of my storage space is full…in my fridge are a few things that I am afraid to look at…it's been longer than I care to admit.

I am compulsive about everything. I am very slow and compulsive in my thoughts and actions when left to my own devices. When I am interacting with people or driving, I am very different than when I am in my home by myself. For me to make a simple cup of coffee can take me so long that I can get very frustrated with myself if I don't practice patience at all times. It is no wonder that I do not want to undertake any activities that take any length of time like laundry! It takes me a long time just to get my brain thinking in one direction. In fact, when I make coffee, I sing the steps out loud and make them rhyme, just so that I can put the ground coffee in the coffee machine, add the water, mix the milk, plain cocoa, and sweetener and put them all together. I turn it into a game so I can tolerate my brain! ◭

Steps 1, 2, and 3

Holiday 2018
Debbie M., NC

Every morning, at the end of my readings and meditation, I pray the first three Steps. This has become a very important part of my day. Over time, I've gained (or, more accurately, been blessed with) some important and useful insights. I confess that these are usually pushed forward by my struggles (and not some deep spiritual state).

For example, through my struggles and readings, I've become aware that Higher Power is in the present moment for me. Whenever I'm regretting the past or worrying about the future, I have shut Higher Power out. The first three Steps have helped me to understand this.

As I declutter, I can be overcome by the pain and horror of the state of my home, that I ever let it get this bad. Step 1 reminds me that I'm powerless over the past, even the current state of my home. "It is what it is."

I've also noticed that there's no room for Higher Power in this despair. It's all about me, me, me. I need Step 2. Being restored to sanity is a process, one day at a time.

When I was new in my other 12-Step program, I remember telling an old-timer that I was really struggling to do Step 3 thoroughly and completely, once and for all. "Oh, Debbie," she said, "you have to do it every day!" I've never forgotten that. I turn my will and life over to Higher Power's care, and that includes the outcomes of today and the worries about tomorrow.

As another example, A.A. and other 12-Step programs talk about the Three A's: Awareness, Acceptance, and Action. All three A's are needed to make a change or to take an action. For me, this triad corresponds with Steps 1, 2, and 3:

- Awareness—I become aware I have a problem with clutter. Actually, one day I realized that my house was out of control, my life was in chaos, and I couldn't seem to do anything about it. No matter what I did, the clutter got worse, and I became more despondent. Nothing I did made any difference. This is Step 1.

- Acceptance—I *accept* I have a problem with clutter. Period. I don't run away from those feelings of shame, guilt, regret, being overwhelmed, etc. Accepting that I have a problem means that I sit with those feelings that I've been doing anything and everything to avoid.

At this point, I'm ready and willing to reach outside myself for help. CLA meetings and members are the first outreach I make. I cling to their experience, strength, and hope. This leads me to thinking about a Higher Power. Members and a Higher Power maybe can help, want to help, and care about me. Maybe with this kind of help and support I, too, could be liberated from the clutter. This is Step 2.

- Action—only after acceptance can I effectively move to action; if I skip this Step, I trip and fall flat on my face. With Higher Power's help and my fellow CLA members' support, I can take action to deal with my clutter. I realize more and more that Higher Power and members are dependable, which reinforces more action. It works, and I keep asking for help. In essence, I'm turning my will and life over to Higher Power's care; this is Step 3.

Naturally, I slip and slide at times, thinking I can do this myself, doing whatever I can to avoid the pain, feeling sick of the whole thing and wanting to quit. This is why I take these Steps daily, more often if I remember. Whenever I become aware of a new challenge, thinking about the Three A's has helped me to focus on acceptance. Often I add this challenge to my "Three-Step" prayer.

As an example, here's my morning prayer to my Higher Power:

One—I admit I'm powerless over people, places, and things, over clutter, over _____ (my other 12-Step programs, etc.), over the current state of my house, and over the past, and that my life is/was unmanageable.

Two—I believe You are restoring me to sanity, day by day. And as I walk with You, I'm getting to know You better, day by day.

Three—I turn my will and my life over to Your care. Give me the willingness and ability to do Your will; to deal with the clutter; to do today's task, physically, mentally, emotionally, and spiritually; and leave the results in Your Hands. Amen.   ◭

Step 4

Step 4 Questions from "Decluttering Resentment: Steps 4-10[5]"

Summer 2019
Alison B., NJ

Note: I did these as Step 8-9 questions, in an attempt to forgive myself.

- *Do we believe we are entitled to the best?*
  No, I don't think so; even though I daydream about becoming a multimillionaire, I don't seem to think that I'm really entitled to it. I have to be willing to take enough of the right actions, and I need a like-minded group of people to join me. There is a part of me that does believe, though.

- *Are we our own best friend?*
  I am my own best friend. I have to be. In the end, I have nobody else. But I am also my worst enemy because I can turn on myself. I always show up to rescue myself before it is too late, even though many times I procrastinate until the last possible minute. I am trying not to do that lately because I really don't like the stress it unnecessarily brings.

- *Do we acknowledge what we do right?*
  Yes, but I need to acknowledge more. I do a lot of things

right. People who judge me by my outside are missing a lot. I found out yesterday in a lecture about interviews for jobs that appearance is still ultra important. I know I don't do that right. I need to acknowledge what I don't do right, too, so I can change it.

- *Do we give ourselves what we need?*
  I try as much as I possibly can. Sometimes what I think I need isn't good for me. But what is need? It is very subjective. I must not get my wants mixed up with my needs. There are physical, emotional, and spiritual needs. I do not have them all fulfilled, but I make the best of what I have emotionally.

- *Are we gentle with ourselves while learning a skill?*
  I am fairly gentle with myself, but I do have to push myself to do my best work and to feel any kind of motivation. I have to do something I am really interested in or know I will be thrilled by the outcome. It is the revision or repetition that I don't enjoy doing by myself. I always prefer to work with the teacher or another person or a group. I feel that somebody else's enthusiasm can bolster me, and I can do a better job.

- *Do we surround ourselves with loving people?*
  I keep myself at arm's length from people because I feel I have been abused too much. I have loving people in my life, but I am not close to anybody. There is nobody in whom I can confide on a regular basis, and I feel that is dangerous. I have nobody to carry out my final wishes when I die.

- *Do we give ourselves the joy of a nurturing home?*
  My home nurtures me in some ways. The rooms are big enough and the ceilings are high. I furnished it mainly from garage sales, and I did my best. I enjoy my kitchen, and I listen to the radio and TV on cordless headphones. I am comfortable with my desktop computer in the living room. I love my bed, which I bought new. When it's quiet, it feels very nurturing to me, but the people upstairs play music, and all I hear is the bass line—thump, thump, thump. I like being alone most of the time, and I do not often allow people in. Most of all, I do not want to be judged—I just want to be loved. ◢

Other Articles About the Steps

Working the 12 Steps

Summer 2017

Kim D., CA

Hi, my name is Kim, and I am a recovering clutterer and grateful member of CLA. I have been asked to share my experience, strength, and hope in working the 12 Steps of CLA. I had practiced the Steps and experienced recovery in several 12-Step programs before joining CLA.

When I recognized that I had a problem with clutter, I was receptive to CLA because it was a 12-Step program for clutterers. I had previously attended organizational seminars, but I hadn't been able to make much progress using them. I had come to believe that my cluttering was a spiritual, as well as an emotional, malady. I was also attracted to CLA because the only requirement for membership was a desire to stop cluttering.

I believe I started my 1st Step when I attended my first CLA meeting and was motivated to come back. I took the 2nd Step by listening to others share their recovery and saying to myself, "If it could happen for them, why can't it happen for me, too?"

I wanted what the recovering members of this program had, so I started doing what they did. I took the 3rd Step when I decided to use the CLA Tools[16] to the best of my ability and be open to doing it someone else's way and not mine. So when I listened to them share what had worked for them, I tried it.

This is how I proceeded:
- I used the phone action line and listened to speakers at the phone meetings.
- I went to CLA events in my area, like all-day workshops and seminars.
- I did service at the group level.
- I realized that having worked the 12 Steps in another program wasn't enough to get recovery in this program. There's no such thing as one size fits all. That's why there are so many different 12-Step programs. The basis of each is one sufferer talking to another sufferer afflicted with the same addiction. So any smugness I had from all my prior years in other programs was removed.
- I started working the 4th Step when I heard another member saying he was available to sponsor people and would take them through the 12 Steps. This was very unusual. I didn't attend the Sponsorship workshop at the 25th anniversary convention in

El Segundo—but I purchased the CD, which I studied in depth.

- I called my sponsor, who said he would take me through all 12 Steps in a very short period of time.

- I did a written 4th Step during that period. I had been in long-term Step study meetings in other programs, and maybe because of my ADHD, I never experienced the spiritual awakening or psychic change described in the Big Book of A.A. Step 4 helped me to deal with my mental clutter and helps me not to reclutter physically (fall off the wagon).

- My opinion is that it's easier to intellectualize if you're not working on a one-to-one basis with another individual who has done all the Steps. I did feel a great sense of relief after this experience. My continued growth has come from taking inventory of my resentments and fears.

- The inventory technique I used was shared by my sponsor at a CLA convention and is available on CD.

- Whenever I am feeling restless, irritable, or filled with "fear, guilt, and remorse," I will pull out a pen and paper and write: "I am resentful at ____ because I have fear of____ . I then, as I did after my written 4th Step, say, "Thank you, God, for revealing

and removing these fears. I ask only for knowledge of your will for me and the power to carry it out. Thank you. Kim." I will then add the person, place, or institution to my 8th-Step list and next to the entry, "My Higher Power is taking care of this."

- This is a program of suggestion. We have 12-Step leaflets that have suggestions on how to do a CLA inventory. I have done a paper inventory based on a presentation given on paper clutter by a CLA member.

Just remember the principles.

- Keep on trying, whenever you fail in your efforts to declutter.

- And—progress, not perfection; easy does it; and let go and let God.

- Finally—clean house and trust God. ◬

How I Work the Steps Every Day

Fall 2020
Susie S., CA

I start my day going through the 12 Steps in this way (it really takes only a few minutes to say all the lines/prayers in quotations below) and will also apply this to a particular situation that might arise during the day, including a challenge I may have in decluttering.

I can feel a complete transformation from this simple few-minute practice, including moving from complete resistance to releasing an item, to complete willingness and excitement for releasing an item! I have included some other notes related to the 12 Steps as well, although I don't reference every Step because they're not all applicable to my quick personal daily practice. (All page numbers refer to pages from the A.A. "Big Book" [*Alcoholics Anonymous*[1]].)

Step 1. "I am powerless over (this person, situation etc.)" (And there is no shame or blame in being powerless).

Step 2. "God, I know you can help me with anything and restore me to sanity. I am asking you to do for me what I cannot do for myself. I am asking you to show off/show up for me or this person and show me that you are here with me. God, I know you are in charge."

Step 3. "I turn my will, my life, my thoughts, and actions over to you, God. I am willing to do your will if you show me how."

Third Step Prayer, page 63: "God, I offer myself to Thee—to build with me and do with me as Thou wilt. Relieve me of the bondage of self that I may better do Thy will. Take away my difficulties that victory over them may

bear witness to those I would help of Thy Power, Thy Love, and Thy Way of life. May I do Thy will always."

Steps 4 and 5. If there is fear, say the fear prayer, "Please remove my fear and direct my attention to what you would have me be." Page 68.

If there is a resentment, I say the prayer on page 67. "This is a sick man (person), how can I be helpful to him? God save me from being angry. Thy will be done."

Step 6. Prayer for acceptance, page 449, Third Edition (page 417, Fourth Edition}, "And acceptance is the answer to all my problems today."

"God, I'm willing (or willing to be willing) to let you remove my (defect of character)." If I provide the willingness, God provides the power. So I can pray for willingness to be willing.

Step 7. "God, please remove my (fear, uncertainty, etc.) and replace it with (peace, serenity, trust, comfort, a decision, etc.—whatever I want to experience)." I can also start to "act as if" I am a person who does not have the character defect that is causing me the challenge. "Humbly" implies that I am not shocked, deflated, or disappointed with any of my defects—because that is lacking humility. "God, I accept myself as I am and I'm willing to change and grow."

Seventh Step Prayer, "My Creator, I am now willing that you should have all of me, good and bad. I pray that you now remove every single defect of character which stands in the way of my usefulness to you and my fellows. Grant me strength, as I go out from here to do your bidding. Amen." Page 76.

Step 10. Ask, "How can I best serve Thee—Thy will (not mine) be done." Page 85. And I do my best to promptly admit when I am wrong during the day. (I like to say a prayer to myself when I get off track into my own will or mentally to another person I may have wronged, "I'm sorry, please forgive me, thank you, I love you."

Step 11. "God, I pray only for knowledge of your will for me and the power to carry it out."

Say Eleventh Step Prayer, page 99, *Twelve Steps and Twelve Traditions*.[14] "Lord, make me a channel of your peace—that where there is hatred, I may bring love…"

"God, please direct my thoughts and actions; what would you have me do next?"

If I have a decision to make: "God, please increase or decrease my desire to take this action or that action."

Step 12. Do some kind of service: Call a newcomer; pray for someone to "have all the peace and serenity I would like to have." Say my version of the Loving Kindness prayer: "May this person be filled with loving kindness, may they be well, may they be peaceful and at ease, may they be happy, and healed, and blessed, and safe." ◮

12 Traditions of Clutterers Anonymous

The Traditions help with the smooth functioning of the group. They work hand-in-glove with the Steps. It is difficult for members to follow the principles in the Traditions without having had the spiritual recovery embodied in the Steps. The Steps and Traditions are the cornerstone of the CLA program.

The Traditions as Part of a CLA Program

Spring 2018
Kathy H., CA

For years I thought that I had a good grasp on the 12 Traditions. I have read extensively on the subject, discussed them with others, and participated in a four-part CLA Traditions seminar several years ago.

Recently, while researching the Traditions for ideas for a skit to be

performed at the CLA 2017 Convention, I decided to read through the Traditions portions of three *Twelve and Twelve*[16] books—those of A.A. and two other 12-Step Fellowships. I read the Tradition 1 section in one book and took notes, then the same section in a second book and took more notes, followed by the third. I did this with each Tradition in order.

Boy, did I find out how much I didn't know! Reading and writing about them in this way, consistently, over a period of a few days, totally shed a new light on how the Steps and Traditions are interwoven and how the Traditions interrelate with each other—they are just facets of one seamless whole. I wanted to share with you some of what I learned.

The basis of our recovery is working the 12 Steps. But how

does this affect the groups, which rely on the Traditions?

Many Steps relate to certain Traditions, but especially Step 12. Tradition 5 tells us that our primary purpose is to carry the message. And what does Step 12 say? "Having had a spiritual awakening as the result of these Steps, we tried to carry the message to others..." It also relates to Tradition 8, which tells us that CLA must remain nonprofessional. All 12th-Step work is, by definition, nonprofessional, just one clutterer helping another.

If we look at the Traditions, we can see how each one is connected to others. And, really, they all follow from Tradition 1, which tells us that our common welfare should come first, that personal recovery depends upon unity. Look at Tradition 5; our primary purpose must be carrying the message because that helps CLA stay unified—which promotes our common welfare.

And Tradition 4, which says that each group should be autonomous except in matters affecting other groups or CLA as a whole. The second part of this Tradition refers back to Tradition 1, in the matter of CLA unity and putting the common welfare first.

From time to time, the specter of using outside literature (and other items) in CLA meetings

crops up. I have had some confusion about this issue in the past: does it break Tradition 6? Tradition 10? Actually, while it does have some bearing on both of those Traditions, it also is in direct opposition to Tradition 5. When our meetings spend any time or space on items that come from outside of our Fellowship or that of A.A., they are taking the focus away from the meeting's primary purpose—to carry the message of CLA recovery.

And even Tradition 7 doesn't stand alone. We can't fulfill our primary purpose of carrying the message or refrain from outside intervention if we don't pay our own way. When others foot the bill, they usually begin calling the shots as well.

Tradition 9, again, harkens back to Tradition 5; we create service boards and committees to carry the message beyond what sharing our experience, strength, and hope; having buddies; bookending; and sponsoring can do.

And both Traditions 11 and 12 relate to Tradition 1. We can potentially destroy our unity and imperil our common welfare by not respecting these Traditions on anonymity. Very few things can break a group apart more than discussing what a member shared in a meeting outside that meeting. Tradition 12 states: "Anonymity is the spiritual foundation of all our Traditions, ever reminding us to place principles before personalities."

My challenge now is to make use of this newfound revelation and to intertwine both Steps and Traditions in my daily life, searching always for that place of serenity and joy that comes through working a good program. There is much more I learned, and I will share some of it in a future article. ⌂

CLA Traditions—Principles Before Personalities

Summer 2018
Kathy H., CA

Tradition 12 states: "Anonymity is the spiritual foundation of all our Traditions, ever reminding us to place principles before personalities."

In this article, I am discussing the concept of "principles before personalities" based on 12-Step readings and my own experiences.

Principles before personalities—what a concept! Without adhering to this principle, a group cannot engender the spirit of loving acceptance that should be an integral part of a 12-Step Fellowship. People will not always agree or like one another—that is human nature. But, in spite of this, we can still meet in a place of acceptance and unanimity. The answer is in the Steps and Traditions of the CLA program.

While the concept of principles before personalities is stated in Tradition 12, the idea is threaded throughout other Traditions and even the Steps. In working a personal inventory (Steps 4 through 7), we learn to find our part in any disagreement. We work to let go of the character defects that keep us from moving on from our resentments. Letting go of our resentments is critical in learning how to deal with others in an accepting and loving manner.

In studying Tradition 1, we learn that we must maintain unity in our groups. But what do we mean by unity? Does it mean that everybody agrees on every issue? Does it mean that members shouldn't speak out if they see something that bothers them or if they see Traditions are being broken? Not at all. In fact, members have a responsibility to discuss their ideas, positions, and concerns with the group, preferably in a loving manner. Unity does not mean uniformity.

Problems arise when individuals, cliques, or rivalries dominate group discussion. It's important to encourage members to give support based on their own knowledge and principles, rather than just voting support for a friend or a clique. This is true whether the decision is for a group conscience vote on an issue or for an election to a CLA position.

On the other hand, respect for unity also means that members should keep to the group conscience decisions even if the decisions did not go their way.

But how do we handle those individuals who repeatedly refuse to abide by the meeting's group conscience and protocols? According to 12-Step experience, they should be dealt with one on one. It is helpful for a meeting to have guidelines which specify which members will deal with the incident and how it will be handled. This helps to avoid controversy among the other members in such a situation. At any rate, we must always deal with troublemakers in such incidents in as loving a manner as possible.

This brings me to a subject I have been wrestling with lately: gossip. I have found myself indulging in it occasionally. When I think about it later, I cringe. I don't want to hurt any other people. This is definitely not placing principles before personalities. It has made me realize that it's time for me to do a deep working of the Steps again.

Of course, there is gossip that does not harm: "John Doe got a promotion with a wonderful raise. I'm so happy for him." I'll pass along that kind of gossip to anyone who's interested—unless, of course, John doesn't want it known. I think my guideline has to be, "Will this hurt anyone if it is known? Is this pointing fingers or passing along less-than-positive news about others?" If so, I want to ignore it and just circulate the positive news. There are better ways to deal with our concerns than gossip. Once again— principles before personalities.

I want to live by what we say in my CLA meeting each week: "Let the understanding, love, and peace of the program grow in you one day at a time."

Clutterers Anonymous Program

While the basis of CLA's program of recovery is working the 12 Steps, there are many other aspects to the program. These include the CLA Tools of Recovery,[16] Affirmations,[17] and Slogans.[18]

CLA Tools of Recovery[16]

Bookending

Spring 2017
Alison B., NJ

Bookending is calling a CLA member before and after I do a difficult task or project. I let the person know I am going to start, and then I call that person back when I am finished. It makes me accountable when I am having trouble getting started. If it is a project or I have a lot of things to do, I break down items into do-able tasks by writing them down and periodically reporting my progress to that person. This is often a reciprocal arrangement.

Recently, I had come home from a three-week vacation and had not wanted to unpack. I'm ashamed to say the clothes were still in two small suitcases (good recovery there!) weeks later, and I could not seem to allow myself to work on emptying them. In complete desperation, I called a CLA phone friend.

She shared with me that she was baking; and when she was finished, she planned to declutter in the living room and then get dressed. I shared that I was going to empty one case and make four phone calls for various appointments. Then I was going to call her back in an hour, so we could report on our progress.

I was able to do those chores, plus the dirty dishes. I called her back and recounted my victories. She shared that she had finished her baking but was interrupted by someone at the door, so it wasn't possible for her to get to her decluttering as soon as she would have liked. We just listened and supported one another but did not judge.

I told her that next I was going to empty the other suitcase and then get dressed so I could go down into the basement and do the laundry. Then, while I was waiting to put the wash in the dryer, I was going to start catching up with the mail I had been letting pile up. Afterwards I was going to make lunch. She told me that she was going to declutter the living room and then get dressed.

The point here is that we were just doing our own thing…it didn't matter that what she was doing was entirely different from what I was working on. The bookending was completely symbiotic and was fulfilling for us both. With the aid of more reporting, I did my laundry from start to finish. Bookending pays dividends!   ◬

Earmarking

Summer 2017
Kathy H., CA

We provide a place for our possessions and return them there. We create a home for anything before bringing it in. When we add a new item, we release an old one. For accessibility, beauty, and peace of mind, we keep some empty space.

The old adage says, "a place for everything, and everything in its place." For years, I tried to live by that. It seems to me to be the key to keeping my stuff organized. But, sooner or later, I would always fall short of the goal.

Until my clutter got to be too overwhelming, I was able to find places for everything. Ah, but my problem was in returning items to their places—the old procrastination demon raised its head once again. Also, as my clutter accumulated, I began to lack enough places to put all the stuff. My life with my possessions was falling apart around me.

Then I came to CLA. Did I magically start returning items to their places? In a word, no. It took some time in the program before I was able to focus on putting things away on a daily basis, although I still sometimes struggle with it. The key for me was focusing on all aspects of the program—but especially in utilizing the Tool of Daily Action, along with the Tool of Earmarking. And getting rid of a lot of the clutter enabled me to set up places for all my possessions.

It's so easy for me to start slipping back into my old ways. In order to consistently take the step of putting things in their designated places, I have to rely on my Higher Power and on bookending with my program friends. Without help, my clutter will once again take over my life.

This Tool also tells us to release an old item before adding a new one. This is one aspect I need to pay more attention to. I don't buy nearly as much as I used to, but when I decide I need something, I often get it without first giving up something else—although I do periodically inventory my stuff and take those items I no longer use to the thrift shop. That's a little backwards from what the Tool directs us to do, though, so that is one behavior I am hoping to change in the future—to not purchase anything until I also get rid of something else. I think it's going to take more work with my Higher Power and my program buddies to attain this goal.

The last part of the Tool talks about keeping some empty space. I can well believe the value of empty space. A room is more visually appealing and restful if it is not jam-packed with stuff. And, if there is room around special items, it is much easier to see and enjoy them. Otherwise, they are lost in the clutter and become just one more part of the visual noise.

So, by working my CLA program one day at a time, I am able to find things after they are put away and enjoy my nice home without all the clutter. Thank you,

CLA—and thanks to all the Tools that help my life. ◬

Focusing

Fall 2018
Adelaide M., IL

I recently moved, and when the movers left, there were boxes everywhere. Some boxes were organized and labeled, such as the boxes for the kitchen or boxes that held books. Other boxes were labeled "miscellaneous" and had been hastily thrown together as I began to run out of time. I had moved into a smaller space, and I wasn't sure how everything was going to fit. I sat down in a chair with boxes piled high above me and goat paths allowing me minimal movement. It felt claustrophobic.

Although I have been in the program for almost ten years, my mind was racing. I felt scattered and overwhelmed. I had gotten to the point where I was doing mostly maintenance. My previous apartment still got messy at times, but everything had a home. I did not know where things were going to go in the new apartment or how much was going to fit. I realized this was how I had felt as a newcomer, and this gave me a renewed appreciation for how difficult things can be at first.

I wanted to call someone, but my phone wasn't connected yet. So I started to change my focus. First, I meditated for a little while and calmed my mind. I followed my breath. I breathed in and out. Afterwards, I felt better able to focus. I started with one box of books.

It was easy enough to put books on the shelf. After I finished my first box, I rested and then tackled another box. It took several weeks to totally unpack the boxes. I finished during the Memorial Day declutterthon. Without CLA, I would still be living out of boxes.

First, I focused on being open to following where Higher Power was leading on a daily basis. This was accomplished by going to the Divine Decluttering line many mornings, where the focus was on beginning the day focused on Step 11. When I couldn't go on the line, I would do my own morning meditation. This would help me focus on Higher Power and on taking a balanced approach. Focusing on this allowed me to not get overwhelmed and stressed. I focused on creating a sacred space for me and my cats.

I started off creating a space where I could comfortably watch TV, eat, and read. I also created comfortable places for my cats to sleep, eat, and climb. Having this

as a focus helped me to create a space that reflected my love for my cats. As I learned in Step 11, I did not just think of my own comfort, but of my cats' comfort as well. Before program, it would never have occurred to me that the cats would enjoy little places to sleep throughout the apartment. Because I focused on God's love, I wanted the cats to feel happy, loved, and comfortable. I was able to create a space that felt sacred. Focus is important in this way.

I believe that, for me, working with others on the Divine Decluttering line helps me maintain a positive focus and keeps me continuing to create a sacred place. When I work with others, I tend to check in every thirty minutes. This allows me to take things in bite-sized portions while feeling I am getting something done. If I lose my focus, there are understanding, caring people supporting me.

In conclusion, CLA has helped me to keep my focus on doing God's will by being gentle with myself but making steady progress. This is the third month in my new apartment, and—while it is not perfect—it works for me. It is my sacred space, formed by focusing on HP one day at a time!   ▲

Telephone

Holiday 2018
Alison B., NJ

"Telephone: *We use the phone to keep in touch with other members of the Fellowship between meetings. Talking on the phone helps both members.*"—"A Brief Guide,[2]" blue leaflet

I believe it is very important to make calls to a number of members on a consistent basis, but do I? Heck, no! There have been many times I have wanted to call someone in the Fellowship to discuss a personal issue that I deemed important, only to realize that I have very few people to call because I am so afraid of reaching out in the first place. And nobody calls me for days on end. I have one good friend who is extra busy—she calls me occasionally. I have another who is busy, too, but usually calls me back when I call her. I can talk to her about anything, but I don't want to burden her with everything—and anyway, I guess I want someone who will be on the end of the phone when I call. In CLA that seems a lot to ask. I made seven phone calls this afternoon and got six voice mails and one person who spoke with me for two minutes. Apparently people were enjoying the nice weather, and I didn't make enough calls!

It takes every ounce of courage I have to pick up the phone. It's a fear of rejection, fear that the person will be too busy to chat, and fear of not knowing how to start the conversation—all rolled into one big lumpy ball. Once I've broken the ice, it's a bit easier. It's much better if I know the gist of what I want to talk about ahead of time, but as soon as I ask the other person about herself, I have a tendency to let her do all the talking. And then there are times I wonder why I come away from the phone call feeling unfulfilled.

Another thing is that I am a needy person to begin with. Sometimes I find it easier to not talk about myself, rather than to start and then be interrupted and not listened to fully. That can hurt more than if I didn't talk at all.

I believe it has something to do with the way I pause between sentences to get my thoughts together. Often it seems the other person thinks I've finished when I haven't. Sometimes just listening to the other person can help me get out of myself, but sometimes that's just not enough. I definitely deserve to be heard, too.

For about three months, I had a co-sponsor. I was calling her on a daily basis, and we were listening fully to each other. There was something very satisfying about that. I was even reporting a written daily 10th Step with everything I did wrong and right each day. I was also sharing my daily resentments, which were coming up a lot because I had just started a 4th Step inventory, and I was getting the present resentments mixed up with the past.

The telephone can, of course, also be used for texting. It's not in the literature because that was created before the advent of texting. It's not really my cup of tea. I began it only when I ran out of excuses and began to feel I was behind the times. Now I dictate the texts, so when the words come out wrong I can have a bit of a laugh, even if there isn't someone immediately at the other end. And surprise—sometimes there is!   ◬

Literature

Spring 2020
Alison B., NJ

Literature: Clutterers Anonymous uses only its own Fellowship-approved literature and that of Alcoholics Anonymous in meetings. Literature is an always-available tool that helps us gain insight, as well as strength, to deal with our problem.

We are a small Fellowship compared to that of A.A.; and, as such, we do not have nearly as much literature as they do. What has been especially helpful to me (since I joined a Step group and have been writing on the Steps in a deep, meaningful, way) has been

portions of *Alcoholics Anonymous*[1] (also known as "The Big Book"), especially pertaining to the 4th and 5th Steps. It talks about all the Steps; and, although I do find it hard to follow in places, it is well worth studying. It also has proper instructions of exactly how to take inventory. And did you know that the Promises are in the Big Book? It is said they actually come about as the result of taking Step 9 with a sponsor (or dedicated group).

Another A.A. book highly recommended is The *Twelve Steps and Twelve Traditions*[14] (also known as the "Twelve and Twelve"). This goes into a lot of detail and explains the Steps and Traditions with care. Many groups and individuals study it. The Twelve and Twelve really is a blueprint for living. I have had occasion to read the different chapters of it many, many times, and yet there is still so much for me to learn. I find I need to read this literature over and over again in order for it to sink in.

The same is true for the CLA literature. We currently have nine leaflets and two booklets. I have the nine leaflets, and the funny thing is that I found an extra set I didn't know I had! In the face-to-face group I go to, we like to pick a leaflet and have one person read the first paragraph. Then that person shares for two minutes, and we go around the room, and each person shares on that paragraph for two minutes.

The different kinds of sharing we get on one small paragraph are truly amazing. Of course everybody is encouraged to share from their experience, strength, and hope, and there is no cross-talk. Then the next person reads the next paragraph, shares for two minutes, and the process of sharing around the room begins again. I truly enjoy these meetings and find them very satisfying. Often, I learn from other people, or I relate to them. I have my own eureka moments, and it is always comforting when I find another point of reference to show that I am not alone.

I admit that I am not voluntarily reading the literature by myself these days. I read it with groups either on the phone or face to face, unless I have homework for my Step group. I have used leaflets for that, too. But I am not very good at pushing myself to do things on my own.

If I had to pick a favorite, I would point to the leaflet "Declutter your Mind[6]" because that is where my worst problem is. I have been known to read that one without being prompted…as long as my mind isn't too cluttered to think of it!

Service

Summer 2020
Kathy H., CA

Service. That word seems to scare a lot of people.

I don't think I have enough time. I would never be able to do that. Someone else will do it. Why should I be the one? I'm a nobody, not a "big shot." These are some of the messages that members may tell themselves when service positions are offered.

And by offered, I mean that doing service in the Fellowship should not be considered an onerous duty—but, rather, an opportunity to grow and be a deeper part of our Fellowship. By helping the program, we are practicing Step 12, which says, in part, "tried to carry this message to others…" Working Step 12 is essential for strengthening and maintaining our recovery. It is much harder to backslide when we are carrying out commitments for the group. In other words, we do service to enhance and maintain our own recovery, not just to help out the Fellowship. And, by the way, we often laugh and have fun while doing so. After all, our literature says, "If you're not having fun, you're not doing it right."

Don't think you have to be a special person or have a special skill to give service. After all, there are no big shots in CLA, and skills can be learned.

What does it take to do service in CLA? It can be as little as setting up chairs in a room before a face-to-face meeting. There are plenty of other service positions with a local or phone group, most of which take very little time for the member doing them. My favorite is newcomer contact.

I am my group's newcomer contact, which means I get to take calls from prospective newcomers to the meeting and also try to keep in touch with them periodically once they have come to the meeting. That's a lot of fun.

There is one very important position that many groups don't fill—that of intergroup representative or delegate to the CLA World Service Organization (WSO).

Some service positions take a bit more work or expertise. Intergroups and WSO have many opportunities available. The positions vary from doing very little work once a month or one time to more complex and time-consuming jobs—but none of them are full time. Most of these positions can be filled by any member. Those who already do the job will be happy to teach you how to do it before they turn it over to you.

And we must never forget the most basic service of all—talking to other CLA members, either through a sponsorship position, as a buddy, in bookending, or just during a program call or after a meeting. I can't think of how many times I have shared something, either in a meeting or in a conversation, when someone later told me that what I said helped their recovery. Most times, I was not even aware that I had said anything special.

I have been in CLA more than 19 years and have been doing some form of service for most of that time. In the beginning, it was just attending a WSO meeting once a month and reporting back to my group—scarcely a difficult job. Eventually, when positions needed filling or work needed to be done, I began to say, "I think I can do that."

Since my first stint as delegate, I have done many different tasks for the Fellowship. Some of them have made use of my professional background, but others have had little to do with it. I have found that, if I am willing to learn and to ask questions, I can get the job done.

My biggest problem is in conquering my procrastination demon. But a funny thing happens when I meet my program commitments: I am better able to declutter—even though I spend time doing my service commitments.

After my retirement, I had begun to feel adrift and incompetent. But doing CLA service helped me gain my self-confidence—which helped me tackle my other problems. I know that my decluttering took a big leap forward when I started doing measurable amounts of CLA service. It's as if I needed something to spur me on to greater achievements—and giving the program some help was just the ticket.

One other way service helped me: while I have non-program friends, it seems most of my friends are CLA members, and I met almost all of them while doing service for WSO. Helping CLA has made my life much richer and more enjoyable. ◘

Slogan

Fall 2020
Ben C., NY

Hi, here is an aid for memorizing the Tools of CLA[16].

Buddies use Telephones to call EarmarKing for Bookending, and Daily Action about Meetings on Trusting the Literature to be Focused on the (3 Ss) Streamlining, Sponsorship, and Service. ◘

Literature

Fall 2020
Kathy H., CA

The CLA Tool of Literature states: *We use CLA- and A.A.-approved literature. Literature is an always-available tool that helps us gain insight, as well as strength, to deal with our problem.*

CLA currently has nine recovery leaflets, a leaflet for professionals, and two booklets. I will briefly discuss how I have used some of the literature to aid in my own recovery.

The leaflet "Home: Our Sacred Place[8]" says "We have lived with these indignities so long that they've become invisible." How often have I sat down to reflect, only to look around and see the mess that had been there so long but which had become invisible to me. Even after many years in CLA and much decluttering, things still can creep up on me. I am working on spending some time each week just to look at my home as if I had fresh eyes, trying to find all the mess I have left.

In reading the "Welcome[15]" leaflet, it hits home when it talks about things like "the fog we create in our heads" and "the emptiness we feel inside." It reminds me that I often clutter because I am immersing myself in distractions, such as reading or playing games, to avoid dealing with these problems. My solution is to talk to others in the program, work the Steps, and get into action.

My clutter is definitely more than physical. My mental clutter consists of resentments and grievances, unfinished tasks and projects, worries, fears, etc. It's a funny thing, but when I allow the mental clutter to build up, the physical clutter does as well. At those times, I tend to spend most of my efforts and times trying to escape that mental clutter. The leaflet "Decluttering Resentment[5]" states: "Just as clutter consumes our physical space, resentment consumes our minds." In fact, the clutter fog and the physical clutter are also connected in reverse. As the "Finding Your Life Purpose[7]" leaflet tells us: "As we declutter our lives, the mental fog that has for so long clouded our minds is lifted." When I am surrounded by clutter, I find it harder to think. So I try to focus on both my mind clutter and my physical clutter, rather than one or the other.

There are several little tips included in the literature that help us with our decluttering efforts. "Finding Your Life Purpose[7]" tells us that: "What we enjoy doing is what we do well." So I am trying to focus on taking care of my house in ways that are enjoyable, rather than seeming like a chore. And I find I enjoy empty space more. "Home: Our Sacred Place[8]" states: "We learn that we appreciate an item more when we surround it with breathing space."

During my first months in CLA, my progress was very slow. I found that, after I began taking on duties in WSO, I began to be able to declutter at a much greater rate. In

less than a year my very cluttered home was almost free of clutter. (I say almost because I still haven't had every little tiny bit of clutter gone.) In the leaflet "Recovery from Cluttering: The 12 Steps of CLA[12]," it states: "One of the ways to maintain a clutter-free life is by being a good example and passing on what we've learned."

And when I feel down because I have let things go, when I wallow in those depressive states and decline to do anything, I try to remind myself that: "It's not the falling down that counts, it's how quickly we get up," as it states in "Decluttering Resentment[5]." That helps me to get up and get moving once again—and once I start, things do get better.

During those times when I'm feeling that I just don't feel like cleaning up after myself or making a needed phone call—or any other task—it helps to remind myself that it's really more important to me to have a clean house or to get a bill paid—or whatever it is that needs doing at the time. In the long run, I'll be glad I did it. That's when I remind myself that: "Discipline is remembering what we want," as it states in the "Declutter Your Mind[6]" leaflet. I take this to mean that I want to focus on my long-term goals rather than momentary impulses. This has helped me tremendously in taking care of both my physical and non-physical clutter. That's why it's one of my favorite CLA sayings.   ⬟

Co-Sponsorship Group

Spring 2021
Alison B., NJ

My Experience, Strength, and Hope

It was just over three years ago that I decided I needed a sponsor in CLA, so I asked someone who had the attributes that I wanted, and she said "yes." Upon further examination, I discovered this woman did not actually have a sponsor of her own. It was my opinion that I could not possibly let her sponsor me without one. It has always been my understanding of the 12-Step programs (stemming from A.A.), that it is recommended that one person sponsors another, who sponsors another, and a chain of sponsors is formed. However, due to various problems in CLA, like not having official literature for sponsors to work with sponsees, for example, people in CLA have been reluctant to sponsor. In fact, it is my experience that many clutterers are afraid of such commitments to begin with.

This other woman had an idea. She wanted to form a group. She knew a group of like-minded women who were interested in having sponsors. There were eight of us. She asked us if we were will-ing to meet. As it turned out, all of us had been in other 12-Step programs at one time or another, so we had all looked at the 12 Steps from different vantage points. This meant we had a lot of information and insight to impart to one another, plus experience, strength, and hope on which to build.

Personally, I have had 35 years in various 12-Step programs. I was in the food program for several years and also in the one to separate myself from the alcoholic. And I tried out other programs. At one point, you could say I was collecting them!

If there is one piece of wisdom I can impart to the newcomer from my own experience, it would be that if you are not familiar with the 12 Steps and have other issues, it would be a good idea to seek out another program and do the Steps there before you do them in CLA. Or maybe at the same time, if you're adventurous. It has been my experience that it is best to get clean in as many areas of my life as possible because it has made it easier to declutter in the long run.

If you have other underlying issues, pick the one you feel is most bothersome, and find a program where you can work on it.

In our group, we came up with a set of guidelines, which we follow very carefully. People from our group have helped other groups to start using these guidelines. Our group is very successful—we have not lost a member, probably because we have been consistent. We have been meeting almost every week for three years. We do homework in between meetings, preferring to use all the meeting time for sharing. If someone cannot make it to the meeting, they let us know ahead of time.

We went through the 12 Steps twice, delving into them very deeply, and learning each other's secrets. We took our time. For a while we were in sync with each other on each Step. We give feedback from our experience, strength, and hope. Now each of us is doing our own work. We truly love each other and call ourselves Step Sisters. We are in touch by text between meetings, although I admit I don't join in much. We even showed each other our homes on video conferencing once, and we plan to do more of that. I enjoy the writing homework so much. It helps me to stay grounded…and sharing it with the group is so cathartic. There is no feeling like it. I have no plans to give it up anytime soon!   ⬙

Bookending

Fall 2021
Alison B., NJ
We bookend when we talk to other

CLA members before and after taking difficult steps in our recovery. This way we can hold ourselves accountable for completing a specific task or project.

Bookending is definitely my favorite Tool, because it gets me moving when nothing else will. There is the spontaneous type where I call a CLA friend on the spur of the moment, if I have a difficult phone call that has to be made, for example; but for bigger projects, I have a special method where I like to make an appointment with a sister-in-recovery, over a two- or three-hour time period. I did it this week. I wanted to work on my kitchen, and in order to get started, I wrote down everything that I wanted to clear or clean before we got together on the phone. We began at 2 p.m. We briefly asked after each other, and then stated our goals for the next half hour. I was going to do my dishes and wipe around my sink and countertop. It just so happened that she was working on her kitchen, too. She had baked cookies and needed to clean up and put things away.

We stayed on the phone for only a few minutes. It is important to both of us that we do not use the phone time for chatting unless one or the other of us is having a difficult time. I agreed to set my alarm and call her back in a half hour. It was amazing how much I got done in 30 minutes when I was focusing! I washed a sink load of dishes; cleaned the draining board, sink, and around the stove; and washed a dirty pan that had been sitting on the stove. I also wiped my countertop like I said I would, but that needs some concentrated cleaning in certain areas. I admit I am powerless over cleaning and that my life has become unmanageable…

At the end of the half hour, I called her, and we reported our progress and then announced what we wanted to achieve in the next half hour. There was no judgment—just praise for what had been done. After two and a half hours of proceeding in this manner, we were pleasantly surprised to find that we had both been incredibly productive, whereas on any other day, I, personally would just be wasting time, as I have done only too often.

It doesn't matter to me if the other person is working on something completely different. I like being listened to and feeling as if I'm not completely alone. It is so comforting to work alongside another person and yet be in a completely different space. I also feel as if I am being acknowledged for my efforts, which is so important to me. Somehow, my self-esteem suddenly becomes much stronger when my work is affirmed, and that spills over into other areas of my life in a lovely way. I become more content.

Well, that bookending experiment was so successful, and we both enjoyed it so much that we did it again in the same week. My willingness took me by surprise because I usually feel like I have very little inner drive or incentive to help myself. It helped even more when I put on my favorite internet music station with mostly familiar songs playing in the background. I don't know exactly how to explain this, but often it seems my mind needs to have a split focus in order to be properly effective.

My new therapist says I have Attention Deficit Disorder, and I'm now reading a book about it—in 15-minute increments! ▲

Sponsorship

Sponsorship in CLA

Fall 2019

Do you need a CLA sponsor? Are you being sponsored—or have been sponsored—but feel unsure about sponsoring others?

Lack of enough sponsors has been a long-time problem in CLA. Some of the folks who attend phone groups have begun a unique approach to this problem: They have started several small Step-study groups, in the hopes that those folks who participate may then feel confident in sponsoring others through the Steps.

But there has been a long-time perception among some members that some literature on sponsorship would be a valuable resource for those hesitant to sponsor. So a few years ago, the CLA World Service Organization (WSO) directed the Literature Committee to work on new literature about sponsorship.

After more than three years in the making, "Sponsorship in CLA" was finally finished and approved by WSO.

How did the Literature Committee write the booklet? First, several written sources on 12-Step sponsorship were gathered and shared with committee members.

These were read through during committee meetings, and parts that were deemed helpful to our own literature were placed into one document and sorted by topic into bulleted lists.

Then members read through each topic area during meetings. They deleted redundancies, things that were considered not appropriate for CLA, and added their own points where it was deemed advisable.

Eventually, members began writing it in paragraph form, using the bulleted lists.

Then they began reading through and amending the document—which happened several times. As new members joined the committee, they often had input which changed what had been written. The content was reorganized into various topics as it made sense. Then it was shared with a few members who had both sponsorship and writing experience—and the document was changed again.

Finally, the committee felt it was ready to submit to the Fellowship for input. Feedback was requested by the end of 2017.

Once the Fellowship had given its feedback, further editing was undertaken. It was difficult to manage because of conflicting answers in the feedback. For instance, one group felt the document was too long and wanted it shortened, while others wanted materials added. It was impossible to satisfy both sets of wants, so the committee decided that it wouldn't shorten the document and would be wary about adding much new material.

Some of the requested additions consisted of good, but not relevant, material, so they were saved for some other document. With each input, the booklet was changed a bit again.

This process is time consuming, but most committee members agree that it's better to gather the collective wisdom of the Fellowship, rather than have a piece contain just a few voices.

With the approval of WSO for the entire document at the June 22 meeting, the booklet was formatted, proofread, and sent to the printers.

"Sponsorship in CLA" is available for purchase at the price of $3.20 each for fewer than 10 copies or $1.60 each for ten or more copies. To order, do one of the following: 1. Visit ClutterersAnonymous.org/store and follow the prompts. 2. Send a check or money order, along with the Literature Order Form (which is downloadable from ClutterersAnonymous.org), to CLA WSO, 184 South Livingston Ave., Ste. 9-203, Livingston, NJ 07039.

The members of the Literature Committee have the fond hope that publication of the booklet will help both those who are willing to sponsor and those seeking a sponsor.

The committee is wishing to begin writing a Step guide or a "Twelve and Twelve" as its next project. They are requesting members to send in their stories of how they work the Steps and how they use the Traditions for inclusion in either project.   ⬢

Affirmations[17]

Fall 2017
Alison B., NJ

I acknowledge and celebrate all my victories, large and small.

When I saw this affirmation, I knew it was what I wanted to write about because, to me, even little victories are large. Relatively speaking. There are various degrees of "large." I am not talking about disasters we have to cope with, just everyday large victories. Life-changing victories, in my humble opinion, would go under the heading of "huge."

The sad truth is that I lack the internal drive to want to make things happen. I have to work by deadlines and pats on the back. I appear to find a little more excitement in my mundane life by procrastinating until almost the last moment with nearly everything I do. I hardly want to do anything that is productive—so, to me, a victory is when I can get a chore done with time to spare. The only time I have any self-proclaimed drive at all is when it is something I am passionate about, like singing or acting—but it seems I don't even want to do that unless there is an audience, or unless I am imagining one.

Even writing this article, which I have been procrastinating on past the deadline, I have to imagine it will receive attention, although feedback is rare. So you see, as long as the spotlight is on me, or I believe it will be on me in some way, I seem to be able to force myself to get moving. Eventually. Grudgingly. But with more love and acceptance, once I get going.

That is why I do my best—and, often, my only—decluttering when I bookend. First of all, it is a large victory to make that opening bookending call. That says I mean business. From that moment on, I can imagine that whatever I am doing on my list is important to the other person, even though it isn't. I can also imagine that I am in the spotlight and that I will pat myself on the back every half hour—which is the time period that my buddy and I choose to call

each other back.

We will have several of these half-hour intervals, during which time I first write down anything and everything that I need to do. Then I try to do the quick ones first, so that I can report some small victories. Once I have gotten myself started, it's amazing how I actually feel like doing more. But for me, it takes a few pats on the back in between victories to keep me going.

There can be anything on my list, from balancing my checkbook to washing my dishes. Decluttering my kitchen table gets more than its fair share of attention because somehow the clutter just gets sucked into that vortex. I need kudos for all these things. I don't take anything for granted because, left to my own devices, I wouldn't accomplish any of them.

A large victory to me is doing my laundry. I seem to have to write it down several times before I can actually bring myself to do it. The most important aspect is that I really have to cheer myself on and have another person around to listen. Someone can tell me I'm doing well, once in a while, but I really have to know it for myself. And I'm still working on that.

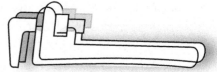

Spring 2019
Claudia P., NJ

I am entitled to surroundings of beauty, harmony, order, and serenity.

First and foremost, the serenity, peacefulness, and calmness must come from within. A certain acceptance of self and putting myself in a high regard—or entitled place—is necessary for this positive affirmation.

I feel it is necessary for my mental wellness and human experience to have order in my surroundings, although a lot of times the order goes out the window when my life seems to be in chaos. I need to slow down and take time to put myself and my environment first in a harmonious way. I need to reflect and ask myself: Is this item necessary for my well-being and is this beautiful? Do I need this item?

To be entitled is to say yes. Yes to myself and yes, it is okay to live with beautiful things. Things that have a balance and order, so that when I walk into my home, I feel it is a place of peace and a place of renewal. When I create a space to live in, I want to create a place in which everything has a place and things can be in harmony with the space.

But what is harmonious with me?—that is the question. Do the things I have resonate harmony in life with them? As I grow to a new stage of my life, sometimes what once served as a purpose of harmony needs to be let go to create new harmony. It is okay to release the things that don't support harmony today. What served purpose yesterday may not be the same things that serve purpose today. Harmony is like music—listen to the harmony of my space and hear the music that is playing.

Is it in order? Is it peaceful? What is it that is me? These are the questions that come to my mind when thinking about being entitled to surroundings of beauty, harmony, order, and serenity. I truly believe that serenity must come from within. Once my own self is in order and I have a plan of living, then I can accept a place of living that is peaceful. ◢

Fall 2020
Claudia P., NJ

I accept my progress as proceeding in my Higher Power's time.

Well, to me, to first admit I am powerless over clutter and my life has become unmanageable—and make a decision to turn my will over to God—pretty much sums up that the timing is then up to God. The willingness to admit that I am powerless about this facet of my life has now given me strength of hope and faith that there is a greater strength within the Fellowship of CLA.

I am thankful to have acceptance that there is a Higher Power,
something beyond me, an energy
field of movement that has its own
speed. I am reminded about the
story of the tortoise and the hare.
Both are part of the race. But the
boastful hare does not win. So it is
in God's time we are all winners. ⏁

Holiday 2020
Claudia P., NJ

*I affirm abundance and prosper-
ity, thus releasing my need to hoard
and control things.*

Hmm, and I mean hmm—this
is a positive affirmation that I need
to say over and over again, not
to convince myself of this but to
affirm that the universe will provide. I do not need to hoard and
control things. I can release and,
when needing an item, it will come
into my path. The more I think I
control, the less control I actually
have. My life is much better when
I release, let it go, let it flow with
abundance thought, not scar-
city. When I live abundantly in
thought, I am able to have faith
that my Higher Power will take
care of me, and this positive affirmation makes a difference in my
life. ⏁

Spring 2021
Claudia P., NJ

*I acknowledge and celebrate all
my victories, small and large.*

This is so very important to me.
The clutter I have did not come all
at once. It came into my home one
piece at a time. Therefore, when
reducing clutter, taking one piece
away or picking up one item and
making a decision—do I want to
spend more energy with this item
in my life or do I want to let this
item go?

Celebrating victories small and
large enables joy to come back
into my life. Many times I look
at things—and I still do look at
things for joy. However,
celebration is an emotion, not a
thing. Celebration is, to me, a
liberating experience, free from
the guilt and shame of clutter. It is
accepting that I can change and it
is okay to celebrate small and large
victories. ⏁

Summer 2021
Mariah W., NY

*"With every item I release, I cre-
ate space in my life for more joy and
energy, as well as new insights and
experiences, to come in."*

I have released a *lot* of physical
and nonphysical items! It is true
that with each and every item—
whether it be mind clutter, spiritual
clutter, time clutter, relationship

clutter, financial clutter, or some item of physical clutter—I do indeed create *space* in my life for more peace and serenity, insights, and experiences to come in. Sometimes I also have glimmers and even waves of joy and energy that come in. I am trusting gently and patiently that, as I continue to work our CLA program, the space of experiencing joy and energy *will* continue to grow and expand right here and now and as I'm moving forward.

Remember playing hide and seek? Maybe that's what releasing every item creates—that space in my life for more joy, energy, and playfulness, along with whimsical and other lovely insights and experiences, to come on in.

Imagine me with my eyes closed, counting by a tree as we play hide and seek together, uncluttering *one* item and releasing *one* item at a time…you're in this game of recovery with me, you know. "Ready or not, here I come!" More joy and energy are so, so very ready to come into my life and yours, as I seek recovery and you seek recovery, and we all seek recovery, by releasing those items that no longer serve and support. "Olly Olly Oxen Free!" Wow! The freedom to create more joy and energy to come on in! I *am* ready! Thank you, CLA and my CLA family! ◭

Slogans[18]

I Am Enough

Summer 2017
Alison B., NJ

I've decided to make this saying my new mantra. If I felt I was enough, I wouldn't have a tendency to collect incessantly, have a hankering to be the center of attention, and think it's normal to fill my plate to overflowing and stuff myself on a daily basis.

I attempt to control these defects in different ways. I allow myself to bring in new things only rarely and then get rid of items taking up equal space. I choose to be onstage as often as possible without stressing myself too much, so I am now in rehearsals for a play. This has meant bringing home clothes for the stage. Now I have to throw old clothes out. I try to stick to a sensible, fairly strict way of eating. Lately, I have been overeating and not wanting to declutter, which can only mean I am clinging to resentments. It usually helps me to stand up for myself when I feel like an injured party, even though it can often take all my courage. Sometimes I overcompensate in relationships. I don't want to be "too much," except when I'm acting. I just want to be enough. ◭

Holiday 2020
Ben C., NY

Using "Action is the magic word" and "the completion cycle." On May 31, while in my bedroom, I heard the clashing of metal, so I went to see what happened. In my kitchen, a cabinet shelf had fallen on to another (bottom ground shelf). The reason for the fall was it was holding metal pots, so after decades the nails gave out.

I decided I would not wait for maintenance to come repair it, so I devised a way of doing it myself. First, everything was moved out; then I took measurements for a piece of wood that would be cut. Next, I clamped in place a piece of wood (that I had had for years that had been found sidewalk shopping) and cut it to size with a handsaw. I used a couple screws to hold the wood flatly against the cabinet wall, and the shelf was laid upon it. Next, my plan was to put the heavy metal on the bottom shelf and most of the light plastic on the top. The handsaw, wood, tools, and parts were returned to their homes; and lastly the floor was swept.   ◮

First Things First

Spring 2021
Vicki V., CA

I use this slogan to guide me in the three areas of recovery: physical, emotional, and spiritual.

When making decisions, I prioritize by importance. Then, writing down a plan for my week that is flexible and based on the idea of First Things First, my life seems to flow.

One small example in my recovery using First Things First is in regard to making my bed. I have already made this a priority. Although it is a simple task, I do this as a start-up action. It gets me going, a common dilemma in so many areas. It makes me feel good that I have kept a commitment to myself.

I have noticed that when I use this idea of First Things First, I am able to accomplish more, feel balanced, and smile more.   ◮

Literature

Literature is one of the CLA Tools of Recovery;[16] it is an important aspect of the program. This section includes articles that appeared in the "Sharing on Leaflets" column in CLA*rity* and other articles about CLA and A.A. literature and writing.

Sharing on Leaflets

Welcome Leaflet[15]–Part Five

Spring 2017
Alison B., NJ

Parts One through Four can be found in Ten Years of CLArity[13]— Editor.

Hello, readers! Please remember to refer to this leaflet for the complete questions.

Question 16: Are you easily sidetracked…? I don't always "move from one project to another without finishing any of them" unless I am really tired or have a lot on my mind. Usually I am

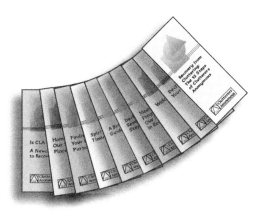

hyper-focused and able to focus on one thing. That makes it fine for finishing a long-term project. I can tire myself out and not finish more important things. I have learned to use a timer and break tasks down into approximately fifteen-minute intervals. That way I can "rest before I get tired."

Question 17: "Are you constantly doing things for others while your own home is out of order?" I used to do that, but I try not to anymore because it drains me emotionally, physically, and spiritually.

Question 18: "Do you often replace possessions…you already have?" Sometimes I still do that, but mostly I know where everything is, even if it's in an overcrowded drawer—because I try to put "like" objects together.

Question 19: "Does perfectionism keep you from doing anything at all?" A lot of the time it does—

until I remember something a therapist once said to me: "If it's worth doing, it's worth doing badly!"

Question 20: "Does clutter cause you to have late charges…?" It has happened, but not lately. I try to be careful.

Question 21: "Do you feel a strong sense of emotional attachment towards your possessions…?" I'm not really sure; I know I don't like releasing them. Maybe that's just because I don't like change in general, and I enjoy doing the work decluttering takes even less. Most of my possessions are not worth much, and those I have already released I do not miss. However, I have to be in just the right mood to let my possessions go.

Question 22: "Do you consider all your possessions to be of equal worth…?" I consider my high-priced items, like the car and computer, to be worth more. But I do consider many of my items to be of equal worth.

Question 23: "Do you waste your valuable time and talents by constantly rescuing yourself from clutter?" I used to have to constantly rescue myself—but now I need to do so only intermittently.

Question 24: "Does clutter keep you from enjoying quality leisure time?" Yes, it does. I sit and stare at the clutter on my kitchen table

that appears to accumulate by itself, and I freeze up until I clear it.

Question 25: "Is the clutter problem growing?" I would not say that the clutter problem is growing because every time it gets to where I can't stand it anymore, I manage to get into action and declutter just enough.

I have reached the end of the questions in the leaflet. I hope my honesty will persuade some of you out there to write for CLArity. ◒

Silence/Emptying

Holiday 2021
Mariah W., NY

Clearing the Cobwebs and Ghosts of the Past in Mind Clutter

Is it ever possible to declutter my mind *completely*? To fully and completely empty my mind to be open to silence? Do I even know what complete silence sounds like? I'm not sure my mind has ever been 100% empty.

As I reflect on our green leaflet, "Declutter Your Mind[6]," I reflect on two aspects: *emptying* and *silence*.

"10. Emptying: At day's end, we empty our pockets, purse, and car and process our input. After an upsetting experience, we ask: "Am I spending $1,000 of emotion on 10¢ worth of annoyance?" We unwind, debrief, write our feelings, and release them. We do not carry today's load into tomorrow."

"13. Silence: We learn to enjoy silence, not merely as a respite from talk, but as a calming, healing force. Silence allows time for deep thoughts to emerge."

One of my questions to myself is: Do I empty my mind at the end of each day so I do not carry to-day's load into tomorrow? Unfor-tunately, the truth is that frequent-ly I do not. I carry the cobwebs and ghosts of the past in my mind clutter, not releasing sometimes really old cobwebby-like thoughts and relationships that have hurt me. I'm the one hurting myself by not forgiving myself and letting go of these sometimes toxic thoughts that end up harming me in my daily living today.

Can I declutter and empty my mind at the end of each day, em-bracing and embodying silence? I'd really like to recover and re-lease these emotions/thoughts/relationships so they no longer get in the way of my daily existence. I have tons of thoughts and thought patterns to empty that create these mental cobwebs:

I forgot to do ——————— and how can I ever fix that? Have I messed up too much?

I'm not good enough. ——————— is smarter than me.

I've made so many mistakes. How can I get out of the mess I've made of my life?

——————— didn't love me, so how could someone else possibly love me?

I'm not perfect and I'll never be. Can someone love and accept imperfect me?

Can I identify what a loving, supportive relationship is if I have never experienced it myself?

Clearly, I am spending $1,000 of emotion on 10¢ of annoyance or—more accurately—I am not being the best, most loving friend to myself. With a great deal of professional guidance to bolster my self-esteem, I have been letting go of toxic thoughts and gently re-leasing the perfectionist tendencies instilled by my family, since this perfectionism is not serving me. As I begin thinking about literal spring cleaning coming up, I know that I intend to clear the ghosts of relationships past and the thoughts of years gone by—even the past hours of my day—that need to be emptied and let go.

My mind has never ever been 100% empty. I'm always thinking, and there are times I'm not sure I even know what 100% silence sounds like, since even in the silence I hear traffic sounds, the sounds of equipment, the sounds of birds and dogs, etc. When I commune fully and completely with my Higher Power—opening to the stillness and silence of my connection with this loving, compassionate, abiding presence—then I do experience peace. This stillness—silence—is a very welcome reprieve. I'd love to experience this peace—this silence—every day.

To one who experiences peace, the entire world is a peaceful forest. May I be a part of this peaceful forest always! My journey of recovery is to continually empty my mind of old thoughts and embrace the stillness, silence, and serene peace of connection with the infinite intelligence we in CLA call our Higher Power.   ⬙

A Brief Gide

Fall 2017
Kathy H., CA

At first glance, I thought, "Why do an article about 'A Brief Guide[2]'? It's mostly a listing of 25 questions, the Tools, the 12 Steps, and the 12 Traditions—and we cover most of them elsewhere." On closer examination, however, I see much that I can discuss.

The first thing I see when I open the leaflet is the Preamble. The messages contained in this section are so basic to 12-Step Fellowships that I often don't focus on them

at all. But while reading it once again, I began to realize that much of it is a restatement of some of our Traditions.

Also, it emphasizes that we solve our common problem with clutter by sharing our experience, strength, and hope. It states that the CLA Fellowship "…is based on suggestion, interchange of experience…." This is much of the reason why CLA works for me. All of my success in dealing with my clutter has come from other clutterers sharing their stories with me—not from listening to a professional giving guidelines.

Don't get me wrong, some of the information I have gained from reading articles from professionals has been very helpful, but it has not given me the motivation to tackle my clutter that going to CLA meetings has done. Listening to many different clutterers in meetings and outreach calls has given me inspiration, motivation, and encouragement to tackle the clutter—also a plethora of ideas on how to do it.

The section, "How Do I Know if I'm a Clutterer?" is included next. These questions are meant to be a resource for newcomers to decide if they really are clutterers or not. But I find that they have other uses as well. While I have struggled with many of the scenarios covered by the questions, there are two that particularly apply to me.

The first is number 3: Do you find it easier to drop something instead of putting it away, or to wedge it into an overcrowded drawer or closet rather than finding space for it? This is one of the reasons I first started cluttering; I tend to procrastinate rather than to take the small effort of storing items properly. Since joining CLA, I have tried to remind myself to put things away—so the clutter doesn't pile up.

The second one is number 8: Do you use avoidance, distraction, or procrastination to escape dealing with your clutter? Yes! Yes! Yes! One of my biggest problems is just this scenario. But that is where bookending and outreach calls have helped.

The Tools of Recovery[16] are also listed. Since we have included articles about the Tools in previous CLArity issues, I will simply say that I use the Tools in my efforts to declutter and gain spiritual recovery—some more than others, but I do use them all. They have helped tremendously in my decluttering efforts. And—as it says in the introductory paragraph—"Action is the magic word." That is important for me because it is in not taking action that I have often fallen short of my goals.

Lastly, we have the 12 Steps, followed by the 12 Traditions. Once again, both the Steps and Traditions have been covered in depth elsewhere in previous issues of CLArity, so I won't say much about them here. The Steps are the whole underpinning of our program of recovery. Working the Steps aids us in our spiritual development—which can lead us to deal more effectively with our physical, time, and emotional clutter. As it is said in the program, we can't make any lasting improvements on the outside until we deal with our insides. And following the Traditions helps our groups remain stable, so that we can focus on our primary purpose—to help the clutterer who still suffers.

I could write much more about the contents of "A Brief Guide[2]"— but there is not room to do so. So I will stop with the thought that, once again, CLA literature has packed an awful lot into one small package. ◬

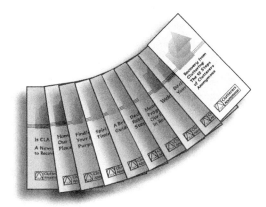

Writing

Decluttering Our Minds Through Journaling

Summer 2017
C.C., CA

In our CLA leaflet, titled "Declutter Your Mind[6]," it states, "Often our minds are filled with trivia; we fail to recognize what is really important. We cannot find serenity because our thought processes are clogged with self-defeating, irrelevant ideas…"

Have you ever found yourself patiently listening to a friend or co-worker talk on and on, in endless detail, often repeating him or herself and not getting to any point? If you answered "Yes," then you've been on the receiving end of someone else's mind clutter. Useless, trivial speech and negative, unproductive thoughts—along with too much information—can be forms of clutter.

Sometimes we just need to talk to someone during times of stress. But, if our everyday style of communication is over-talking and giving too much information, we are cluttering up our speech.

One powerful tool to help in decluttering our words is journaling. Just as "we empty our pockets, purse, and car and process our input," we can empty our minds by writing daily about what is going on in our lives. Putting our thoughts and feelings down on paper helps us to process what has happened during our day and can be a stress-relieving activity. Journaling can discharge or lessen negative emotions and allows room for clarity to enter. It can help us organize our thoughts and feelings about a certain event or person and helps to simplify how we want to proceed with a situation.

The physical act of putting pen to paper and releasing anything and everything that comes to mind is a form of emotional expression that may be sufficient, so that when someone asks you how you are doing, you don't give them the blow-by-blow account and overwhelm them with trivial information (clutter).

So the next time when you find that you need to express yourself, first try journaling about it. Then when you talk with that friend or co-worker, you may find you have less need to clutter up your speech. You may have more energy and clarity in your mind to concentrate on building the relationship.

"Emptying: We unwind, debrief, write our feelings, and release them. We do not carry today's load into tomorrow."

Some tips:

- Just start anytime and anywhere. Over time, your journaling will naturally fall into a good time of day that works for you.
- Free journal: Just write whatever comes to mind. Forget punctuation, grammar, or being politically correct. Just let it rip!
- Then tear it up or shred it and declutter it!   ◭

Clutter and Decluttering

This section contains articles about clutter, including categories for Shopping and Collecting, Paper Clutter, and Nonphysical Clutter. It also has articles discussing our efforts to declutter, including Focus on Decluttering and Getting Unstuck and Motivation.

Getting Unstuck and Motivation

Focus on the Dreaded Task of...

Fall 2019
Alison B., NJ

Laundry! I don't simply dislike it or despise it. To borrow a phrase, I recoil from it as if from a hot flame! I write it down in my weekly face-to-face group as a commitment, knowing full well I don't intend to follow through. This goes on for several weeks…. Meanwhile, over time, I've bought

oodles of underwear so that I may rationalize my procrastination. To my credit I've thrown out all damaged underclothing, so when I get desperate, I'm left only with something uncomfortable. I re-wear my other clothes. My excuse is that I don't go out a lot, and I can air out the clothes by hanging them back up. Besides, I wear them for only a couple of hours at a time. I just give them the old sniff test—they're fine! (Really?!)

I've done everything to push myself. I've put it on my daily list, read it to my daily buddy, and ignored it relentlessly. I've talked about it in great detail. I've determined that my mother did all my laundry. Ah, yes. I've made a list of all the good things I could think of about doing laundry. I found 12—it didn't help.

Finally, I ascertained while writing on something else I was having trouble with, that I needed permission, instruction, encouragement, and applause. Permission from my trusted buddy and from myself, instruction on decluttering my mind by talking about taking physical steps, and also reasons why my mind was going around in circles. So after I got out of my head, I wrote down a numbered to-do list. Eventually, I had no more excuses—I just had to follow the list to take the first set of actions, which was the hardest part. I texted my victory to my buddy and she texted back with applause and encouragement. I didn't think texting would satisfy me but it did! Did you know there's actually an applause emoji? Receiving several in succession had me laughing through feelings of inferiority! Below is everything I discussed with my buddy:

I live in a 30-unit apartment building, and there are four washing machines and two large dryers in the basement. I wear a housedress, so I need to dress to see if two washing machines are available. I never know what to wear, and that contributes considerably to my mind clutter. Then I can handle only two loads, even if there are more. What will I wash? What's in a pile on the chair that I choose to ignore? More mind clutter!

I go downstairs with my quarters and detergent, put those in the machines, and close the lids to start them chugging away—empty, except for the cold water and soap. Then I rush back upstairs and put every dirty thing airing out in my closet in the laundry bag. I drag the bag down the steps, thanking my HP that it's only one flight. I don't really sort the clothes—maybe light and dark—but with cold water it doesn't matter.

Part of my dilemma is that I won't start unless there is time to complete the process. So I've made that really simple. I time the washing, then the drying. When the clothes are dry I drape them over a chair in the laundry room in preparation for hanging. Nothing gets folded—not even the undies—I just throw them in a big transparent plastic bag, which I reuse, and I don't even care if they're inside out. I can straighten out each one as it's time to wear it.

All my socks are the same so even if I lose one to the sock monster, I know it will get matched eventually. Now I need to take the stuff upstairs. I lay everything over a chair and hang it in my closet immediately. My other rule is there has to be room for all the clothes in the closet. I think it's overflowing slightly again, so it's time for another cleanout.

By the way, I had a big victory. I did it all in 2 ½ hours!   ▲

Focus on Decluttering

Holiday 2017
Alison B., NJ

My bed is in my living room. Why? That's a good question. I tried to live with it in the bedroom when I first moved into this apartment approximately 23 years ago, but I wasn't comfortable there for many dysfunctional reasons.

One reason is that I used to live in a studio apartment and *had* to live in one room besides the kitchen, but that isn't all of it by any means. The person who lives beneath me snores so loudly that I can actually hear him through the floorboards! Why haven't I moved? Oh, I have all kinds of excuses for that, but the easiest is to blame it on the clutter.

The bedroom has been the worst because I deliberately turned it into a kind of junk room. Every time I had an item I didn't feel like putting away, didn't have a place for, or didn't know what to do with, it went into this room. I was not using the Tool of Earmarking or the concept of releasing items before bringing in more of equal value and space. I thought I was only bringing in things I needed, yet it was getting extremely messy, with no space on the tops of dressers and the floor like an obstacle course.

I knew I couldn't declutter it by myself. I needed help. I wanted someone from my face-to-face group to come over and do it with me. I thought someone could give me a couple of hours, and then I could reciprocate at some future point. That's hard because I don't really like the intrusion. But I was talking to my fairly organized and not-so-cluttering sister on the phone, and she volunteered to talk me through it.

We started with one item on a chest of drawers. She asked me if I had used the item recently. I said that I hadn't, but I liked it and thought it was decorative. So she asked me to put it on a tray for the time being. We went through every item like that. She asked me to bring in a plastic shopping bag and hang it on a door handle to collect garbage. Some things I threw away immediately.

Some things belonged in other rooms. I walked them there immediately, sometimes stopping to put things away and sometimes leaving them in another pile to be dealt with later. It's amazing to admit that a space that had been bothering me for a year took 30 minutes to declutter and 15 minutes to dust and decorate.

I spent about five hours with my sister on the phone. I now have spaces for eye rest all around the room. I can walk all around my floor, my laundry stays in a bag instead of all over the floor, and I have given two bags of clothes away—which was easy once I took them to my car and forced myself to drop them off into one of those bins in town which takes clothes. I don't mean it was easy to give the clothes away. I mean it was easier than usual to get them out of my apartment once I made a commitment to take them to the car.

I could have used a clutter buddy, but using my sister was helpful because the focus was on me. Five hours was a lot of time, but there's more to be done in that room. I did take a break in between to eat, and I don't necessarily recommend such a long period because we are supposed to rest before we get tired. But it worked for me, and it taught me that we don't have to go into one another's homes to be of help!

Spring Cleaning, Spring Festival

Spring 2019
Anonymous

An Eastern/Western approach to my creating a sense of urgency in working the 12 Steps

The holidays and spring cleaning are frequently times when people consider clearing clutter. At least that was, and is, true for me. I have chosen to create and integrate a fun hybrid of Eastern and Western traditions. This means that I choose to begin making changes over the autumn holidays and choose to make my resolution prior to the traditional time of a New Year's resolution.

The winter holidays and long, long nights of extreme dark are super tough for me. I've experienced depression and despondency at this time of year in the past. All my clutter within and without made the winter holidays even more challenging. This year, I decided to make even a small change, so I started attending CLA phone meetings. I decided to think of my winter holidays as spring cleaning and to clear my clutter within and without. This comes from our American western tradition of Thanksgiving/Christmas/ Hanukkah/New Year.

I have—over the years—integrated the Eastern (Asian) tradition into my own ways. I love anime and manga, and had seen storylines that included Spring Festival that I only now understand to be the Chinese New Year, which is frequently celebrated in February of each year. Here was a solution to my problem of having a hard time in the winter—Spring Festival and the Chinese New Year have given me another excuse for a sense of urgency. You see, if I create a sense of urgency, I seem to be more likely to change and take action.

So here I am today, working the Steps and Traditions of CLA and sometimes sobbing and crying through activity sessions or meetings where I just have to breathe deeply and take one moment, one thing at a time. In this way—one moment, one hour, one day at a time, and the amazing support of our CLA Fellowship—I was able to clear enough clutter out of my hallway, my bathroom, my foyer, my refrigerator, and freezer that I can now really eat, live in, and enjoy my home. What a miracle! There is space enough to savor these new clutter-free parts of my home again.

I now celebrate two New Year holidays: the Western New Year and the Eastern New Year/Chinese New Year (typically around Valentine's Day). The Chinese New Year/Spring Festival has inspired me to also keep coming back to CLA meetings, as I gently heal from physical, emotional, and spiritual clutter.

I'm very grateful to CLA and the Fellowship, which helps me gain experience, strength, and hope to recover from physical, emotional, and spiritual clutter—in ways that work for me by trying things on for size to see what fits for me in recovery. ◬

The Cemetery of Forgotten Decisions

Holiday 2019
Anonymous

Some in Clutterers Anonymous share that clutter is simply unmade decisions. Hmmm…well, what I have is a veritable cemetery of not just unmade but also entirely forgotten decisions! It's not exactly that I meant it to happen, but one thing led to another, and stuff that I meant to deal with when I had more time was put into a room as I pressed on to matters I felt were more important *right now*. I totally forgot about it…all that stuff.

Alas, more and more stuff ended up in that room, which is now what I call the morgue or the "cemetery of forgotten decisions." Morgues are probably better looking than my cemetery of forgotten decisions: layer upon layer of unmade decisions clutter my mind and my space! Blech!! So I take several deep breaths—reach out for support from CLA members—then galvanize with our CLA Recovery Affirmations[17]—two in particular:

17) *I participate with my clutter by putting my attention and action on it in the present moment.*

Little by little, moment by moment and in relationship to the cemetery of forgotten decisions facing me, I reconnect to that which was forgotten—dead and gone—to respond to each matter/project/object to bring it alive again, which may mean honoring and releasing it to some other home or place (including the trash/recycling). One moment, one hour, one thing, one project at a time.

24) *With every item I release, I create space in my life for more joy and energy, as well as new insights and experiences, to come in.* ⬢

Spring 2020
Kathy H., CA

Throughout my years in CLA, I have made a great deal of progress in decluttering my home. But I still struggle with procrastination and maintenance. This is why I still need CLA and probably always will. I can lean on my program in my efforts to keep my home the way I want it.

Here are some of the things that have helped me to declutter:

Bookending: When I want to accomplish something but have that resistance to getting started, I can pick up the phone and call another CLA member to share my goal. Then I call back later to let them know how I've done. This helps me to get going when that little part of me is saying, "Wait just a little; I don't want to face doing anything now; I can read or work a

puzzle to distract myself." Unfortunately, there are times when I am resisting the bookending call itself. It helps to have bookending relationships with several clutterers. A few times when I just wasn't able to get started, a bookending buddy has called me to bookend—and that's just what I needed.

Handling Overwhelm: When everything seems like too much and feels too daunting to complete, I try to focus on just one bit at a time. Like the time when my bedroom had gotten so cluttered I couldn't face it. So I began working just on the stuff piled up on my dresser. I was able to clear the dresser that way, before I tackled anything else. This is also a good time to bookend, to talk to my buddy, to read program literature, and to lean on the Steps.

Ten Things: When the clutter starts piling up, I like to commit each day to picking up at least ten things to take care of—to put away, throw away, place in the recycle bin, or place in a box to donate to the thrift shop. It's amazing how doing this can jump start my decluttering efforts. And, since I usually take care of each item as I am passing by, it feels like no work at all. I generally keep a count in my head until I reach ten. Sometimes I can accomplish a lot more than taking care of ten things, but some days it may be just the ten.

Daily Action: Taking care of ten things a day also speaks to the Tool of Daily Action. I find that taking care of at least a little bit each day keeps me in the habit of taking care of my house. And it also means I don't have the large piles that overwhelm me.

Steps 1-3: While working all the Steps is important (and I like to dwell on Step 10 for at least a little bit every day), I find I need to go back to the first three Steps daily to avoid cluttering again. It's when the house is in good shape that I have one of my biggest challenges: how to keep it that way. When I am feeling good about the house, my emotional self seems to say, "It's done, and I'm happy; now I can rest and not worry about it." That's fine for a few hours, or maybe a day or so, but I need to be careful to avoid slipping back into my old ways. This is when I really need to focus on Steps 1, 2, and 3: I am powerless over clutter, and I need to let my Higher Power lead the way.

Through all of my struggle with my clutter, I try to focus on the place in our CLA literature which says: "Discipline is remembering what we want." To me, that says that I should keep my long-term goal (a decluttered, clean house) in mind, instead of focusing on the short-term gratification (ignoring my clutter, having fun instead of doing housework, etc.).

FOCUS:
A Clutter Jack-in-the-Box

Fall 2020
Mariah W., NY

My cluttering—physical and nonphysical—seems to be a product of distraction and procrastination or extreme time clutter/busyaholism. Sometimes my clutter is from experiencing pain or being in fear. If I ignore it or forget about it, maybe somehow, someway it will magically go away—POOF!!—by the declutter fairies, who will magically whisk it away while I'm sleeping. Sometimes I think that way—that there is this same fantasy I have that magical declutter fairies will fly in while I'm sleeping and clear away all my clutter so I have a magnificently sparkling clear and beautiful home—like the magical beings who came into the cobbler's shop to repair and make shoes while the cobbler slept to help the cobbler be successful. This is a children's fantasy, and yet I play with that fantasy when I feel overwhelmed. Playing with fantasies may be fun; however, staying in fantasyland doesn't get my decluttering accomplished: engaging fully in a direct relationship with my clutter does help in my recovery to clear clutter.

How do I engage fully in decluttering? *Focus.* Focusing means I'm putting my attention and action on a project (my clutter) that I choose to declutter in *this* present moment. I'm learning that emptying, along with focus, makes a difference in my recovering from clutter. I've learned that focusing on *focus* at a gentle pace with a decluttering project makes quite a difference in supporting my success in actually *completing* my decluttering project in a way satisfactory to me. I know we have quite a bit of CLA literature on the topic of focus, yet I'm not sure I've focused on the quality of *focus* in my recovery. I can go at a breakneck speed or I putter around in decluttering, being attracted to the next shiny object or distraction. It's no wonder I'm not experiencing any sense of accomplishment in my decluttering journey.

What would *focus* look like?

Hmm...maybe it's in recovery affirmation number 17: "I participate with my clutter by putting my attention and action on it in the present moment."

Here's an example of this *focus* in my life (participating with my clutter by putting my attention and action on it in the present moment). I've been avoiding/procrastinating on decluttering my hall closet for a long, long time now—treating this hall closet like a recycle bin or catch-all by throwing/stuffing stuff in there for "later." (Later never happens, by the way...until now.) Later never happened, and it became so overstuffed that the closet doors no longer closed all the way, and I had absolutely no idea whatsoever what was in there anymore. I became afraid to deal with decluttering it and, by God, those little declutter fairies never did fly in to do anything about it.

So one day I resolved to focus and empty everything out to start discovering what was actually in this hall closet. Wow! It sucked!! It was like a big clutter jack-in-the box popping out and exploding into the larger space—a Mount Vesuvius-like profusion of bags of bags of bags poured and oozed out of the hall closet: trash bags of bags, smaller plastic grocery bags of bags, decorative gift sack bags of bags, fabric bags, gift wrap, and massive amounts of other fix-it kinds of stuff—flowed out of the hall closet. *Yuck!* Blech! I sat down and took a break. I had saved all these massive amounts of bags thinking I'd use them later; then I clearly totally had forgotten about them! Do I discard them or begin using them for actual trash until they're gone? I'm not sure yet; however, for now I've gathered them together in one smaller container to clean the closet so it is functional again and can actually fit my vacuum cleaner, mop, and cleaning supplies. By focusing and emptying (looking at what I emptied) and getting like with like while deciding what I'd do with what used to be in this space, I can declutter this project—my hall closet—to create the space that better supports my life. I'm delighted to share that, after a lot of focused decluttering and elbow grease, I now have a clean and far more tidy/decluttered hall closet. I totally celebrated the fact I could close the closet door, and it comfortably actually stayed closed. Woo hoo!

Focusing on *focus* as I gently declutter helps me make more supportive choices one bag o'bags, one moment, one hour, one day at a time. Emptying and focus are making a great difference in my recovery right now. Thanks CLA! ⬤

Holiday 2020
Alison B., NJ

It was time, as usual, for my yearly housing inspection. I promptly delayed it an extra two weeks so that now I had five weeks to either be nervous or take things one day at a time. I am an "all or nothing" kind of person, and it is usually a full-time job for me to keep my mental health in check—therefore, I do a bare minimum of maintenance because I can't seem to manage decluttering on a daily

basis. I also admit that I am powerless over my clutter. I have just started tracking my daily movements with a sponsor, and one thing I have noticed is that I go to a service meeting almost every day. However, I go to only one recovery meeting per week.

I love helping people in CLA—just not myself. But I digress...I started by promising myself I would go to the phone lines daily...and so every morning I was on the Divine Decluttering line at 10:30 a.m. Eastern Time. I liked it so much, but I would become mesmerized. I would stay on it most of the day and get one thing decluttered. Progress, I told myself.

Also, I would call and make daily commitments to a buddy. Then I would call back the next day and report on whether I had done them or not. Most of the time, especially in the beginning, this did not work for me; but I kept trying because I had to. I spent one week on the phone checking in on the half hour with a buddy for three hours every day. That was when I seemed to get the most done.

I started decluttering in the kitchen, where I sit most of the time. I looked around. I tried to picture my kitchen the way I wanted it to look. I took notes. Then I stood in the doorway and looked from a different angle. I broke it down into numbered, doable parts. I was able to shift, declutter, and clean in sections—and also clean out two entire cupboards. This was done very slowly. When I tried to scrub my stove and my sink and they weren't getting clean enough, I knew I needed help. I made a decision. I was going to hire a professional cleaning service.

But a cleaning service does not do all the work. I still had to declutter the other rooms so that they could clean easily and so that I would be comfortable letting them in. My apartment was not that cluttered—it was just single-layer surfaces, except for the spare room. My challenge was to get clutter off the floor. I did the best I could. I also managed to declutter the surfaces, but there is one surface that is now even more cluttered with supplies that I don't have storage space for...

Some evenings I would go on the 8 p.m. phone meeting and listen to it like a radio show while I decluttered—that worked for me. For some reason, I seem to work better in the evenings. I had to clean my bathroom before I felt comfortable letting the professionals, well, clean my bathroom. I bought the strongest cleaners I could find and did a little bit at a time. I did not bother to clean my tub because I have a back problem—and, after all, it was be-ing done for me. What a treat!

My living room/bedroom was in fairly good shape. I didn't have to do much.

So finally I ordered my cleaning crew of two to do a deep cleaning. They arrived the day before my inspection and stayed for four-and-a-half hours. They even cleaned my microwave, fridge, stove and sink for $30 extra. It was expensive but well worth it. They took away tons of dust! I know CLA has no position on outside issues, and I did feel like I was cheating. However, having an incentive like that helped me to declutter when I couldn't muster up the enthu-siasm, and I was completely and utterly exhausted and discouraged. Now I am in maintenance mode, and I feel like I have been on vaca-tion ever since! ◬

Focus on Decluttering

Summer 2021
Rosie, NY

As I continually work this pro-gram, the issue of fear versus trust always comes up for me when I have to declutter. For me, when I'm doing the physical declut-tering, I notice my mind clutter often boils down to whether my thoughts focus on fearful or trusting thoughts. My negative self-talk, thoughts that distort the value of objects and a lot of my resistance, very often come from when my fears win out over trusting in my Higher Power.

I'd like to share some questions that help me declutter by making me aware of the thoughts and mind clutter that get triggered by my physical clutter. In this way, I can see how my thinking and my beliefs are affecting my behavior. Before and during the action I take to declutter, I can look at my mind clutter by asking myself the following:

Do I release objects and trust in my Higher Power to provide me with what I need when I need it—or do I compulsively act out of fear and hold onto things I'm not using that don't support the life I want to live now?

Do I trust that my choices are guided by my Higher Power because I seek my Higher Power's guidance daily—or do I compulsively act out of fear and let my mind clutter keep me stuck in indecision?

Do I trust my Higher Power wants to bless me with a future that's beautifully fulfilling—or do I compulsively act out of fear and cling to objects from my past because I'm afraid to let go and move forward into the unknown?

Do I trust in my Higher Power that this program will work if I work it—or do I give up on my practice of willingness to change out of a fear of failure because I'm still trying to do it on my own? Do I trust my Higher Power will see me through this and bring good people into my life and my home, who accept me as I am—or do I hide in fear behind the clutter wall?

One thing I heard recently has been inspiring me to work through my mind clutter as I free myself from physical clutter—and I'm going to paraphrase what it said here: "When the clutter wall is no longer needed to hide behind, the wall will come down."

For me, that's freedom from fear and clutter. ▲

My Sewing Room Revisited

Holiday 2021
Kathy H., CA

Many years ago, while fairly new in CLA, I had decluttered and reorganized my sewing room. After that, it worked well for me for quite some time. However, due to my changing needs, as well as letting materials sit wherever, it had become somewhat cluttered once again. I knew I had to tackle the large task of decluttering and organizing it once again—but I was busy, so I let it sit.

Then things got worse. Mice moved into my house. I promptly purchased and set out glue traps, which had worked many years ago when I had had mice. I found a trap with tufts of fur stuck to it, but no mouse. So I purchased the old-fashioned spring-loaded traps. The mice removed the cheese without getting caught. In all, I tried four different types of traps, and caught only one small mouse. Finally, I resorted to poison, which I had not wanted to use. After a couple of weeks, all the mice were gone.

I had avoided going into the sewing room because I could hear that they were spending a lot of time in there. Those pesky critters had not only messed up what had been in the sewing room, they had also dragged items from other rooms to the sewing room and left them in the mess. Their droppings were everywhere, even in the folds of the fabric.

Once the mice were out of the picture, I got started on the sewing room. I spent an hour or two on it most days, and it took about a month to get it where I wanted it to be. After sweeping up mouse droppings off the floor, one of the first things I did was to gather all the fabric that was stacked up and wash it. What fabric I decided to keep got measured and marked and stored in the fabric cupboard, which is in another room. When I came across notions or tools, I set them aside for later.

Once the fabric was taken care of, I began to organize the cupboard, shelves, and drawers. I did one step that I had not done the first time. As I organized the room, I noted the contents on the outside of each drawer or box. This should help me when I have to find supplies or tools that are used occasionally—since one reason some of these had not been put away properly in the past is that I could not remember which compartment they were supposed to be in. Once the organization was complete, I put away all the notions and tools I had set aside.

I was able to release a lot of fabric, about one third of my sewing and craft books, and miscellaneous supplies and notions. These were given to the sewing and craft classes at the senior center. Everything now fits into its designated space, and I should be able to easily find what I need for sewing and craft projects again.

I could not have done this without CLA and my program buddies to lean on. Upon reflection, I realized that I used several of the Tools (including Buddies). I tried to work on it for at least a while every day (Daily Action). I shared my goals and successes with my home group and my co-sponsoring group (Meetings). I used the Tool of Bookending several times. I made a place for every item and put it in its designated place (Earmarking).

The work I was doing with my co-sponsoring group also helped. We have been working on Steps 5 and 6—and the reflection and soul-searching needed gave me some additional awareness of my procrastination issues that helped me to continue with the project—even when I just wanted to quit.

Thanks to CLA and the support of fellow members, I should be able to use my new functional sewing room without a major reorganizing effort for many years. ⬭

Various Articles on Clutter

Multigenerational Clutter

Spring 2017

Kat/Seven, NJ

From Legacy to Letting Go

This year brought more decluttering challenges to my life and home than I ever envisioned—pre- or post-CLA recovery. You see, I am my mother's legal guardian. She resides in a facility, occupying one large room. One large room needs very little to fill it. I share a two-bedroom condo with my son. One two-bedroom condo does not need much to fill it, either.

My mother has clutter issues. As far back as I can remember, she surrounded herself with paper—piles of it. As a teacher, she saved education articles, students' assignments, bulletin board construction designs; she even saved her teacher evaluations!

When I was a child, we spent most weekends shopping for… more. If it was on sale, Mom bought it. My childhood home was filled with the best of clearance racks, end-of-season specials, reduced-price clothing, unmatched furniture, and tabletop tchotchkes. Driven by childhood poverty, Mom stuffed every nook and cranny.

Fast forward: my dad died, my mom still shopped, then married my well-off stepdad. He bought a "McMansion" and—you guessed it—she filled that too. In 2004, he died. Two years later, she returned home, laden with new stuff, boxed stuff, and business stuff (she was a silk floral designer), adding to the stuff of her original house.

My mom has dementia. In 2013, I entered an uphill court battle and was awarded guardianship. The lawyer congratulated himself and me, but I knew this was not a "win" in any sense of the word. Now I was responsible not only for her, but for all her stuff. I was court-ordered to sell the house (owned for 55 years), disposing of its contents through auction, sale, donation, distribution to family members, or the trash. (Notice I said trash last. Do you know any clutterer who "tosses" things first?!) It took three years to empty my parents' house and sell it. What did not go relocated with me.

In 2010 I found decluttering help, but no matter how I tried, I could not get rid of stuff without replacing it in some way. Adding my mother's clutter to my own pushed me over another edge. Thankfully, six years ago, I found CLA.

As part of my healing process, I shared Step and Tradition writings with a partner. To help me avoid clutter behaviors, I also use the Tools and leaflets. I check in with a declutter buddy most days.

If I spend my time doing Step and Tradition writing, I am grounded spiritually but still sitting in clutter. If I only declutter, I am taking action but may not be connected to the healing God that fills the empty places in my heart. Real recovery balances the facets of my recovery: physical, mental, emotional, and spiritual. I integrate the Steps, Traditions, Tools, Literature, Writing, Prayer, and Action to move through the clutter.

In applying these principles to my parents' things, different emotions have surfaced.

I feel:

1. Guilt: I feel disloyal, as if I am rejecting my parents and relatives. I am not! I am letting go of things they do not use and I do not need.
2. Sadness: I reflect on my childhood. I release the items and cherish the memories.
3. Anger: I spend so much time with my mother's unending stream of stuff. Lesson: The sooner I let go of it, the quicker I reclaim my life.
4. Concern: What unhealthy messages do I send future generations? Do I want my son consumed with stuff? What legacy will I leave him—living

burdened by my clutter *or* living unencumbered? I hope he will be free. I hope to be free.

5. Shame: When people visit, I say "this stuff is Mom's," but my clutter lies beneath hers.

Can I say I am clutter free, that my mother's things no longer occupy my space? The dining and living rooms say otherwise. But I am in process—selling, donating, and giving stuff away. In another article, I will continue describing this process and my conflicting feelings as I let go. Multigenerational clutter is deeply rooted, more than a tug-of-war between stuff and me.

For today, I am:

a. Learning what to keep and what to release;
b. Answering the question "How important is it?" honestly, fairly, and practically;
c. Creating a clutter-free life vision, still respecting my parents' efforts;
d. Retaining the best values my parents taught me, letting go of those that once served them but no longer bring joy;
e. Defining abundance in ways that do not involve the number of shoes in my closet, filled bookshelves, or home décor; and
f. Being gifted spiritually by

finding meaning in relationships, interests, and connection to God.   ⬙

Giving Thanks for CLA Flexibility

Spring 2017
Kathy B., NY

The Telephone is one of CLA's Tools; using it can be very helpful in a clutterer's recovery. But this article shows a situation in which a member is sharing her phone number with only selected members.—Editor

I do not give my phone number during meetings because of previous phone trauma. I don't relish the idea of someone hearing something I share at a meeting and calling me with their idea of how I could solve that problem or improve my output or be more efficient, etc. I can tell myself all those things on my own.

Clutterers Anonymous is where I learned how to stop trying to be perfect. It's where I learned mistakes are not the end of the world. And if I no longer have to listen to myself tell me what I did wrong, (what I could have done better, how I should have done more), I don't see why I should have to listen to it from anyone else.

The "Decluttering Resentment[5]" leaflet says "We no longer need to fix anyone or prove them wrong....We don't need to fight

to prove that we can." So I am protecting myself from others who aren't in that place yet and still feel the need to "try to help."

When I hear myself say, "I am/was just trying to help," I say "Uh-oh." It's not my business. If someone asks what I would do or how I handle a situation, I tell them I ask my Higher Power. If I don't ask to be guided by Good Orderly Direction, I'm continuing the behavior, the mindset of the past—that I can (or have to) figure out what to do or how to do it or when. And I have proven my life is unmanageable when I try to control, so doing more of what I have done will get me more of what I have gotten—unmanageability!

I have listed the ways I have tried to control things—all the books, magazine articles, and seminars—shaming myself because I couldn't do it according to what worked for someone else.

But when I let go and ventured into the territory of "allowing myself to be led," I found more success, completed more projects, and no reason for shame. What works for someone else doesn't work for me. So what? I'm happy they found something that helps them. I no longer see myself as a failure! Shaming myself, blaming myself, and/or feeling guilty did nothing to accomplish change. In fact, I think part of my addiction was due to that brain chemistry. I did not know how to succeed. I did not know how to apply myself to a task.

CLA taught me to go against all I've ever done in the past. It tells me it's beneficial to "Celebrate all my victories, no matter how small." The small victories add up to larger ones. And my brain chemistry changes. It feels foreign and every so often I find myself in the old neighborhood, but now I know there is another way.

So I do not try to find the right street out of the dangerous neighborhood; I go up. I go straight up to my Higher Power. The helicopter is right there, dropping the ladder. I climb onto the rung of gratitude, and I'm on my way. ◢

At a Crossroads

Spring 2017
Ruthe S., PA

I am at a crossroads. I have spent the past 13 years in CLA decluttering, recluttering, and decluttering again. I have a second bedroom that has become a storage space (my husband has clutter in there, too), and I have storage spaces that I pay for, thus wasting money. I now understand how much I really hate clutter!

To be fair to myself, I have made tremendous progress in CLA. I have been able to stop picking up as much paper information as I used to. It has gotten easier to throw things out. I purchase fewer physical books and magazines than ever. I have been able to leave things in a store when I didn't really need them. I am better at putting things I need regularly in the same place, so I can locate them. I have been using files and other systems that work more than they don't. I no longer compulsively audiotape and videotape. I cancelled my subscription to the newspaper. I am able to get my hands on what I need quicker. I can miss things and not get as upset or for very long. At different times, I have been able to throw out or give away books, magazines, paper, food, broken or useless objects, makeup, and clothes that are old or don't fit. I have even started to declutter on a regular basis.

I understand clutter in a way that I never have before, and I truly believe that you have to get rid of the old in order to make room for the new. But I still have clutter. What is it that I'm missing?

How could I have worked on this for so long and still have a lot of/so much clutter? I have pondered this a lot during the past year. A piece of this is related to having ADHD and being in menopause, as I've heard that ADHD symptoms can get worse then. I have also not been attending meetings, calling people, and using our new leaflet, "Measuring Progress on Our Journey in Recovery[11]." But there is more to it than that. I have come to the conclusion that, although I am now more willing to part with things than ever, I am really not getting rid of enough. Our wonderful literature states that we should have faith that God will provide what we need when we need it, and I am not doing that.

I went to two meetings during the New Year's Eve Declutter-thon on the telephone. One of the speakers was talking about this very subject, and it clarified what I was already thinking. Having the faith that God will provide what I need when I need it means I have to get rid of everything I don't need or use. The speaker shared that she has done this and has had a transformation. Although I have used that phrase to help me declutter in the past, I never really made it a way of life. I see now that it is about turning it over to God. If I am keeping a lot of things, I am not doing that. All I am doing is trying to organize my clutter.

So it is time to take a leap of faith. I have learned that I will survive if I miss something. In fact, I usually move on to the next thing pretty quickly. Nothing will happen if I throw something out,

then need it later. If I lose or can't find something, which happens more than I would like, I will forget about it. I have learned these things in increments, and now it's time for it to become a way of life. I have to rid myself of everything I have been holding onto. I used to say that my life was under my piles, and I still believe that is true. This means that I don't try to look at everything; I just throw it out or give it away. If I haven't used it, worn it, or read it in the past year, I probably don't need to keep it. I have heard it said that "faith is the opposite of fear." It is time to live my life out of faith. And if I do that, then maybe one day my second bedroom will really be a second bedroom!   ▲

My Romantic Clutter

Holiday 2017
Anonymous

Most of us have experienced the heartbreak of a failed romance. Besides the emotional fallout from a breakup, we can be left with the physical reminders of our exes. For me, for example, that would be the necklace he gave me, the college t-shirt of his that he loved seeing me wear, the millions of photos of us on my phone, etc. All shared during happier times and now just memories.

As a clutterer, I already have enough trouble trying to decide what to do with the "things" of my life. But the physical leftovers from broken romances are double trouble. They are triggers that remind me of my latest ex-boyfriend and of love lost. Or, in a couple cases, they reminded me of how happy I was to be out of bad relationships. Ah, silver linings.

Yet the thought of getting rid of this clutter terrifies me. So I do what any good clutterer would do and hide it somewhere where I don't normally look, i.e., in a box at the back of the hall closet. It's an out-of-sight, out-of-mind approach that I've found to be quite helpful. As I haven't yet decided what to do with it, I'll call it "romantic clutter" for the purposes of this article.

The thing is that these sentimental things serve as proof that someone chose to be in a romantic relationship with me. And ultimately, it's visible proof that I'm lovable. The inherent problem with all this romantic clutter is that if I donate it or throw it away, I can literally *never get it back*, just like my exes. Of course, I don't want most of my exes back, nor can I ever get back the happy times when I got these things.

It's important to note that mind clutter may accompany this romantic clutter. I am referring to the messages I might tell myself during and after a breakup. Things like,

I'll never get over him...I'll never meet anyone else who will love and accept me like he did...He was the best I'll ever have...What will I do without him?...I blew it and now I'll be alone the rest of my life. And on and on. If and when I'm able to answer these questions with confident answers, i.e., I'm lovable and someone else will fall in love with me, then I'll leave this sort of clutter behind.

It's important to note that the loss and grieving a clutterer like me experiences probably isn't that much different from what a non-clutterer goes through after a breakup. As I can speak only for myself, I'm guessing that, as a clutterer, I might hang on to more of my romantic and mind clutter for longer than a non-clutterer would. But I've known plenty of non-clutterer friends who grieved their failed romances just as much as I have.

But being in love feels so good that I'm willing to look for it again, and I can already guess the name of my next CLA*rity* article: "Love as a Clutterer." Fingers crossed!   ◬

512 1/2 Boxes

Holiday 2017
Susan, OR

Hello, fellow Clutterers! While new to CLA, I have been a clutterer since I was a child, when my father told me that I could not go out to play until my desk was clear. After a quick thought, I found the perfect box, put everything from the top of my desk into that box, hid it in my closet, and went out to play! Fast forward to April 7, 2017. A neighbor's tree fell on our house and slid down the side, effectively shearing off our outdoor faucet.

I had already left for work, and when my husband returned from walking the dogs, water was spraying everywhere. He had to quickly turn off the water—which, unfortunately, was located in my over-crowded "Christmas closet." My husband had to quickly unload much of this stuff to reach the faucet turn-off knob.

If this were our only concern, there would be no story. The problem is that I also have stuff packed into the basement, spare room, office, etc. I learned at the convention that I am a "closet clutterer," as public parts of our home are free of boxes, just cluttered. My husband had had enough. He got on the computer, found several decluttering methods, e-mailed them to me, then called me at work and asked that I "pick one—starting tonight!" Luckily, I chose the Westside Center CLA meeting in Beaverton, where I immediately felt at home.

I learned about the 12 Steps, 12 Traditions, bookending, and so much more. Other people did not laugh at my confession of taking shampoo/conditioner and even used soap from hotel rooms.

After hearing about the CLA Convention, I felt encouraged to go. I skipped out of "kindergarten" and now feel I jumped into 2nd grade! I got in-depth explanations related to the 12 Steps and CLA program. I also connected with others who had similar issues or were ahead of me in their progress. Jane said she "unloaded 512 and ½ boxes" and had only about 100 to go—how encouraging is that? I love quotes like this one and heard many other great ones throughout the convention. I posted all of them together so all my fellow attendees could see them. So many people came up to copy them that I decided to share them in this article.

- Use it or lose it.
- Let go of the criticism, let go of the praise.
- Guilt leads to self-destruction. Pride leads to the destruction of others.
- Cluttering is a dis-ease.
- It is impossible to be grateful and resentful simultaneously.
- Don't just do something, stand there!
- Progress, not perfection.
- Work the program, not the

problem.

- The disease is progressive... but by the grace of God, we are all here because we are not all there.
- When you say "yes" to something, you say "no" to something else.
- I'm dating my clutter.
- What we resist, persists.
- People are more important than clutter.
- Do not bring in more than you can release.
- Staying in the solution, and not the problem, aids in our recovery.
- Create a Clutter Free Zone.
- Focus on what you want. What you focus on grows.
- The only one I can control is me.
- Use 12 Steps: Non-resistant, non-judgment, non-attachment.
- Regarding why we clutter, don't spend too much time on this. It does not matter why we do it, it is that we are doing it!
- Take pictures of clutter—before and after.
- If you are burning out decluttering, then the motivation might be wrong.
- Ask yourself what is the intended purpose of the room.
- Physical decluttering is different from emotional decluttering.
- Inside the will of God, there can't be any failure. Ask, "God, do you want me to own this?"
- Have God remove stuff. You are the pencil God has. Ask God for help, but you have to do the work you are directed to do.
- Hold on to the memory, not the object.
- I am grateful for this program.
- My home is transformed and I am transformed.
- Take a photo, let it go.
- Think of the 12 Steps every day. Do 12 focused minutes (for each of the 12 Steps).
- Ask yourself "How would a mature person handle this?"   ◬

Fermentation

Spring 2018
Terri J., OH

In my early days in CLA, I had a massive "clean out" of my clothes. But for whatever reason, the clothes did not get to the trunk of my car, the thrift store, or out of the house. Bags and boxes of my unloved clothes sat by the back door waiting for their new homes.

Out of the blue, a lightning bolt hit, and it occurred to me that I could easily and gracefully move bags and boxes of my old loves to the trunk of my car. I noticed this was easier than I had anticipated.

Somehow, in the corners of my cluttered and overwhelmed brain,

I realized that moving these old loves out of their usual home (my bedroom closet) to a different location in my basement created an easier release.

The idea of "fermenting" and moving things out of their somewhat earmarked positions does an energy shift, and helps make the releasing of clutter less painful.

I also experienced this in releasing items of deceased family members. I hurried to empty my childhood home in order to sell it before the Cleveland blizzards slowed down the real estate market in their usual way. Mom and Dad's house sold pretty quickly, but the sad news was that so did their garage and nooks that had held some of my overflow. I had to bring home my large ceramic tile saw, my pub table and four chairs, a few ladders, and many gallons of paint that had stayed warm and cozy in my parents' basement.

The bad news is family photos, tools, and houseware treasures have entered my present home from my childhood home. The good news is that I have the Tools[16] of the program and my CLA action partners and action lines to conquer this generational clutter. My fermenting process continues, and released items are leaving as I slowly detach from memories. I realize I can remember my parents' love without keeping every item they ever owned. ◬

Are You a Binge Declutterer?

Summer 2018
Sean M., HI

A fun and satisfying part of my CLA experience has been participating in the multiple day declutterthons we organize throughout the year on the telephone bridge. They are held mostly on consecutive days during American holiday weekends. I call in at the beginning of any one of these sessions at the start time and make a commitment to myself to stay on my speaker phone, muted, for this 5- or 6-hour time slot. Sometimes I will unmute and announce what I'm working on and how much progress or completion I am experiencing or perceiving. Listening to what others are doing is very motivating and enlightening.

These declutterthons are announced several days to weeks beforehand, so I usually plan to stay home for a couple of those days during that weekend to tackle a specific project or work on a specific area of my house that I want to maintain or change into something new. Sometimes I will prepare my food beforehand and spend a few of the declutterthon hours listening, relaxing, eating, and cleaning up after my meal before getting back to my planned decluttering project. This is a description of only what I sometimes do. There may be times I might listen and/or participate for only one of the session hours. I may not even have a planned action and just listen and become acquainted with other clutterers from around the world. There are no rules about having to stay on the phone line throughout the entire declutterthon or participate on multiple consecutive days. It's not a race. Easy does it.

So what I want to emphasize is that it's fun to push myself to focus on a multi-hour work session dedicated to fixing up an area of my house. It can be compared to taking a long-distance run where I turn around at some halfway point and have the energy and stamina to be able to comfortably run back to my starting point. It's an opportunity to discover who I am and what I am capable of doing. I treat this type of declutterthon work as a special occasion, a holiday. Playing the long game, what I find the most valuable is developing the ability to do a little each day in specific areas and work in a slow, steady, and consistent way.

I believe everyone may get bursts where we do more than we thought we could, surpassing expectations. Though far and wide, we are operating on a normal day-to-day rhythm, which may not be so energetic and/or efficient as these

rare instances. It's so important for me to have a realistic and humble vision of what I want and when it can be accomplished. During these declutterthon weekends, I discover more about myself and reality. I find that setting the bar comfortably low and slowly raising it is the way I can see and feel a joyful sense of progress away from an unmanageable, clutter-filled life. ⬕

Radical Decluttering

Holiday 2018
Wendy L., IL

It took the shock of learning I could have uterine cancer to jolt me into thinking about my clutter differently and more, well, radically.

While my immediate reaction to possibly having cancer was to wonder how my body could turn on me like that, it then occurred to me that my life could end prematurely. I was scared but didn't panic, as cancer is only one possible cause of my symptoms, and this type is usually very treatable.

As I considered my mortality, a few thoughts bubbled up. One, I don't want to spend nearly as much time decluttering as I am currently doing. Instead, I want to spend the rest of my (possibly shortened) life doing fun things, and I don't consider decluttering a fun thing to do. So I will need to find a more efficient way to deal with my clutter and/or try to avoid cluttering in the first place.

And two, that dating, and online dating, have basically become clutter, as they are taking up too much of my time and mental energy. None of the men I've dated in the last few years has worked out, so either I'm choosing the wrong men or I need to look more internally for the answers. Either way, I don't want to spend the rest of my time alive trying to date, so I've stopped online dating, at least for now.

Finally, I need to find a faster way to declutter so I can spend more time doing what makes me happy. Which is spending time with my friends and family and doing things like being out in nature, writing, etc., (while I'm still able to, that is).

Heck, maybe I should just clutter whenever I want to because I won't have to have to deal with my stuff once I'm gone. Okay, so that's pretty childish, plus I don't yet have a cancer diagnosis, and I hate having clutter around. So scratch that.

What I've finally decided to try is what I'll call radical decluttering. For example, the scrapbooks I've never filled will go, as will the purses I rarely use. No more saving coupons because I hardly ever actually use them. If I don't use my health club membership at least five times this month, I'll drop it.

All those pretty journals I've saved over the years but have barely written in will be donated, as will the books I own but have never read and know I probably never will.

Since I began writing this article, I learned that my biopsy results were negative, meaning I don't have uterine cancer. Although I still need a follow-up test, this great news is clearly a huge relief. But I still plan to try some radical decluttering, as I'm hoping it'll be good for me anyway. Of course, I haven't started yet because at the end of the day, I'm still a clutterer.

In my next CLA*rity* article, I'll report back on my progress. Until then, happy decluttering, and it was great to see those of you who made it to our CLA annual convention, held in my beautiful hometown of Chicago.   ◬

Radical Decluttering: The Saga Continues

Spring 2019
Wendy L., IL

In the last issue of CLA*rity*, I wrote an article called "Radical Decluttering" and promised that I'd report back on my progress. The following is my report.

Basically, I'd had a cancer scare that ended up not being cancer. But had it been the Big C, my potentially much-shorter life called for doing what I enjoyed, and decluttering definitely did not count. At that point, I couldn't have cared less about keeping those cute clothes that were still too small, or all those bank statements I'd been dutifully saving. Imagine the joy and naughtiness of shredding tax documents that were less than seven years old. It was supposed to be a sort of radical, mass decluttering that would leave me the time and space to live, laugh, and dance—as if no one was watching. I do that already, but at least now I won't run into my clutter.

As you can imagine, this approach didn't work. At all. You'd think I was being asked to give away some of my vital internal organs or, say, my mom. My sister, yes, but not my mom. Just kidding, but my point is that even in the face of death, clutter still had its steel grip on me. The silver lining was that it had caused me to ponder this sort of decluttering that I could still use, even in the face of, um, life.

My clutter is mostly paper and physical things, e.g., too many trinkets, jewelry, clothes, linens, pens, etc. I'm still experimenting with it, but here's what I've discovered so far. I've been able to throw away a couple boxes of old cards and letters, without much remorse. Most of the letter writers were people I haven't spoken to in years, and some went back to my preteens. Remorse scale: zero (for no remorse).

Now, throwing away a hat cleaning kit caused me quite a bit more angst than the card purge. The hat was relatively new, and the cleaning kit hadn't been cheap, nor had the hat. I actually fished the kit out of the recycle bin in the basement of my apartment building, I was so wracked with remorse. Literally, the only people who could possibly relate to this disturbing behavior would be other clutterers.

My people, like me, have also probably never thrown away a can of leather or suede protection spray, which was pretty much most of what the hat cleaning kit consisted of—although for felt, I think. Whose sick idea was it to invent this spray, that we pretty much use only once, if that? I started wondering whether vegan leather (pleather) also needs to be sprayed. Remorse scale: 10

Finally, and please don't tell them, but my neighbors recently left for warmer climes for the winter—three months. I was having company over and needed to get my boxes of clutter out of my home. Now, I'm only talking maybe four or five boxes and things. Yes, you can see where this is going, and I temporarily moved my stuff into their apartment. During the move, other neighbors saw it sitting out in the hallway and asked if I was moving. Nope, just, uh, moving things. Hmmm, did they know how to reach my next-door neighbors in Costa Rica? I thought irrationally. Nah, keep it moving, and I did. My home looked, and still looks, marvelous, and my friends next door are none the wiser.

Obviously, I'll move the boxes back in two months and 29 days. Ideally, I'll go through each box before it gets moved. Ideally…

Recently, my dentist gave me a mold of my mouth that he used for some dental work. Really?? Clearly, he'll only need it again if I throw it away. Obviously, and enviously, he's either not a clutterer, or he's a really good one. Remorse scale, for my dentist: 1,000,000

In closing, let me say that I just opened a fortune cookie in which this fortune appeared: "Your present plans are going to succeed." Obviously, that could apply to, literally, any of my plans, but, because of my timing, I'll take it to mean that I'll eventually sort through my moved boxes. Perhaps fortune cookies should be added to our CLA Tools of Recovery[16]? Seriously though, I'm determined not to have to bring those boxes back to my apartment.

To be continued, again, three months from now…   ◬

CLA, You Are Not Crazy

Holiday 2019
Anonymous

Why do I clutter? Why is it that when I see something I want it? Not only do I want it…I have to have it. That chair on the side of the street with a wiggly leg next to a trash can could be useful. It could be fixed, repainted, transformed into to an object d'art. It could be broken down and made into something entirely different.

All those clothes in clothing stores are must haves. They are on sale. They may never be that cheap again. Clothes don't spoil. Eventually every item will be worn or it will make a great gift.

At the grocery store, the sales are irresistible—2 for 1—and there are coupons on top of them. That is a great way to stock up and save money. Sales must be taken advantage of because money is tight nowadays and it is food, so of course I will use it.

Often, when I don't take advantage of a good deal or an item that may never, ever, anywhere on earth be available again, it makes me feel physically sick.

What in the hey-all is wrong with me?! My brother and dad hardly ever bought anything. Once my brother used cardboard boxes for end tables for two years, waiting for the perfect end tables, and then instead of buying them moved to where he didn't need them.

I have had a theory that I am pretty sure would be backed up by known history and science. People who clutter or people like me (who are on the hoarder side) are experiencing a natural inclination.

When we humans were running wild in the woods, each person had a purpose. Some were hunters. They went out and brought their tribe food. They stalked, trapped, and killed meat and fish for their clans to eat and provided the animal hides used for warmth and shelter. They traveled light because speed of movement was important in hunting and for safety. While out on their treks, they looked for where the food was in order to remember where to return.

Others were gatherers. They explored the world looking for things of use to maintain life and to make life more comfortable; or they gathered food growing on the ground, on trees, and on bushes. They brought their people berries, nuts, fruits, vegetables, and wood for fires and branches to make shelters.

Others were the nesters. They collected anything and everything they could to make comfortable homes. They made warm beds, shelters safe from animals and weather, and areas to protect and prepare food and water. They were the savers, who saved things to make sure all their clan's needs were met. Eventually, they began to collect the luxuries—the things that made life more enjoyable, like pretty things and comfortable things.

We human beings are hardwired to hunt, to gather, to save, and to nest. Those of us who are clutterers embody all of these basic human tendencies for survival of our species, and it's thriving on our beautiful planet of endless abundance. But as we now know, we no longer need to do these things to survive, and this creates our problem.

A member pointed out that originally one of the reasons we couldn't accumulate too many possessions was because we couldn't move them easily. We had to carry what we owned by hand or in a cart or, at best, a wagon. We didn't drag around unnecessary things. We regularly had to move to find food, work, or safety.

Also, at one time we could not afford enough things to clutter our lives. Now there is a dollar store, thrift store, or the endless bounty of castoffs on the curb to keep even the poorest of us in homes full of unnecessary possessions.

I am poor; I know for a fact that is true. So what to do? Purge the unnecessary so we can clear and clean the way to enjoy and use the things we need and love. Fortunately there is a program to help us do that, and it is called CLA, Clutterers Anonymous. Don't worry, you are not alone in your struggle. Together we can help each other clean house.   ⬖

A Reformed Lifelong Clutterer

Spring 2021
Sheryl B., MI

I am a lifelong clutterer! I have a picture of my bedroom when I was ten. My unmade bed is covered with junk, and clothes are hanging from my dresser drawers. An old radio from the trash sits on the floor. If I tried to clean, I usually got distracted and never finished. My mom was too busy to realize that I didn't know how to be organized. In my family, I was "the slob," and I accepted that in the same way I accepted having brown hair.

Not only was my bedroom a mess, but so was my desk at school and, later, my locker and dorm room. When I bought a house, I continued my messy, disorganized ways. I used to mow the lawn with a flashlight at 11:00 p.m. because I never planned anything, and I procrastinated on anything I disliked doing. To me, lawn mowing was right up there with laundry.

I married at thirty; and after my honeymoon, I handed my husband my paycheck, saying I never wanted to see it again unless he was dead. I don't know how many of you have been asked (very nicely) to leave a bank, but I had already—twice!

Being married helped me realize that I was helpless to change my ways; my efforts were met with failure over and over. I had small children, and when my grandma visited, I'd use a leaf rake to make a path through the toys to her favorite chair.

My husband, who ran a child welfare agency, would come home at noon, look around, and say, "Sheryl, two out of three Protective Service workers would let you keep your children."

As the kids grew older, I wanted to get involved in our new community. Since failure in housekeeping wasn't something I could control, I decided to "Play to your strengths!" Do what you do well, and forget about the other stuff!

As president of a disability group, I was sent a $7,000 check, which I promptly lost. The money was needed for campers, and I knew I had a snowball's chance in hell of finding it, so I called the nonprofit organization it came from and had it reissued. They asked that I bring it in when I found it, which I did—eight months later!

I had 35 books on cleaning by age 40. My 70 year-old neighbor said, "Sheryl, if you spent a quarter of the time doing the cleaning that you spend reading about cleaning, you'd get ahead!" Good advice, but—like all good clutterers—where would I begin? I knew I couldn't win at this thing. If anyone was coming into my house, I'd always say, "I'd apologize for the mess, but the next time you come, it could be worse! Then you'd think I was either insincere or a liar!"

Life went on, and nothing changed. I worked full time. I never did correspondence. I never finished projects. I was bored by the monotony of laundry, cooking, cleaning, or paperwork. Every surface was covered in clutter, and the floor was an obstacle course. I became sick of it.

When I retired, I decided I was not leaving this mess for my kids to sift through after my death. Since I had over 2,000 books, I decided to go through those first.

In October 2019, I found a little book which opened with "What makes A.A. work? The first thing is to have a revulsion against myself and my way of living." Wow! That's how I feel about being a slob! I wondered if someone had applied these A.A. principles to being disorganized.

On the internet, I quickly found CLA! I listened to the phone meetings. I read the literature and offered to do service. I had been close to God since childhood, and He had helped me countless times. But I never knew that He wanted me to live a life of order! I knew He'd urged me to do things many times, but I'd ignored that voice. I knew if I asked, He would tell me in a quiet, inner way what I had to do. And now, finally—I was ready to listen!

As I write this, I'm sitting in a neat and orderly living room. It's only one room, but it gives me hope. Someday, I'm sure that everything in my home will have a place, and I will live in peace and order the way God intended. I am very thankful that God has led me to CLA! △

Moving at Last!

Summer 2021
Betsey K., NJ

One of the most stressful experiences in the life of a clutterer is moving to a new home. When I moved out of my parents' home at age 25, my mother said, "This is the easiest move you'll ever make." The truth of her statement has become even more evident over the years.

More than a year ago, I decided to sell my very cluttered house and move to a continuing care retirement community. I put down a deposit in January 2020 and was hoping to move in on June 1. I was on vacation for the month of February, and when I returned in March, I was ready to start preparing the house for sale. I had lived there for 47 years, and my son had lived there for his entire life (45 years). He had even more clutter than I did.

Just as I was about to start the process with a downsizer, whose services were provided by my new community, the pandemic shut everything down. Ordinarily I would have been able to donate many things to my church's annual sale, but it was canceled. I was able to donate some items to other charitable organizations but had to throw out a couple truckloads of clutter, and on many garbage collection days put out a dozen or more large bags. It was amazing how much I was able to get rid of.

One week in July, a crew of teenagers and adults from my church came over and did a lot of work outdoors. There were six people at the beginning of the week, but there were twice as many by the end of the week as other crews completed their assignments. The place had never looked so good! They even cleaned out the garage, which was already cluttered when my husband and I moved in 47 years ago.

By August, my new apartment was ready, and I could have moved in; however, I needed the proceeds to pay my apartment entrance fee. Two months later, they allowed me to move in when I paid an additional deposit. I moved in two days before Thanksgiving. Selling the house was not easy. There were many complications, but the closing finally happened at the end of March.

I am working hard to keep my new apartment from getting cluttered. My biggest problem these days is paper clutter, and I need to use the CLA Tool of Daily Action to make sure I put things away before they get a chance to pile up. That way I should be able to find them when I need them.

I have often been asked how I like it here in my new apartment. I say, "What's not to like? I don't have to cook, I don't have to clean, and I don't have to nag my son to mow the lawn or rake the leaves." There are many amenities and activities here. And I will never have to move again! ◭

What Does the Beginning of Recovery Look Like?

Summer 2021
Sheryl B., MI

This is new for me since I've been in CLA for only a year, but

I still want to tell others who may just be starting down this road, too, about my beginning of recovery.

I am able to accomplish things now that before I would never have thought even possible! Clutter had robbed me of my initiative and any ambition. I could never get up the gumption to start working on the simplest task. I would look around myself, shaking my head and think, "Where to begin?" or "Why bother?"

Now I can do things. I can clean off a table (even if it takes three days!). I can make an appointment. I can even finish the laundry. I may even start a new creative pursuit now, without the fear that it will wreck the beginnings of my new-found peace and order.

I understand what God wants for me—to have life and to have it abundantly. Thank you, God! Thank you, CLA! ⬮

Nonphysical Clutter

Emergency Versus Peaceful Routine

Fall 2018 and Spring 2019
Sarah L., NY

I recently returned to CLA after a several-year break. I had begun working the Steps with a sponsor. As a result of a renewed relationship with my Higher Power, I was changing my mindset and outlook towards clutter. One of the messages/thoughts that came to me was that "life does not have to be an emergency every day." By this, I meant that things like laundry, supper, and bedtime come around regularly and are not necessarily an emergency every day.

One day as I was coming home from the supermarket at 6:00 with raw food to cook for supper, I was having the thought, "life does not have to be an emergency every day." I wondered why supper wasn't ready already and why I was starting to cook so late. My life that night felt like a mini-emergency. Then I had another thought and came to the realization that all I'm hearing is the word "emergency," and it is subconsciously giving me a message that life is an emergency every day. I had the idea that, rather than using the word "emergency," I should try to state it in the positive.

After some contemplation, I came up with, "Life can be a peaceful and calm routine (a safe haven), where needs are predicted, anticipated, and expected. Needs are proactively met."

I see this as a hierarchy of three levels:

1. Predict the needs. This means that if I needed to eat supper yesterday, predictably, I will need to eat again today.

2. Anticipate needs. Anticipation is a level higher than prediction and connotes a positive sense of looking forward to the need.

3. Expect the need. This means having a readiness and pre-paredness. I am looking forward to meeting the need because I am ready for it. It connotes calm and serenity.

This was a paradigm shift for me, that I could proactively meet regularly recurring needs like supper and laundry for myself. I could plan and take action each day to meet expected needs so that life would not be an emergency every day, but rather one of peaceful and calm routines that foster serenity.

This analogy to an emergency was especially poignant because I had spent three-and-a-half years caring for my elderly father, who was not well. (I had regularly cooked for him but was not so good at caring for myself.) This was true, especially in the last year of his life, when he was in and out of hospitals, had many visits to the emergency room, and spent six weeks in the ICU with several life-threatening situations occurring there.

My father passed away this past November. I am adjusting to a new life, where life is not an emergency every day, but rather can become one of calm and peaceful routines.   ▲

Living Within Our Means

Fall 2018

Barbara B.

One of our recovery affirmations[17] says, "I set reasonable goals, remembering that my first priority is my well-being." I have been thinking about how this affirmation might apply to our Fellowship as a whole.

Are we planning more events than we have the resources to pull off serenely? Are we leaning heavily on a few members? By our actions and inactions are we creating fertile ground for caretaking, control, dependence, laziness or negativity to take root?

Do we put the values of serenity and inclusion ahead of getting things done? Is each of us willing to do our part so that newcomers can see how physical, emotional and spiritual recovery are compatible with getting enough done so that the Fellowship can function?

Finally, I am left with a wise question I heard at a meeting: What is the most loving, life-giving action I can take right now?   ▲

Automatic Thought Patterns

Summer 2019
Dody W., PA

When doing a 4th-Step personal inventory some time ago, I discovered that I had a whole new area of mind clutter that was undermining my progress: my core beliefs and automatic thought patterns. I discovered these when I was doing a 4th-Step inventory on time clutter. I began asking myself why my schedule always seemed too packed. I soon realized that I had some automatic thought patterns that were telling me what I ought or ought not to do. I had recently been trying to release activities and obligations which were exacting a cost to my self-care but without much success.

My "shoulds" and "oughts" probably formed at an early age, and many of them were interfering with my progress with both physical and nonphysical decluttering. Here are some examples:

- If Mary—an 87-year-old chronically ill homebound friend—has a need, I should try to meet that need ASAP. (Yes, I "should" on myself.)

- If someone invites me to do something new and novel, I should say "yes," or my world could become smaller and smaller.

Pride and fear are at the root of so many of my flawed beliefs. In regards to my friend Mary, I hate to admit how much of my prideful self is wrapped up in being so indispensable. Unfortunately, I've caught myself having a God complex far too often. For the second example, not wanting to refuse an invitation is obviously FOMO, Fear Of Missing Out.

My inventory also revealed my fear of feeling guilty. I often avoid releasing items that I don't really like because they have some use left in them and I don't want to feel guilty. A significant portion of my time clutter resulted from my hyperfunctioning in many areas so that I could avoid guilt from "not doing enough."

I am doing my 10th Step now, so I am forming the habit of "spot checks" and being open for solutions to be free of these negative patterns.

I try to nonjudgmentally observe any nonverbal negative narratives about myself or others that are going on in my mind beneath the surface. If one pops up, I try to ask most of the following questions: "Why did I have this thought? Do I really believe it's true? Why or why not? How does this thought or narrative serve me? Does it hinder or enhance my recovery? Does it keep me in my familiar habits of pride or fear? What would I say to a treasured friend to help them succeed?

A person in recovery will grow in the capacity to not believe their mind's stories right away.

The 12-Step recovery slogan "Think it Through" has also been very helpful to me in this matter.

We are advised in *Alcoholics Anonymous*[1] (known as the Big Book), p. 84, to "Continue to watch for selfishness, dishonesty, resentment, and fear. When these crop up, we ask God at once to remove them."

Wise teachers from different cultures have observed that we will get more of whatever we focus upon. Allowing negative narratives to make a home in our minds attracts more negative thoughts, making reversing their course much harder. Antidotes to negative thinking could include meditating on our affirmations[17], expressing thanks for five different things, situations, or people, and as often as you remember throughout the day every day.

It is also important to remember that not all of our automatic thoughts are negative and to acknowledge the ones you have that you are happy about and align with your values. I have a core belief I think is true, and it also helps me in preventing resentments, and that is that every person, including me, is created in the image of God and has infinite worth and dignity. We are God's children and loved beyond our comprehension.

I feel so grateful for the blessings of this simple program and all of our members who are so different from one another and have so much in common!   ◒

Recovery Stories

Recovery from cluttering can be many-faceted: recovery from both physical and nonphysical clutter. This section deals with recovery in CLA not covered in other sections. It contains two categories: Qualifications and articles that appeared in the "Recovery Moments" column of CLA*rity*.

Qualifications

My Qualification–My Journey With Clutter

Spring 2017
Kathy H., CA

I didn't grow up with parents who cluttered, nor did I grow up in an abusive family. I have only myself to blame for my cluttering.

When I think about reasons why I began cluttering, they come down to two main ones: procrastination and a desire to avoid boredom. When I lived at my parents' house, I hated to have to stop an activity to clean or do other chores. I remember telling myself that when I was an adult and lived on my own, I would do the chores at a time that suited me. Of course, I envisioned myself as maintaining a clean, attractive living space. I never realized how procrastinating would negatively impact that vision.

Fast forward in time. My apartments were always messy. When I was younger, I would take a few hours on the weekend to do household chores, and it would be passable—although I never really maintained the standards I would have liked.

By the time I'd decided to move from the apartment where I had lived for about 20 years, it would have taken weeks to clean it up. My procrastination had led me to a place where it was just too overwhelming to tackle.

About 17 years ago, I bought a mobile home—and for the first

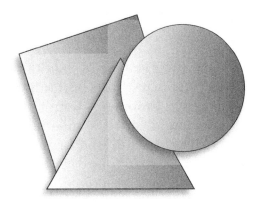

time, I lived in a place that was totally mine, that I could change and rebuild as I wished. I was so happy about my new situation, and I remember telling myself that I was not going to mess it up as I had done to all my other homes. I was all unpacked and moved in within two weeks.

Two years later, my home was even more cluttered than any previous abode. I seemed unable to get the motivation to take care of it—which sent me into a big depression. I had hit bottom.

That is when I came to CLA. While I made minimal progress in decluttering for the first couple of years, I did find ease by going to CLA recovery meetings.

It was when I began doing more service at the World Service level, attending Clutter-Free Days, and listening to more members' shares, that I was finally able to make major progress in decluttering my home. My progress has not been smooth. Sometimes, I seem to be on fire and do a lot of decluttering. Other times, I can barely keep up with the maintenance—but, at least, when I do that, the clutter doesn't get worse.

I did have a CLA sponsor for a while, but I am currently without one and need to find another—especially since I feel the need to do another deep working of the Steps. But I do try to keep the Steps in

mind in my life, and I follow what my previous sponsor told me. Upon retiring, I review my day and particularly think on whether I need to make any amends. Upon awakening, I review my plans for that day.

I use all of our CLA Tools of Recovery[16], but the ones that have been the most helpful are Sponsorship, Buddies, Bookending, and Daily Action. In fact, Daily Action has been the biggest reason for my success in decluttering. I am trying to set the habits that lead to my success, and that takes daily effort. If I miss a day, I try not to beat myself up over it but, instead, work on getting back into the swing of things the next day. I am trying to beat the demon in my life—procrastination.

I still struggle with maintenance. But there is not much clutter left, although I still have the need to take care of it every day, or my stuff will start piling up again.   ⬘

My Qualification

Spring 2019
Ruthe S., PA

When I was younger, I didn't understand that I had a problem with clutter. I thought I wasn't cleaning up because I wanted to go out and have fun, and I figured that I would do it "one day." I also thought it might be a reaction to my pathologically neat mother. It wasn't until I started in recovery that I realized I had a problem. I started in CLA in November of 2003.

I started with the nonphysical clutter. I had a lot of mental compulsions that were keeping me stuck and led to physical clutter. I couldn't stop getting the newspaper because I was afraid I would miss something. I taped television shows because I was afraid that if I had a bad time, I would be upset that I hadn't stayed home to watch them. If I was invited to more than one event in the same day, I would go to all of them because I was afraid I would make a mistake and attend the wrong event. I would attend the same events year after year and couldn't miss them because I was afraid to stop. I was addicted to information, which led me to buy many books and magazines on the same topics. I was stuck in a box and had no freedom to move.

I now understand that I was afraid because I didn't know how to deal with the disappointment, upset, sadness, and anger that might come up around missing something or making a "wrong" choice. I was trying to manage everything in order to avoid these feelings.

I was able to stop these behaviors a little bit at a time. I book-ended my actions. I started to notice that I didn't get upset when I didn't receive the newspaper or miss a show. I also began to realize that after I got rid of something, I barely thought about it. I was on to the next thing. This gave me the courage to keep going. It took some time, but eventually I was able to stop those behaviors.

After I dealt with the nonphysical clutter, there was a family emergency that ended up being an ongoing crisis. I did some decluttering, but it was challenging. I've heard it said that all clutter is unmade decisions. I have to decide what to keep and what to throw or give away. These decisions are difficult for me under normal circumstances, and they are even harder when I am under stress, and I was under a lot of it. This is why, although I have been in CLA for 15 years, I am not completely done decluttering.

After I got through the worst of the crisis, I began seriously decluttering physically. I have done some of it on our Divine Decluttering activity session and some with help from a professional organizer. (CLA has no opinion on professional organizers.) This organizer had training in chronic disorganization (which is what our illness is called professionally) and understood that I had to be the one to make the decisions about what goes and what stays. She is there to consult with and to help me figure out how to organize. I have been seriously decluttering for a year and a few months. I have made tremendous progress, and it is wonderful to see so much open space in my apartment.

Releasing the nonphysical clutter gave me more space in my brain to know what I was feeling and thinking. Releasing the physical clutter has allowed me to start to know who I am and start to live my dreams. Most importantly, I am a happier person, and I feel good about myself.

CLA is an amazing program. Meetings have shown me that I am not alone. In them, I have found "action partners" to book-end with. I have also heard people talk about things that I have never heard people talk about before. Our literature is amazing. It is where I learned the idea to have faith that God would provide what I need when I need it. I have held many service positions over the years. This has allowed me to fulfill the purpose of our Fellowship—to help the clutterer who still suffers, and it has also brought me friends in this Fellowship. Our action lines have helped because I can declutter with others, which is very supportive.

And, of course, the Steps. The Steps are the foundation of our program. I have been in a Step group, and we have delved much deeper into the Steps than I have ever done before. I am learning so much about myself. We don't have a lot of sponsors in CLA, and by working the Steps in a group, I will be able to be a sponsor when I am done.

There are no words for how I feel about CLA. I have met so many wonderful people and continue to learn so much about myself. I now see that being a clutterer was a blessing in disguise.   ◔

My Qualification

Fall and Holiday 2019
Laura Z., NY

A friend had told me about a declutterthon, and I called into it in November 2016. What spoke to me was the literature that was read. This is how I came to Clutterers Anonymous.

What I heard was a spiritual solution. Who knew there was one for this problem? I never thought of it, and I am in other 12-Step programs. The fact that I didn't think of it speaks to me very clearly of the nature of the illness. The powerlessness and unmanageability of this illness is real.

Had this been a problem only of collecting too many things, being messy, not organizing or cleaning well enough, or not knowing how to do these things, I would not have needed a spiritual solution.

In the course of my life I tried various tools, read self-help books, even sought outside help. The process of change that I have embarked on in CLA is a journey I never could have imagined. For me, the clutter and disturbance in my home and life are the symptoms that drew me to call into that declutterthon. But my need was beyond that. I felt hopeless about what I saw around me and, above all, had an overpowering shame.

My mother had died in 2015. I brought some of her furniture to my home. I already had enough furniture for my needs. The extra furniture caused me to feel powerless in itself. Over time, I accommodated things but did not give anything away. Beyond that were the boxes in the living room, papers, and more. My powerlessness partly was in hanging onto these things, thinking if I had them, I had a piece of my mother. She was my friend and I had lost her, my only relationship with immediate family. It was one we both worked at, and it had grown out of that mutual effort. It was special but the things I brought are just that, they are things.

I had been here and lived with boxes, walking on a carpet of papers, and it had been very painful and difficult. Over the years, I coped with my cluttering by having a cleaning person. Although I had in the past kept my home clean, I had noticed I would clutter it up at stressful times. Then there came a time that I was unable to recover from. The cleaning person took away my responsibility in this. She picked up my clothes, did the dishes, and cleaned. This kept me functioning. It didn't do anything for the clutter. Boxes and piles she did not fix.

I came to CLA five months after the cleaning person quit. I had retired from my job and had to limit my expenses. I was unwilling to have the cleaning person cut corners. I wanted more from her, and she was unwilling to do it. I see my generosity and willingness to settle for less than adequate work as part of my illness. Even after 20 years, each time she came I felt tremendous shame. So this is why I came to CLA. I used to be able to care for myself and my home, but I had become dependent on someone else to do it, and now I couldn't. How could I have done this to myself? Why don't I care enough for myself?

I called into a phone meeting. I felt desperate. There was no one to lead the meeting. I was scared there would be no meeting! So I volunteered to lead that meeting for three months.

Service is the first Tool for a reason. People were generous and helped me. I found by doing this service, the shame was lifted. Activity lines did not work for me. I couldn't trust myself to do what I said I would. I was powerless. I had no ability to be trusted, to trust myself to take action, never mind not knowing where to start! So I listened in meetings and began to pray, asking for guidance as to how to begin. I had to do what I truly was led to take on but not procrastinate. How to do this?

The literature was especially meaningful, giving me permission to be where I was, to take things on as I became able and willing, to give me comfort that I am not a shameful and lazy person who just doesn't want to take care of responsibilities that for other people are a matter of routine. As I listened and read, I kept my mind and heart open to the guidance as to how to do this new program. Here is what happened. I have learned that all action I take comes as a result of a spiritual process for me. I had so much shame that I could not take action. What emerged for me was the healing of the shame as a result of meetings and contact with other clutterers. Only then was I able to start taking action.

I put my desires, goals, and visions in my HP's hands. I left them there and remained open to guidance. I was led to establishing maintenance habits. This is where I started; not with piles or furniture but with the question: how do I live? I began using mindfulness in mundane activities. This helped me to take actions. I began listening to my feelings, conflicts and fears, letting them give me information to give my HP about the roadblocks I had previously experienced. I began to trust the guidance as to how and when I would be able to take action. I was grateful for where I was and gave myself the peace of mind to let go of where I "should" be.

I started trusting and giving to HP what I could not yet do.

I gave to my HP my inability to plan ahead for events, my lack of follow through on projects, and my inability to work towards my goals. My ability to plan became more logical. I was able to get things done on my list by allowing myself the dignity of choice. I began to experience spiritual timing. A wonderful example of this process came to me in the area of the kitchen, the dishes, the counters and using the kitchen. The sink was full, counters piled high, and I had not cooked in years. I used the microwave and got out of there as soon as possible.

Here and there I would clear everything; this in itself came only as a process of whittling down the counter clutter, thanks to CLA, but I couldn't sustain it. I kept putting the sink, dishes and counters on my list and never taking the actions. I finally decided what belonged on my list was to give the kitchen to my HP. I meditated and prayed on this. This was my action. So I kept putting the kitchen in my HP's hands. An opportunity came up to go to a Clutter-Free Day and give service. I showed up, did my service, I listened, I was present, a different experience than my previous Clutter-Free Day. The following week I cleared the sink, put the dishes in the dishwasher, cleared and cleaned the counters. I felt strongly that I would keep this up. I really have kept up with the dishes and counters. I have even done a little cooking. It's not been perfect, but I have not let things get to the level I had before. This is a miracle.

As a result of this miracle, I decided to go to the CLA Convention. If showing up and doing service while praying and meditating on a project or action I am unable to take—and bringing it to a Clutter-Free Day—gave me that miracle, can you imagine what can happen as a result of bringing it to a convention? And I signed up to give service. This is truly amazing; I am most grateful! ⧫

Holiday 2020 and Spring 2021
Doris D., NY

I looked up a definition for the word "qualification": a quality or accomplishment that makes someone suitable for a particular job or activity. The word, when defined, made me even more uncomfortable, but here I am with my story.

I came into the loving arms of the CLA Fellowship on August 20, 2018. My life was totally out of control: financially, physically, and emotionally. The only constant was that my spiritual life was intact, as I had a strong belief in a power greater than me, God.

In May, I drove to Florida to take part in a cruise that would go to Cuba for a couple of days. I travelled with my (former) professional medical group and earned continuing education credits as well. Really, I just wanted to see Cuba. On the drive back to New York, I had planned a stop in Daytona Beach for a two-day seminar for my professional certifications. I never made it to Daytona Beach— for after the cruise, I got into a terrible car accident which totaled my car. How could I have risked anyone's life on the road by my inattentiveness? I wondered what had distracted me, while at the same time thanking God no one was injured. How out of control had I been and what happened? Did I momentarily black out? I had no clue, but I was devastated. By the grace of God, both driver and passenger walked away without a scratch. Unbeknownst to me, this was to be a life-changing event.

With the money from the insurance company, I bought a used car and drove it back to New York. I didn't realize how out of control my life was until I got home. I found out I was six months behind in rent! My landlady laid into me. I was shocked and ashamed. I had been blinded by the density of the clutter fog I had been living in. I went on a cruise and drove to Florida without paying rent for six months! It took me a year to catch up on my rent! I now have been paying the rent in advance of the due date for the past four months.

Five months after the accident, I joined CLA, and that was the beginning of my long journey into recovery. A journey to where, truthfully, I saw no hint or glimmer of light at the end of the tunnel. Still, I knew I needed help, and so I faithfully began attending the five face-to-face meetings in New York. After about a month, I learned about the nightly phone meetings, started attending, and volunteered to moderate three of them—sort of a total immersion, I guess. As winter began, I began to drop off from some of the face-to-face meetings.

By Thanksgiving, I was almost exclusively attending the nightly meetings because of the cold weather. Also, I wasn't finding a comfort zone or potential sponsors at any meetings. I decided not to visit my family in Michigan for Christmas. Instead, I volunteered my service to moderate for the month of December to give other CLA members a Christmas vacation. "Service" was the keyword and the mantra that I heard from the beginning of my joining CLA. Moderating was the best experience I had. I know it gave me back so much more than I gave.

I received an unexpected invitation to stay for three months in Costa Rica as a family houseguest. After discussing it with program people, I accepted this offer from my hostess, who said "Just get the airfare and come," even though I was still playing catchup with my rent.

During those three months, while I was off in Costa Rica, my CLA recovery was on hold. I read CLA and A.A. literature—although the A.A. literature became irrelevant to me. All I did was maintain a watchful eye on myself for purchasing "stuff." I basically lost my recovery momentum while I was there. At the end of May when I returned to New York, it was like starting all over. I couldn't get my footing for several months.

My thinking was disjointed; I was feeling disconnected with CLA; and my home was cluttered.

I returned to my home with sugarplums dancing in my head about Costa Rica's countryside, animal life, and experience of microclimates and volcanoes. I was wishing "clutter fairies" would get to work and free me of my clutter, so I could figure out how to get back to Costa Rica and reside there for a spell. But, alas, no "clutter fairies" came to my rescue. So I floundered, depressed, doing nothing constructive for days, weeks, months. I wallowed in my clutter, participating minimally as a moderator during a couple of holiday declutterthons, so unlike my previous enthusiastic participation… clearly, I had lost my way. However, after a time, I did make myself go back to the face-to-face and nightly recovery meetings while I continued searching for a sponsor. I was hoping to find someone who could explain to me this spiritual program of CLA.

My search for a sponsor continued to elude me. None of those 5- to 10- to 20-year CLA veterans that I was meeting in face-to-face meetings were interested in being sponsors. Then one bright evening in January, I heard a familiar voice on the 8 p.m. recovery line say something about the Steps that helped me understand. I began to see a glimmer of light at the end of the tunnel.

After calling and talking to him the next day, I knew immediately that he was the one I wanted as a sponsor. So, stammering, unsure of myself, I asked him if he would sponsor me—and he said yes. "When the student is ready, the teacher will appear," as the saying goes, and that is exactly what I experienced in that encounter.

It marked the beginning of my journey through that tunnel of recovery and personal transformation through a 12-Step program.

I couldn't believe that someone would take me so seriously and was willing to help me: I did not know then that my addiction was and is to the unloving and negative thoughts I harbored all my life against myself. I couldn't believe I was worthy of such care and consideration. My addiction was not about the clutter. Clutter is just a symptom of my lack of love of myself and lack of love in my life.

My sponsor asked of me only one thing—that I call him once a day. I jumped at the chance because he wasn't a stranger. I felt comfortable with him. We had corresponded and occasionally talked on the phone in the past. He had even sent me recovery literature. I knew it was a good fit.

After he took me on as a sponsee, I saw that he continued to speak truths to my questions and gradually began to shed light into my darkened, cluttered mind… the fog was beginning to lift. Yet, admittedly, I didn't understand a lot of what he said. Oh, so many times he had to repeat himself, and he did so, time and time again, without rancor or judgment, and always with patience. He seemed to anticipate what I couldn't understand or immediately grasp and knew just why I couldn't grasp the meaning of the words he sometimes said. Still, no matter how long we talked, his only request was that I call him daily. When I didn't call him, I felt like I was a child playing "hooky" skipping away from school.

One day he said in a very, very serious tone that I needed to be calling him every day. At that moment, I knew he meant business and that he was seriously concerned with my welfare. I realized instantly that I was being disrespectful, as I wasn't holding up my end of the bargain and, yes, I needed to call him every day if he was going to be my sponsor. After all, I was the one who had asked him to help me. So I darn well better do what he told me! And, for the record, I did not resent him "pulling me up short" about calling him every day. No, I needed to know why we were talking. I had to be reminded just why I asked

for help. It is, as he said, "recovery is serious business, life is play." And, if I was going to get well, I needed to honor his only request, call him every day. He never had to say that to me again, as I have called him faithfully every day, except for one day, when my family was in town. Each time I called him after that, I called in gratitude. I knew just how much he cared about my recovery and was there for me. Yet, of more importance, was that I never realized seeds were being sown every day that I made that phone call. For whether we spoke or not, with every call I made, I was cementing my commitment to my desire to truly recover while showing him respect. Those realizations came only months afterward. As time progressed, I came to feel that I wanted to call.

It seemed like forever that I was taking tiny baby steps as I moved to reach for Step 1. My recovery came about only as I came to understand and work the Steps through my writing and with the guidance of my sponsor.

One morning about six months after we had started, I had my first real and dramatic spiritual awakening. I suspected the cause was the "action" I took the day before, working twelve hours in the bedroom while listening to an extended action session. For, as we say in CLA, "Action is the Magic Word!"

The actions I had taken were probably a catalyst to unleash my newly transformed positive and happy attitude. My changed attitude was also the culmination of my writings and the dedication I had to working the Steps with my sponsor. My writings had cleared up so much of my cluttered mental fog that I had made room in my mind for new ideas and creative actions. I awoke elated that morning, so proud of myself for all the work I had done the day before in the bedroom. I was transformed in how smoothly I moved through those actions. Those actions made me happy!

I was puzzled about my newfound euphoria, although my sponsor wasn't puzzled at all. He knew what had happened to me and my thoughts. I heard his laughter and his chuckling, as I was dancing around excitedly. He knew that I was having a really true, big, bona fide spiritual awakening. I had achieved a true release from bondage of some of my negative self-destructive and addictive self-loathing thoughts and was reveling in blind, blissful joyfulness. The clutter fog that had held me hostage for so many decades was gone. I didn't recognize myself: I was so gleeful. I felt as if I was flying high as a kite in the sky. I was so happy. I know now that the euphoria I felt was a direct result of the cumulative efforts on

my part to be committed to my recovery. It came about only as I came to understand and work the Steps through my writing and with the guidance of my sponsor. I was seeing me begin to love myself, embrace hope and life again, and start to live my life in a state of happiness and gratitude.

I could not have achieved this happiness alone and still did not fully understand my surrender to God. Working the Steps is a dynamic process, ever changing as I change. The spirituality of this recovery process is still unfolding, and I am learning how it is unfolding. I had to surrender and ask God to help me. I continue to ask and to receive that help. I also came to understand that I need to give back what I am getting, participate in giving service, and to share the help I receive. I see my life changing for the better every day.

I cluttered my life to avoid the fact that I felt unloved, unworthy of being loved, and injured by those I chose to give my love to. Additionally, my disease is one steeped in lack of self-love, negative and wrong thinking, harmful and damaging self-talk, and fear. All of these bad thoughts and my fears only hurt me, and that is why I was surrounding myself with so much physical and material clutter; cluttered thinking; living in a clutter fog; and, more recently, accumulations of digital clutter. I have made profound realizations and changes in my home life. Now I am finally making my home a sacred space, a safe haven for me, a place where I want to spend time and invite friends over again as I did before my clutter fog destroyed my sanity.

Recovery is a life-long process. I will always need to attend meetings regularly, maybe not as many, but still I must attend meetings. Meeting attendance ensures that I never ever forget the depths of clutter fog from which I escaped. Surrounding myself with CLA supportive literature ensures that I stay and maintain my focus. I am reaping the benefits by keeping my attention on CLA. With the help of my sponsor, I have stayed focused on the *truth* of my addictive disease and disorder.   ⬭

Recovery Moments

Spring 2018
Betsey K., NJ

A number of years ago, as we were preparing for a Clutter-Free Day, someone suggested we provide a support for attendees to write on as they took notes at the workshops. I said I had a lot of old magazines that could be used for that purpose. Further, I indicated that once Clutter-Free Day was over, these magazines would not come back into my house; they would go right to the recycling center. When someone wanted to take one home, we refused the request, as we didn't want to add to anyone else's clutter.

Before the next Clutter-Free Day, we purchased clipboards, which we continue to use to this day.   ⬭

Fall 2018
Kathy H., CA

As I sat down to write this article—late, because I procrastinated—I had an epiphany about procrastination. As those of you who have read my articles in the past know, I call procrastination the demon in my life. Working my CLA program has helped me to procrastinate less—but I still do it, making problems for myself and others.

Over the past few months, I have had a very crowded schedule. Besides my usual travels and my regular CLA volunteer work, I had two jobs outside the normal spectrum of my activities, which took an enormous amount of my time.

During the last few weeks, I was extremely busy getting ready for and attending my family reunion. Since I had so much work to get ready for the reunion, I procrastinated in writing this article, telling myself I would finish it after I completed work on the reunion. Of course, once those time-critical jobs were done, I totally forgot about the article until it was a week late. Had I taken a bit of time to write it earlier, I would have happily submitted it to the editors on time.

This has brought home to me the fact that even when I have a good excuse for my procrastination—such as this reunion job that had to get done—what I am still doing is procrastinating. The effect of the procrastination is still a less than desirable end result. What it means to me is that I need to get stricter about using my CLA program to avoid the procrastination—especially using the Tool of Bookending. Had I shared my commitment with my bookending buddy early on, the article probably would have been done on time.

From now on, I will try to bookend my articles with my buddy. CLA does have useful tools, if we are willing to use them. ◮

Holiday 2019
Alison B., NJ

I have been seriously working the Steps for over a year and a half in a small phone Step group. I have been enjoying it immensely. We have homework on each of the Steps for several weeks, and we meet once a week to share our writings and get feedback.

We are on Step 12. Apparently, I have to go over some of the Steps again because there is a disconnect for me between reading about working the Steps and actually doing things in real life, like decluttering and cleaning—I don't wanna, I don't wanna, I don't wanna!

Recently, I had to get my rent-subsidized apartment in shape for its yearly inspection. With every fiber of my being, I did not want to work on it, but I did give myself extra time this year. I am a person who likes face-to-face meetings. I am not a phone meeting person, but yet I needed a huge amount of extra encouragement because, as usual, I didn't seem to have the incentive or drive to declutter and clean on my own. I didn't wanna.

So I made daily commitments to my phone buddy to go to morning and night meetings, and I pushed myself to go every day for a few weeks. It was difficult to get myself to show up at the meetings because my comfort zone is to watch TV every chance I get…I had to force myself not to turn it on and instead record favorite shows. The people who do service on the meetings are dedicated and cheerful. That helped, but I am anything but dedicated and cheerful when it comes to decluttering and cleaning. I don't wanna, I don't wanna.

At first I was making commitments to my clutter buddy and just not doing them. This happened day after day. Then I was talking about them and doing a couple of things. Then I broke down my decluttering and cleaning into manageable parts on paper. I ordered heavy-duty cleaning supplies online to make cleaning less effort. I didn't have a vacuum cleaner, but I found I had an electric carpet sweeper, in the box, unopened. My buddy on the phone helped support me in putting it together. It served its purpose. A friend from my face-to-face group came over and spent an hour with me while I decided to throw away about a dozen handbags and put some things in order. The fact that she was coming over forced me to declutter and clean before she arrived, especially as she had never seen my place before. When I was on the phone meetings, I began to declutter while I was listening, even if it was just a regular nightly meeting and not a decluttering session. I did it in hourly parts and stopped before I felt tired. When I got stuck, I just switched to another room. Giving myself extra time allowed me to think clearly about what I needed to do next.

When the guy came to inspect, it wasn't perfect by any means; but I had been relaxed about the process instead of being completely stressed, almost to the point of panic, as in previous years. And guess what? He stood in the clear hallway, didn't even peek into the whole apartment, asked me if I had any complaints, then went merrily on his way.

As for the phone meetings, how easily I "forgot" about them. It's so comfortable to revert back to my former self. Will I ever learn? ◬

Fall 2020
Alison B., NJ

The problem: A paralyzing fear of going food shopping because of what's going on outside. The solution: applying the Steps to this one problem. So it was told to me by one of my Step sisters in my weekly group. It seemed unorthodox, but I was willing to try anything. Apparently I could complete the Steps in a few hours.

I started in March, when the chaos was happening. By July, I had done several weeks of Step 7! I have gone through the Steps before and thought I'd delved deeply into them, but there had been a disconnect when it came to decluttering. This time I was determined to declutter as part of my homework.

As the weeks went by, I decluttered my kitchen table, my kitchen counter, a box on the floor, a nook, a pantry shelf, and a fridge door shelf...one at a time, before my meeting. Then I wrote about each experience and how it pertained to my problem.

I kept digging and digging until finally I had an epiphany—I was using a neck-scarf instead of a mask...it kept falling down! I ordered some proper masks online and received them a week later. My fear hasn't gone...but it's certainly abated greatly! ◬

Holiday 2020
Ruthe S., PA

The CLA leaflet, "Recovery from Cluttering: The 12 Steps of Clutterers Anonymous[12]," states: "Our clutter seems to have a life of its own, to multiply without effort on our part." I used to describe that as my clutter "having babies." I couldn't understand how this happened. The clutter seemed to reproduce on its own, and I felt helpless. I had heard others on the lines talking about this too, although they may have described it differently. It has taken me almost 17 years in CLA to understand this phenomenon.

I have sorted through everything in my apartment once. I don't know if I would have figured this out if I hadn't done that first. This insight started to form before the virus began, but being home more often solidified it. What was happening was that I was not putting away what I took out. I would suddenly decide at night that I was tired and wanted to go to sleep, but I didn't set aside time to put away what I had used or was working on. This was the reason my clutter was multiplying. And every night I left more clutter out, and every morning I would come out, and there it would be. Thus my clutter appeared to have had "babies."

Then I had another insight, and leaving mail and packages out for a few days due to the virus clarified it. I have started to understand that it is important to neaten up at least every few nights. I find it amazing that I can straighten a pile, put some things back where they belong, and open mail and packages, and my apartment looks a million times better. I've started doing this, and I have noticed a big difference. It also makes me feel better because I now understand that I do not like clutter.

It gives me great satisfaction to see open spaces that didn't take me long to create. I now leave time to put away what I take out before I go to bed. And if I miss something, it gets taken care of when I do my neatening up. Now, I have a fail safe, so to speak. Since I have started taking these actions, I have noticed that my clutter does not multiply. In fact, I get to see open space and decluttered surfaces more often, even if I haven't spent hours decluttering. It takes at the most two minutes to put away what I take out. It can take a little more time to neaten up because that now involves opening mail and packages, and putting away nonperishable food that I left out, rather than wiping it with alcohol. But that does not happen all the time.

So there it is—put away what you take out! It stops the clutter from reproducing. Neaten up at least every few nights. I cannot tell you how much a little time goes a long way towards sanity. Even if you are just starting out with decluttering, it is worth doing this. It takes some time to develop this habit, but it will give you a head start. Somehow I vaguely remember my kindergarten teacher telling us that we should put away what we take out. Maybe my mother said it too. As it turns out, this advice is one of the greatest clutter busters there is.   ⬖

Summer 2021
Rosie, NY

As I continually work this program, the issue of fear versus trust always comes up for me when I have to declutter. For me, when I'm doing the physical decluttering, I notice my mind clutter often boils down to whether my thoughts focus on fearful or trusting thoughts. My negative self-talk, thoughts that distort the value of objects, and a lot of my resistance, very often come from when my fears win out over trusting in my Higher Power.

I'd like to share some questions that help me declutter by making me aware of the thoughts and mind clutter that get triggered by my physical clutter. In this way, I can see how my thinking and my beliefs are affecting my behavior. Before and during the action I take to declutter, I can look at my mind clutter by asking myself the following:

Do I release objects and trust in my Higher Power to provide me with what I need when I need it—or do I compulsively act out of fear and hold onto things I'm not using that don't support the life I want to live now?

Do I trust that my choices are guided by my Higher Power because I seek my Higher Power's guidance daily—or do I compulsively act out of fear and let my mind clutter keep me stuck in indecision?

Do I trust my Higher Power wants to bless me with a future

that's beautifully fulfilling—or do I compulsively act out of fear and cling to objects from my past because I'm afraid to let go and move forward into the unknown?

Do I trust in my Higher Power that this program will work if I work it—or do I give up on my practice of willingness to change out of a fear of failure because I'm still trying to do it on my own?

Do I trust my Higher Power will see me through this and bring good people into my life and my home, who accept me as I am—or do I hide in fear behind the clutter wall?

One thing I heard recently has been inspiring me to work through my mind clutter as I free myself from physical clutter—and I'm going to paraphrase what it said here: "When the clutter wall is no longer needed to hide behind, the wall will come down."

For me, that's freedom from fear and clutter. ⬣

Clearing Out

Summer 2021
Anonymous

I am reminded that clearing out is not just a process of identifying and disposing of items that take space or time and provide little value—but also of locating each valuable item and putting it in a state

in which it can be most useful. If I may use an agricultural metaphor, decluttering goes beyond sorting the wheat from the chaff. It also includes cleaning, grading, shipping, and milling the good stuff—in other words, putting the good stuff in a condition and in a place where it is likely to be useful. ⬣

I Am Accepting of Change

Holiday 2021
Mariah W., NY

Ahh. This is an affirmation I say at least once or twice (sometimes more often) daily; however, I realize this is a major area for me to be in recovery in my little world. Am I really accepting of change? Hmm. I say it, and yet I clearly don't fully embrace and embody change. *Life* is all about change. The seasons change four times a year in the paradigm I grew up and learned: winter, spring, summer, and fall. *All* of life changes every day in every way, so why is it that I can become so bleepity bleep stubborn about wanting my little world to never, ever change? Eep! That's a super sucky realization.

My relationship with stuff is always changing, as are—sometimes—my mercurial sadness, grief, and relationships with people. I am unsnarling my relationship clutter just like a ball of yarn. I am willing to be willing about being accepting of change in human relationships.

Most recently in my recovery work in Clutterers Anonymous, I have been taking a very deep dive in uncluttering my relationships with my family. I have been in individual and group therapy since I was a teenager, dealing with major family issues, traumas, and scars. There was much manipulation and controlling behavior from my parents and family as I grew up. Without going down the rabbit hole of my childhood, I am keenly aware that I need to look in the mirror—connect with my Source (Higher Power)—and be open and available to accepting change.

Along the way, I learned something called unconditional positive regard, and I'm trying to have that concept for myself and all others (yes, including family) to gibe with being accepting of change *and* accepting of another person—including my family—as they are right here and right now. That's not always an easy journey, I'm telling you. I am not in the driver's seat of their lives. I am only in the driver's seat of my own life, and I am in recovery with the unconditional support of the "Infinite Loving Presence" that we call Higher Power.

I am choosing my life, moment by moment, and sometimes even the loving members in CLA can

push my buttons, as it were, and I realize I have more recovery work to do in releasing and being open to change. We all have different perspectives; an array of different ways of doing things; and a rich rainbow of how we think, feel, and choose to act. I am accepting of change, changing perspectives, and honoring all—ideally with unconditional positive regard, which includes myself.

As I strive for accepting change, I am releasing my need to feel as if I should keep things the same all the time, while setting boundaries about what behaviors I am comfortable with from my family, friends, and others. I can more fully lean into the concept of accepting change in all areas of my life.

Like the seasons, I can—in the winter of life—release all the flakes and, maybe as I spice things up in the other seasons, I can release the mean people, the bullies, jerks, and controlling and manipulative people (or at least set healthy boundaries), so I make space for nourishing and supportive family, friends, and others who are on my side and guide me to be higher and better every day in every way. I am then truly on the journey of uncluttering relationships. I am accepting of change. I am creating the life of my dreams.

"People and relationships are more important than my lifeless

possessions."—from CLA "Affirmations[17]"

▲

Spiritual Recovery

CLA is a program of spiritual recovery, based upon the 12 Steps. Our experience has shown that without working on our spiritual development, most of us are doomed to clutter again, even if we have had some success in decluttering.

Regaining Self-Love

Summer 2017
Judy K. FL

[Author's Note: I was raised agnostic, so spirituality doesn't come naturally to me. The paragraphs below are the result of prayer and meditation with my Creator (you can use whoever your Higher Power is) and co-sponsoring with my CLA 12-Step partner. The lists below are suitable for me. If you are a list maker, you can develop lists that work for you.]

There has been a shift in me. It pertains to how I see myself and my possessions.

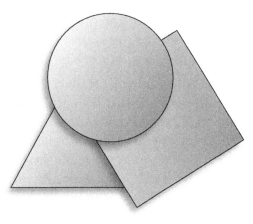

Self-Love. My neighbor asked if I love myself. She thinks people who love themselves don't create homes that produce guilt and shame. (What a concept!) Through communication with my Creator and guided research, I'm regaining that loving feeling. Do you love yourself enough to provide a nice home for yourself?

Priorities. The following intangibles are important to me.
1. My relationship with my Creator
2. My health
3. Myself (I'm faking it until I make it.)
4. My other relationships
5. My creative/enriching pursuits

What are your priorities?

Visioning. The bane of my existence is paper. During meditation, an image came to me that described paper in my life. For me, it's a hailstorm. It's white. It comes unbidden. It is destructive and makes my footing unstable. How do you see your clutter?

Paper Limits. My Creator and I have come up with the following rules about which papers I may keep.
- Tax-related (includes financial and charitable documents)
- Legal
- Medical
- Current creative/enriching pursuits
- Sentimental (Fortunately, I'm not excessive about this category.)

Which papers may you keep?

Other Limits. We've come up with the following guidelines about what other tangible items I may retain.
- Do I use it?
- Do I love it? (Fortunately, I'm not excessive about this category.)
- Is it irreplaceable? (**Very** little falls into this category.)

Which other items may you retain?

Slogans. Because I'm easily distracted, having a very few meaningful slogans helps me focus and get back on track. I have been using the following.
- If I can live without it, I will live without it.
- Every paper diminishes my happiness.
- Everything I keep makes my life worse unless it supports my priorities, paper limits, and other limits.

What slogans help you?

I hope that you will make an effort to love yourself enough to work on your home, get a CLA 12-Step sponsor or co-sponsor someone, work on meditation and prayer, and let it change your life. ◬

Grief, Acceptance, and Letting Go

Summer 2017
Anonymous

A few months ago, I attended a workshop on acceptance. Participants were asked to write something, then burn it to symbolize letting go. I wrote, but I did not burn. As a clutterer, I suppose I could be accused of holding onto my issue. That may be part of it, but I want to share this experience of hope with others first.

That week, my daughter would have celebrated a birthday, but she is not here. I filled the day with events, perhaps to avoid sadness, perhaps to grasp as much life as possible. Either way, I find myself reflecting on the purpose that physical clutter and over-scheduling serve in my life.

I fill my days with activity and my house with stuff. I'm attempting to fill a void that cannot be filled—not with events, not with stuff. By dragging my heels, I hold on to the dream that my stuff will be enough.

It's not enough. Actually, it's too much—too much of something that does not soothe, sate, comfort, fill, or renew. Clutter drains and fuels fatigue. I feel powerless to combust, tackle, or remove it. My issues are buried within and beneath the clutter, and they emanate from it.

What do I want? Release, but maybe without effort. What do I seek? A solution in the moment, a quick fix. All that lies within, around, over, and through these mounds of clutter suggests this: I must be willing to let go. If I unleash guilt, shame, sadness, and grief and embrace all I keep hidden, I can rise to the surface, discard the clutter, and walk free.

What lies beneath the clutter may not ever totally leave. I live with a measure of grief, mourning loss in quiet moments, each day that I live. It does not need to define me. I can embrace life with its full range of emotions. What is pure, rich, and beautiful will lie parallel with sadness and sorrow. This is acceptance—life on life's terms.

The Steps present a path for healing: surrender/relinquish (Step 1), reclaim (Step 2), reconnect (Step 3), reveal (Steps 4-5), release (Steps 6-7), reconcile (Steps 8-9), review (Step 10), renew (Step 11), and relate (Step 12). Joy can outweigh grief if I choose to say yes to this simple, but not easy, process. ▲

Where There Is…

Fall 2017
Laike {aka Kat}, NJ

[Writer's Note: I attended CLA-East's Clutter-Free Day this year. In one workshop, the presenter read the St. Francis Step 11 prayer. I wrote my own thoughts afterward. May you each find your own meaningful "where and when."]

Lord, make me an instrument of Thy peace, that…
– where there is mess, may I strive to be neat;
– where there is chaos, may I seek order;
– where there is conflict, may I offer resolution;
– where there is confusion, may I bring clarity;
– where there is angst, may I extend calm;
– where there are wounds, may I manifest healing;
– where there is dissonance, may I compose harmony;
– where there is burden, may I lighten the load.
When overstepping occurs, may I practice healthy boundaries.
When indecision paralyzes, may I seek Divine Guidance.
When disagreement abounds, may I find common ground.
When shouting occurs, may I utter a whisper.
When others turn a deaf ear, may I endeavor to listen.
When stagnation pools, may I

participate in movement.
When insensitivity dictates, may
I practice consideration.
When unrest prevails, may I pray
for and live in contentment.

In all my affairs, may I follow
my God.

I am imperfect, so these
thoughts reflect my hope of recovery. I may not attain them all,
or have them at the same time,
yet they offer me a guide for how
I want to live my life. What are
yours? ⬤

Overdoing Versus Spiritual Timing

Fall 2017
Terri J., OH

I used to take pride in overdoing and busyaholism. How many
things I could do at once in a day
was a skill I prided myself on. I
never realized I was cluttering up
my mind and life with activities.
Before CLA, I understood only
possession or "stuff" clutter. Now
I understand the cluttering disease; it is so much more involved
than just too many possessions
in my physical space. Cluttered,
overactive thoughts in my mind,
cluttered emotions, overdoing
life, busyness stash, and a spiritual disconnection were adding
a component to my life I did not
understand.

Before CLA, I had compared
myself to the plate spinners that I
used to see as a child on a popular
TV show. Plate spinning is a circus
manipulation where one person
keeps plates spinning on sticks at
fast speeds, usually by themselves.
Usually, in the beginning all is
well, but when the plates start
crashing it gets quite messy....
Welcome to my life before CLA.

Without getting into messy
plate-breaking details, I will simply
state I could swirl many plates at a
time, almost magically. So when I
got to CLA and heard what I considered to be two of my greatest
character assets—those of overdoing and busyness—were not on
the list of actions that would aid
my recovery, I had to admit I was
skeptical.

So you get the picture in all its
cluttered details. I would rush
around keeping all my plates spinning. But when one plate would
spin too fast and another too slowly (because of the attention I was
giving my faster-spinning plate),
it could get messy. Oh, and when
the menopausal hormone sprinkled
my plates and became active, you
should thank HP you weren't in
my life.

I truly didn't know I shouldn't
be a human doing and should be
a human being. I felt my value
came from my doing. Every once
in a while a plate would crash. If
everything didn't crash together,

I thought life was doing just fine. I had a refrigerator magnet that actually said "a clean house is a sign of a misspent life," and another magnet read, "I never needed a man to make me happy, but a maid would help."

My internet research for a solution led me to the Clutterers Anonymous web page. Oh, how I celebrated! How come I never heard of this before? My clutter issue was over. I would be saved by another beloved 12-Step group. In the beginning, I thought my home would become decluttered by osmosis. I could sit in on a meeting and hope the magic CLA clutter fairy would do what retirement had failed to do. My hope for a clutter-free environment began.

My social life clutter slowdown was spurred on by wanting to attend the 8 p.m. meetings. I couldn't go out so much in the evening and seek recovery. I even got aggravated if friends would want to come to visit during my 8 p.m. meeting.

CLA has helped me slow down. I don't spin as many plates. I try to spin only one plate at a time. I believe my HP intervened to help me find CLA. I have to make a concentrated effort not to overdo. I have become aware of experience greed in my life and the adrenaline rush that busyness can cause.

I am working on staying in balance, harmony, and well-being with our recovery program. I have been looking at both my assets and defects of character and working the Steps, with the help of God. I am striving to find answers to physical clutter using a spiritual solution.

I am healing nonphysical triggers and emotions with my Higher Power. My Higher Power lets me know I am on the right path by synchronicity and coincidences, intuition and dreams—if I listen.

When I get out of the inner battle and struggle of overdoing and listen to God's messages, my life becomes more manageable. Slowing down and loving myself in my nonperfect human being (not doing) state has helped me along.

I believe that clutter holds me back from becoming all that I can be and living the life I really want to live. There is more to clutter than just the physical manifestation. I have learned that I need to love myself—my imperfections, clutter and all.

I have found a CLA promise in our literature. I have quit overdoing more than I am capable of doing in a healthy manner. My busyness stash ceases to be a distraction as I open up my overloaded schedule and pay attention to my experience greed.

I have become selective in my experiences. My experience greed is slipping away as I decelerate. I am giving up wanting to try everything possible to fill a void. I refuse some invitations and let go of my fear of missing something. I am letting go fearing the one fact I think I need to make me whole, which will be replaced with knowing HP's love, and then I will release my need for perfectionism.

My overachieving plate spinning is slowing down as I grow in realizing that I am a perfect human being, just as God created me, and I don't have to be a human doing to be validated. ⬭

Chaos

Fall 2017

Andrew S., MD

The Oxford Dictionary defines chaos as "complete disorder and confusion. A state in which behavior and events are not controlled by anything." It's a fascinating word with a long history. For it derives from the Greek word for void or chasm and also refers to the state of the universe before creation. That's the history and the broad definition of chaos.

For me, in the present, chaos is primarily a feeling of disorder or disorganization—an absence of orderly arrangement. Personally, I think chaos clearly relates to a loss of a sense of control.

Generally, the overall quality of this bundle of feelings is negative or undesirable, but can also be neutral or positive.

It's fascinating that sometimes, while in the midst of a physical project, it might seem uncontrolled, disorderly or disruptive, though it does not feel to me as unpleasant, confused, or negative. The neutral or detached point of view seems to be connected to being able to be in the present, without expectations, and accept things as they are.

Is this an example or illustration of the statement in our Fellowship that clutter is defined by the individual's attitudes and feelings toward it, rather than others' attitudes and feelings? Today I'm not understanding chaos as CHAOS (Can't Have Anyone Over Syndrome) but much closer to the classical definition above. Yes, at one point years ago, I felt much more uncomfortable having company in my space. Somehow, I broke away from the worst of it: the feelings of shame and embarrassment. And I also spent a lot of effort clearing up certain areas of the house where I expected to be receiving guests. Letting go of perfectionism was a huge component on the path to good enough. Sometimes I would prepare visitors with a brief conversation before they arrived, and that seemed to work for both of us. This led me to self-acceptance and helped me to be comfortable inviting people to my house.   ⬙

Living in a State of Anxiety

Holiday 2017
Ted S., NY

My mail gets delivered to an address in the State of New York, which is considered my residence. An awareness has come to me that my body may reside in New York, but my mind lives in a State of Anxiety. The anxiety is an environment which has enveloped me since the age of two.

I distinctly remember lying to my father while standing in the basement as he called down and asked if I had broken an adult-type metal desk airplane. Standing there in fear, I said "No."

My father believed me, and nothing was ever said about it. That episode, as I feel and think about it in recovery, taught me behaviors. I learned that lying was a way of getting out of trouble, also that lying gave me anxiety, knowing that it was wrong. It became a heaviness over me that I was eventually able to live with, but the anxiety grew heavier with each succeeding lie throughout my life in all types of interactions.

The behavior became an everyday way of life, and I eventually became comfortable feeling comfortable. One can become blinded to certain things in one's life. I ignored the deprivation around me, existing with an anxiety that, because of its duration, actually became tolerable and a normal feeling. Whenever I would start to feel comfortable about being comfortable, with something nice happening to me, then there inevitably would be some sort of behavior to sabotage.

People would say things about my living situation, and I would hear the words—but the real meaning of them never got through the cloak of denial. For each of us, there either comes a day of awareness—truly seeing the light the new day brings—or each day renewing the dawn of denial is filled with ignoring what is in plain sight. An extraordinary person introduced me to recovery but didn't push me.

On a particular dawn when I awoke and looked around, things didn't look normal any more. They looked in disarray, and I remembered saying, "Oh my God, what have I been doing?" I was able to ask this person for help. He took me to my first meeting and showed me a better life, one with color and vitality, not the one I lived in with the dreariness of a black and white world encompassing a total lack of self-worth.

My first Step, admitting to being powerless over clutter and having an unmanageable life, was completed in a flash. It's just that it took my whole life to get to that flash, the starting point of my recovery. Finding out there was another way felt redeeming to me.

I embraced this new way of being with the same enthusiasm and energy as it took to keep up my secret life of a clutterer. Having a Higher Power gives me the self-esteem, self-love, and self-respect that was lacking in my life. Now feeling good about myself compels me to treat myself with dignity. One of the ways I accomplished this is by being on time for appointments.

In the past I was always late for anything: work, social gatherings, picking up an unemployment check, a date—anything and everything. This behavior kept me in a state of anxiety while racing to the particular destination. Now, because of self-worth due to the Steps, it is a pleasure getting somewhere, knowing I'm on time and able to be calm all along the way.

I don't plan on moving out of New York State anytime soon. I'm leaving the State of Anxiety, though. I have a one-way ticket to the Land of Serenity—a peaceful land just down the road, not far, only takes 12 Steps to get there. △

My Relationship with Clutter

Summer 2018
Debbie S., CA

While we were reading the Steps at a recent meeting, my attention was caught by Step 6, "Were entirely ready for God to remove all these defects of character." One of the consistent features of my recovery is that I learn things, then forget them and have to learn them again. I was frustrated by my lack of progress in dealing with my clutter—I was thinking that I have to fix it. I know that God is the one who will fix my problems, but I had forgotten it (again). For the rest of the meeting, I had Step 6 at the back of my mind.

Toward the end of the meeting, we read the Affirmations[17], and one of them stood out for me, "I am…willing…to change my relationship with clutter." What? Relationship with clutter? Really? Relationship??? What an odd idea! But my house is so filled with clutter, I guess I must have a relationship with it. Then I connected that with Step 6 and came up with "I am ready and willing for God to change my relationship with clutter." Hey, I like that. I need to look at it for a while, but I think it's good.

For this to work, I need to keep it at the front of my mind instead of forgetting it. So I will say it several times in a row, several times a day— like a mantra. Then I thought: It's going to be interesting to see how God does this. Sometimes when I turn a problem over to God and it gets fixed, then I can look back and see how the pieces of the puzzle have come together—somebody says something in a meeting or a conversation, then I read something in the literature—so I was looking forward to seeing how the pieces of this particular puzzle would fall into place.

Then I remembered that when God fixes a problem that I have turned over, it involves pain. Always. So I had to consider: When I say I'm willing for this to be fixed, am I also saying that I'm willing to experience the pain that will be part of the process? I don't think that recovery itself is the direct cause of the pain. But there is pain in life, and pain in me, and recovery means giving up the dysfunctional thinking or behavior that I have used to cover up the pain.

My first two years in 12-Step meetings were incredibly painful, but when it was over, I felt better about myself than I ever had before. I kind of got dragged into it, I didn't really have a choice, and I'm glad about that. Even knowing the outcome, I don't know if I would have had the strength of character to choose to go through the pain. But this time

I had a choice, and after thinking it through, I decided that I'm willing. An important difference is that now I have Tools for dealing with the pain—the Steps, Meetings, Literature, the Telephone— and my relationship with my Higher Power.

After a couple of days I went online to look up the exact wording of the Affirmation and found that I had left out a few words. What it actually says is, "I am ready, willing, and able to change my relationship with clutter." But I have a problem with the word "able." It contradicts Step 1, which says I'm powerless, and ignores the Steps that say that God is going to restore me to sanity and remove my shortcomings. So I like my version better: "I am ready and willing for God to change my relationship with clutter."

Over the next week or so, I kept getting irritated at all sorts of things, but they were really just minor annoyances and inconveniences, and my anger was out of proportion. And sometimes I was just irritated—not irritated at something or someone, just irritated. One of the important changes in my life as a result of recovery is that now I'm aware of this feeling of irritation and understand it. It means that something is coming up, some feeling that I don't want to feel, and I'm using anger to cover it up. It seems likely that this irritation is connected to my new commitment to changing my relationship with clutter, but I don't yet know that for sure.

Right now I'm waiting to see what happens in the next chapter of this story. As I've been told, more will be revealed. ⬤

Life Is About the Journey

Summer 2018

Ted S., NY

Four railroad tickets have been in a small tub with my New York City maps. They were worth over $150, some being multi trips over 3 years old—and all had gone past their expiration date. Still, the money had been paid, and using an expired ticket didn't mean someone else would not have a seat, such as on a filled airplane. Seemed logical to me. The train had plenty of seats; and, once again, the price of the ticket had been paid. Not wanting to waste the money spent, I planned to get on a train and use one of the expired tickets.

Once the train started down the tracks, anxiety would travel even faster throughout my body, while waiting for the conductor to ask, "Tickets please." My mind would wander back and forth, wondering if he would notice the outdated ticket. Inevitably, the attempt-

ed ruse would be noticed and prompted a planned explanation that the tickets had been paid for. "I'm not trying to ride for free." The conductors seemed to take it personally that someone was trying to get one over on them for a free ride. One conductor made me pay for a ticket, another hovered over me and had me get off at the next stop. The stop was at Atlantic Avenue in Brooklyn.

Later on, sharing with my sponsor about the rejection...

Stop the Story, Stop the Story! That word rejection has made a thud in my chest. Have I been trying to use the railroad tickets to save money or set myself up for rejection? Being rejected is a familiar feeling and something that has happened often. It has become a comfortable feeling to be with but only because it is familiar. I say to myself, "Oh, I'm used to this feeling."

Now, let's take peace, serenity, calmness—what strange acquaintances they are. If those feelings start a friendship with me they can be shed faster than a runaway locomotive. I have been sharing for a while that life is no longer black and white. The phrase used is, "There are many spokes on the wheel." There are many reasons for my railroad ticket behavior. Trying to save money, creating an accustomed experience of conflict with someone such as the conductor, making sure I don't have a serene ride without a care in the world. The reasons could go on, similar to one of those western 100-car freight trains. All on one track with the sound of rumbling wheels jostling its cargo, just as my insides are tossed around to the habitual feeling of stress.

Back to the story…he said, "Atlantic Avenue! The cops don't even go down there." Now the situation had become serious, as the station area was unknown to me, being from a different part of New York. Luckily, not knowing the area, I wasn't aware of the potential for crime.

There was no fear but actually a relief as the stress of waiting for the conductor to come down the aisle was over. There had been the back-and-forth explaining to him that there were plenty of empty seats and the money had been paid. There was no submission on his part, and the threat of police waiting for me at the next station convinced me to get off at the next stop. A subway station was close by. And with the fare paid, my journey was completed a few stops down the line. Riding on the subway car was noticeably different; the jostling was a massage.

The ride was peaceful, and I didn't have a care in the world. ⏺

Self-Care Is Non-Negotiable

Summer 2018
Anonymous

Why is it I have to work at self-care? Sometimes it even feels like working so hard. I'm aware that it's important, yet it ends up frequently coming in dead last in my life and in my world. Why is it so challenging for me? Let me take two aspects of our CLA literature (which abounds with the importance of self-care):

"Reparenting: If we didn't receive healthy parenting, we can give ourselves the acceptance and encouragement we never got. The more we nurture ourselves, the less need we have to resent."—Healing Grudges, "Decluttering Resentment: Steps 4-10[5]," CLA pink leaflet

I was not parented in the healthiest way and was actually physically and sexually assaulted as an infant in my crib through young adulthood. Since my primary topic is self-care, I will say that I have worked in other 12-Step groups, and in intensive therapy, through these family issues. My own journey to better self-care may be in my increased awareness that I must reparent myself, nurture myself, and give myself the acceptance and encouragement I rarely had at home. Okay, so this likely does help me understand why—for me—I have to work at self-care.

Reparenting myself and nurturing the inner kid in me is one of my paths in recovery of self-care in CLA.

"Healthy Relationships: When we release resentments, our need to cling to hurt is gone. We have no need to 'fix' anyone or prove them wrong. They're attracted to us because we seem more empathic and forgiving, and we are! They sense that we'll accept them as they are because we accept ourselves." —Rewards of Recovery, "Decluttering Resentment: Steps 4-10[5]," CLA pink leaflet

I have released resentments but maybe—just maybe—I have yet to release my own resentments of the mistakes I've made myself and keep trying to "fix" me. I no longer cling to hurt or "victimhood;" rather I embrace my gentle journey of recovery. I'm passionate about healthy relationships, perhaps because I long to learn and embrace what healthy relationships look and feel like. I've experienced glimmers of healthy relationships, and conceptually I understand that a healthy relationship starts out with me having a healthy relationship with myself.

Why do I say "self-care is non-negotiable"? Because I believe my recovery requires me to focus on self-care and getting better one moment, one hour, and one day at a time with CLA self-care. I must take care of myself or there is no "me" and no recovery inside or outside CLA. While CLA is a "we" program and not a "me" program, I am keenly aware that the "me" that fully embraces recovery via self-care, and working our 12 Steps and 12 Traditions, brings a healthier "me" to our awesome CLA "we" program. And for this, I'm grateful. Thank you, CLA!

"Our first priority is always our well-being." —5. Prioritizing, Toward Healing, "Declutter Your Mind[6]," Clutterers Anonymous green leaflet   ◬

Rest As My Clutter-Free Zone

Fall 2018

Anonymous

"Time is a precious gift, so I use it wisely."—Recovery Affirmation[17] No. 23, "Is CLA for You? A Newcomer's Guide to Recovery[9]," p. 21.

As I journey on the road to recovery in decluttering every aspect of my life, I am aware that rest is my heart's desire of a centerpiece for my primary clutter-free zone. In our CLA Recovery Affirmations, No. 11 says "I create at least one clutter-free zone or room in which I keep only items I use and love."

Could the concept "rest" be my clutter-free zone? Could I keep only habits that serve me, such as an attitude of gratitude each day and meditation and connection with my Higher Power in my "rest" clutter-free zone? Sure would like to do this and have an amazing "rest clutter-free space!"

I choose to have rest be the centerpiece of my clutter-free zone, at least in my ideal recovery vision. There are 168 hours in any seven-day week. My centerpiece clutter-free goal of rest is to have 56-60 hours of rest in any 168-hour week. So I'll round it up to 60 hours a week and then understand that the remaining 108 hours are for God, work, family, life, etc. Can I find a way to get rest before I'm tired and create centerpiece clutter-free habits for good sleep hygiene? That's my vision.

I currently feel very over-cluttered, with too much work and, certainly sometimes, too much mind clutter. I must release this work clutter and the bordering on obsessive focus on working so much every day. Work is my current centerpiece, since I work multiple jobs. I feel like I'm addicted to work and addicted to busyness. I long to unplug, unwind, and clear away some of these habits that no longer serve my recovery. Time to brush that away to a more balanced perspective that replaces it with the centerpiece of restful clutter-free space so 60 hours each week are for rest. This might

include focusing on gratitude (at least five things I'm grateful for each day), making space for meditation with my Higher Power, as well as making ample space for general rest and even nourishing, restorative sleep as a precious CLA gift towards my recovery. I feel calmer and more focused with ample rest, too. Rest—it does a body and my recovery good! I'll start today with my new "rest" clutter-free zone! Sweet dreams— dulces sueños—now and always in our recovery! ▲

My Thoughts on What I Would Do if It Were My Last Day on the Earth

Summer 2019
Vicky V., CA

When I heard this topic in the Self-Care meeting, I was overwhelmed with fear that I had not taken the 9th-Step actions that I needed to do with my two brothers. Then I was angry at myself that I had allowed a very important action to fall into the endless list. I have a firm belief in my Higher Power and that death, for me, is graduation. And that my spirit will continue to learn in a different school.

Where to start on almost any project is difficult. I started writing some of the positive times in our family life. Then I wrote the hard items. Being in the meetings and being of service gave me courage and energy to continue. On Saturday, January 6, 2019, the letters were complete. As happens many times to me, they were misplaced. I called on the Action Line for prayers. It felt so good to have a recovery family that knew how this could happen.

Taking a few more searching movements, the thought came that I needed to write a couple more ugly stories. Then the letters were found. Three more pages would cover it. Thanks to CLA, I closed my letters with "God forgives everyone; please forgive me and God is love."

This has been a mental, emotional, and spiritual cleansing. I feel right with God.

Thanks to my sisters and brothers in CLA.   ⬭

Divine Decluttering Prayer

Fall 2019
Tatiana

Dear God,

I am awakening to life again as the magnolias and the cherry blossoms release their burdens under the trees. I very much want to do the same, releasing all I do not need in my home. And as I create more space, I use it to care for my health and wellbeing, to exercise,

to have tea with my friends, and to read the books I love that are lying on my sofa.

Please, dear God, help me put my daily needs first on my agenda and support me in repairing patterns of self-neglect that I carry for a lifetime. I want to accept the responsibility that I have toward myself and create a sacred space in my home where I can grow spiritually, emotionally, and mentally. Help me to be happy with fewer objects and more awareness of peace, harmony, and serenity in my life, my home, and in my relationships.

Thank you, Amen.   ⬭

Divine Decluttering Prayers

Holiday 2019
Tatiana

Dear God,

I feel overwhelmed about spring cleaning.

Being surrounded by an accumulation of books, clothes, and memorabilia, I find myself unwilling to separate from them. The books have a better home in the nearby library; the clothes are small, and I can't wear them any more; and the memorabilia can't go with me in my grave anyway— and nobody else is interested in them.

Please, dear God, help me

lighten up my burdens and leave an empty house before I leave this planet. Help me separate from all I can't take with me in the next dimension. I don't want my daughter to be left with all she does not need as a memory of who I was for her. Help me travel light on my last journey to you, as I leave my boxes behind, under the grass. Let me be fully present in the here and now and do my spring cleaning with your help and with the help of all CLA declutterers who show up daily to do your will. Help us to simplify our lives and to let go of all that we do not need for a daily organized life.   Thank you, Amen.

Dear God,

Some days the sky is gray, and as it rains heavily outside my windows, my heart is wet with tears and sadness. A desire to release a very long-lived relationship fills my soul with heavy-duty mixed feelings. Please, dear God, help me release all items, bad habits, and people that do not add to my well-being and serenity. Help me to also release the emotional attachments to others who exhaust my vitality and leave me depleted and absent from my own goals. This leads to my ignoring my daily responsibility for my self-care, my health, and my desire to grow, to learn, and to open new vistas of experience in my life. Make me strong and

grounded in the daily reality of a productive and continuous search for an authentic spiritual path of self-discovery, of self-acceptance, and of sharing what I learned with those around me who can benefit from it.   Amen. ⬥

Serenity, Kindness, and Tolerance

Spring 2020
Mickey M., AZ

What to do when your serenity, kindness, and tolerance seem to have disappeared? I have been experiencing negative feelings, negative thoughts and, worse yet, I acted on them in meetings, in talking with other members. The worst part: I went on and on in front of two new attendees!

I get so irritated when people show up late. I get irritated when someone speaks out, chiding another member for what they believe is inappropriate behavior. Excuse me?! What happened to our group conscience that no one is to do that?! We discussed and agreed to adopt the CLA Group Code of Conduct (which includes a paragraph about showing up on time), and we discussed and agreed that no member has the right to speak out to another member in the meeting. We agreed that the facilitator would do that.

Five positive things for me to

think: I can think of peace, I can think of serenity, I can think of kindness, I can think of tolerance, and I can think of unconditional love for my fellow human beings.

Prayer and meditation: Wish me luck. Wish me serenity, kind thoughts, tolerance, and love for all. Pray for me. Pray that I am being led (yes, I am). I am being led to my highest good, despite this temporary appearance.

Serenity, Courage, and Wisdom △

Labyrinth Rescue

Summer 2020
Ted S., NY

Editor's Note: This event took place during the Clutter-Free Weekend in Florida earlier this year.

A labyrinth is a walking experience in the shape of a curved spiral path, or it can be elongated 90-degree angled aisles within a square. It is a focused and purposeful walk, moving in a clockwise direction to the center. Once there, one may pause, then reverse course returning to the entrance.

Walking the labyrinth path while staying within the lines actually helps the mind be in line with the exact moment—not an ordinary experience for many. One thought is that this walk helps one become grounded, calm, and serene. The person is asked to concentrate on the now and allow the everyday

thoughts of life to step aside, focusing only on each step as it is taken. At the end, after this brief walk of mindful focus, one may leave the area emotionally refreshed, feeling less burdened—pleasant but certainly different.

The day of the labyrinth walk, I awakened with plenty of time for my usual routine. Then it was time to leave the cabin and do something that was out of the norm. Walking briskly towards the appointed place, it was comforting to know that a first-time visit the day before had allowed me to be certain of where the labyrinth was located. The feeling of not having anxiety wondering where I was going and not being late is still strange sometimes. There was enough anxiety wondering if the leader would be there, as nothing was spoken about it the night before.

As I rounded the corner, our dependable leader, Lisa, greeted me and offered encouraging instructions for the walk. I was the first participant and delighted to be alone without distractions. A short pause at the entrance; then, with a methodical walking pace, the shapes of the round edged blocks became noticeable.

After some time, a man and dog appeared out of the coconut tree-barked forest. It was annoying to see an unleashed dog wander across the dark colored border blocks, not honoring the lined boundaries and, even more so, coming towards me. I'm a cat person; they can lie all over me, but a dog's nose on my pants and leaning up on me seems invasive and overbearing.

Putting those thoughts aside and my best pleasantry forward, I asked the stranger what the dog's name was. He said, "Mary Lou." As I bent down, my arms embraced this sweet black lab, who had the eyes of one who had never barked with meanness. Ken, the owner, said she was a rescue. Mary Lou had been a guide dog but had developed health problems. He mentioned she went only towards people whom she deemed good. This was a powerful acknowledgement from Mary Lou.

There was a time in my life when anger was a weighted cloak attached to my shoulders. Dogs became the target of any venting and were wary of my venomous stares and silent rebukes. Mary Lou brushed against my leg, tail touching last, as she walked off to give an affirmation of goodness to another human creature.

Standing upright, ready to continue the walk, I realized that I had absolutely no idea which way to go, left or right. I was totally lost and uncentered, yet fully present in the experience. It might've been possible to trace the lane with my eyes to see where the start was, but it's similar to following a crease in the bark of a tree. It would have made me brain crazy. It felt better, when not knowing what to do, to stand still for a while. I felt safe doing nothing by just being in the moment. Soon another path walker, Eloise, came along. She had entered after me, so following her towards the center was the way to continue the journey. My heart was full and eyes near tears.

It's common in CLA for people to say they haven't been in program long enough to offer guidance or help another. Eloise, besides entering the labyrinth after me, had also entered CLA after me, and only recently. Yet, this woman knew the way to the center and gave me her wisdom. She guided me to where I was headed and asked for nothing in return.

Just as it is in CLA, we help others because that's how we return the help to the ones who helped rescue us. Mary Lou? She's still rescuing people. She absolved me from a past that had dogged me for years. Maybe that's why dogs are called "man's best friend." Thank you, Mary Lou, may you walk unleashed. May we all walk untethered from our past, free to detect the goodness and offer love to all. ⏶

Motivation Six

Summer 2021
Mickey M., AZ

The Fall 2019 issue of CLA*rity* was read by my group at our meeting a couple of months ago. The cover story, "Focus on Decluttering," written by Alison B. of New Jersey, caught our attention—and for me, I was so inspired!

Subsequently, I spoke with Alison about her story. I asked her: Where did you get the formula—Permission, Instructions, Encouragement and Applause? She said she made them up. Yes, I thought, a great way to follow a path to move forward with a difficult project.

Alison also had a bookend buddy to call to check in with while she was progressing. Oh, yes, and she said she has to give herself permission, instructions, encouragement, and applause to proceed.

I asked her if she minded if I added prayers before and after to the formula. She said she prays all the time. But for me, a person who has to remember to pray, beginning and ending a project needs prayers of thanks and gratitude.

So for me, I would begin, once I had my bookend buddy expecting my calls or texts, by saying a prayer of gratitude:

"Thank you, my Higher Power, for this guidance. Thank you also for my friend (let's say Wendy), for agreeing to work with me today. Thank you for permission to begin. Thank you for the instructions I need to focus and move forward. Amen." Then it's time to start; to take action; to progress through to find the places to put things away, encouragement; and, of course, applause that the project is going forward!

Then the project. Over the course of an hour or two, depending on the magnitude of the project and on the limits of my motivation and energy, I call my buddy or text her. Hurray, here's what's been accomplished. And so forth, until I've gone as far as my energy allows.

So how would this look as a set of easy-to-follow directions?

1. Prayer of gratitude
2. Permission
3. Instructions
4. Encouragement
5. Applause
6. Prayer of thanks.

I am so excited by this set. Here are our instructions. We already have permission, some of us. We have our clutter buddy offering suggestions, encouragement, and applause that we are moving through this project—or any project! And we have our Higher Power residing within and without leading us to *action* and recovery.

Thank you, Alison, for this wonderful idea. I hope I've been clear as to what inspired me to feel this set is a how-to for projects. ◬

Prayer

Summer 2021
Lisa G., FL

Dear God, Higher Power, Loving Divine Being,

Please continue to keep me safe, and let me be aware, at all times, that I am safe—especially during times of inner or outer turmoil, fears, uncertainty, instability, and feelings of lack. Please reinforce that those are just feelings, and feelings are not facts. Continue to remind me that while those thoughts and feelings made me safe as a child, they keep me stuck as an adult.

When I have these feelings, please let me know through your loving, kind, and gentle life lessons, that you are in charge. Let me be reminded that my thoughts won't harm me and my fears are unfounded. The only certainty and stability is within you.

The only lack is my own lack of knowing your infinite wisdom, kindness and love. That includes your love for me, all humankind, all animals, and this beautiful planet.

Please continue to keep us all safe and sound within the embraces of your infinite love and wisdom. Amen. ◬

Powerless Over Clutter

Fall 2021
Jane D., CA

The medical references in this article refer to hoarding primarily. Although many CLA members are hoarders, some others, while still clutterers, are not hoarders. However, the CLA program of recovery as discussed in the article does function for all clutterers.—Editor

Alcoholics Anonymous (A.A.) co-founder, Bill W., sought help from Dr. William Silkworth—who later became A.A.'s great medical benefactor. Bill learned from Silkworth the key to Step 1: "We admitted we were powerless over alcohol and that our lives had become unmanageable." "The Doctor's Opinion," a chapter in *Alcoholics Anonymous*[1] (the Big Book), was written by Silkworth. In it he proposes that alcoholism is "an obsession of the mind, coupled with an allergy of the body." The Big Book states on page xxvi, "[Dr. Silkworth] confirms what we, who have suffered alcoholic torture, must believe—that the body of the alcoholic is quite as abnormal as his mind. It did not satisfy us to be told that we could not control our drinking just because we were maladjusted to life... [This was] true to some extent, in fact, to a considerable extent with some of us. But we were sure that our bodies were sickened as well. In our belief, any picture of the alcoholic which leaves out this physical factor is incomplete."

Unlike A.A., Clutterers Anonymous (CLA) lacks a medical benefactor. Our literature doesn't mention anything about the physiological factors contributing to our state of powerlessness. Yes, CLA says A.A. literature is applicable to our circumstances. But what does it really mean to have, "an obsession of the mind, coupled with an allergy of the body," when it comes to clutter?

Suddenly, I had a stroke!!! I worked with neurologists to recover. They underscored how my Higher Executive Functioning was now impaired. It turns out that neuroscientists have also been researching the relationship between physiology and Hoarding Disorder (HD) or clutter. Shockingly, people with HD are almost universally impacted in their Higher Executive Functioning, which guides many skills, including:
- Paying attention
- Organizing, planning, and prioritizing
- Starting tasks and staying focused on them to completion
- Understanding different points of view
- Regulating emotions
- Self-monitoring (keeping track of what you're doing)

Researchers conducted brain scans and discovered people with HD have lower glucose metabolism in the Dorsal Anterior Cingulate Cortex—the area of the brain that controls attention, cognition, error detection, motivation, executive control, response selection, and decision-making. The information processing center of the brain is also affected, which impacts categorization, perception, and associative or complex thinking.

After my stroke, the words in "The Doctor's Opinion" rang in my ears: "It did not satisfy us to be told that we could not control our drinking just because we were maladjusted to life...we were sure that our bodies were sickened as well." Finally, I understood that there truly is something different in my body/brain from non-clutterers, and it fills me with self-compassion. Thanks to the Steps, I know I indulge in the dubious pleasures of my character defects of pride, greed, anger, envy, lust, gluttony, and sloth, etc. But I now believe that my clutter is a manifestation of an obsession of the mind (fueled by my character defects) and an allergy of the body (fueled by the hardwiring of my brain). Thus, I am admitting that I am powerless over clutter and that my life has become unmanageable.

Ultimately, it doesn't matter why I'm bodily and mentally different from my fellows (just as alcoholics are). What matters is that I surrender to this truth and utterly abandon myself to working the remaining Steps. Biology is not destiny. Character defects can be removed. God can, and does, restore clutterers to sanity. I know this because I've been blessed to witness the miracle of recovery in others. Hence, I'll keep coming back…because it works! △

The Power of God's Sprinkler Head

Holiday 2021
Sheryl B., MI

If I were to draw an analogy of what God's power must be like for a clutterer vs. an alcoholic, I'd say it was like a hand-held sprinkler head on a garden hose, and the power of God would be the force of the water.

For an alcoholic, the sprinkler would be set for "jet" and all the power of the water on full blast is going toward not taking that next drink.

But, for a clutterer, that setting isn't on jet at all, it's on "spray"—because we all know that God's

power needs to be spread out over a lot of areas!

Many areas are deficient—daily routines, paperwork, bills, relationships, the physical state of my home, my yard, my car, my mail, my appearance, and my health. This is not one big stream in one direction—but a stream that's divided into many areas—all deficient, all needing help and healing. When you look at this comparison, for the clutterer, it sounds like a losing battle.

Luckily, God's power is not like the force of water in a garden hose. Even if God's power is divided up into the many areas of deficiency in my cluttered life, it does not become any less powerful, any less miraculous, or any less healing. God is omnipotent—all powerful. If I seek God's will for each new day of my life here on earth, God will help change me and my behavior so that I am doing God's will, not mine!

I trust that is exactly what God is doing—leading and guiding me to make real and lasting changes. I would have no hope were it not for this still inner voice that tells me what the next right thing is for me to do. If I keep the eyes of my heart firmly looking to God for help, then I know in time I will no longer live in chaos and brokenness. I will live in peace and order, and even beauty—the way

God made the world and the way God made, really, all of us! Thank God for God! ⬭

Enthusiasm for Recovery

Holiday 2021
Mickey M., AZ

Recently I was reading an article about a famous musician. During the course of an interview with a longtime contributing editor from a well-known magazine, the musician said that the word "enthusiasm" was derived from the Greek adjective entheos, meaning "having the god within," with its attendant sense of "living without aging," as did the gods on Mount Olympus.

I like that part: having the god within. When we act on our enthusiasm, I believe we are acting on God, our Higher Power, within. We are "living without aging'" in the sense that we are outside of time, moving forward to an organized life of peace, serenity...and leisure time!

I have waxed enthusiastic relating to my recovery, my recent recovery, I might add. Sometimes my enthusiasm is warmly accepted and sometimes...not so much. Timing is everything. I tell myself to curb my enthusiasm when in the middle of a business conversation. Sometimes I remember...and sometimes I don't.

The musician went on to describe his lifelong passion, that of teaching young people to love music. He said that he understood that love and learning are inextricably linked, that learning is a kind of love and love a kind of learning and used his robust and radiant enthusiasm as a force of illumination.

Robust and radiant enthusiasm for love of recovery and learning is what that means. This is what I'm taking from the musician's interview. We learn to recover and we learn to love recovery with robust and radiant enthusiasm as a force of illumination.

We have the Tools of Recovery[16], Service, Sponsorship, Meetings, Literature, Bookending, Buddies, Daily Action, Earmarking, Focusing, Streamlining, Telephone, and Trust. Anything we can do lovingly can become a prayer of action. There's our magic word and there's love. My motivation of six actions: prayer of action, permission to proceed, instructions about what's next, encouragement to continue, applause for proceeding on these actions, and lastly a prayer of gratitude.

I also believe that God is present in the loving attention I give to the work entrusted to me.

That's why I included two prayers, one at the beginning of a project and one at the end of my motivation six. With closer and conscious contact with our Higher Power, we know we are proceeding with our recovery—not alone, but with our God within.

But I was writing about enthusiasm. I apologize to those I might have bored with my happiness describing my progress. Those who listened with acceptance and joy, thank you for your kindness. ◓

Procrastination

Procrastination is one of the biggest common character traits among clutterers. It exacerbates all types of cluttering problems—physical clutter, mind clutter, time clutter, and relationship clutter.

Procrastination: Isn't It Normal?

Spring 2018
Alison B., NJ

I'm sitting here with three days to go until the deadline for CLA*rity* submissions. I like to write for each newsletter, and I had three months to do it, so why am I waiting until the last possible moment? Because I have been going through long periods of procrastination, meaning that I

watch TV from the time I wake up until the time I go to bed, pausing only to make meals and take bathroom breaks. I'm completely addicted—after all, there is no clutter in TV land. Unless that's the topic of the show.

The times when I have been more successful in my CLA program are the times when I did more service in WSO because I had to go to business meetings and create a timetable for myself, and I have also put myself on limited TV watching in the past. There doesn't seem to be a TV Watchers Anonymous!

Procrastination for me is like that game where you stack the wooden blocks to make an unstable tower. Then, with a group of people, you go around the room and, one at a time, each person pulls a block out and tries not to topple the tower. I have gone along quite happily, many times in my life, doing nothing to help myself until that "tower" is ready to topple and I have to rescue myself.

I am a master at rescuing myself at the very last minute. I will often do it by calling a bookending buddy, and I like it best when we can spend the whole day checking in every half hour. It is amazing the number of things I can easily get done in one day!

It does not seem to matter how much time I have in program. If I am not doing the Steps with a sponsor and making use of the Tools, I am not in balance. Nor do I want to be. At this point, I am just "willing to be willing." The sub-freezing weather just makes me not want to do anything at all. Another excuse to watch TV.

Saturdays are not my day for watching the usual TV shows, and one Saturday I finally went on the Action Line, which worked amazingly as an antidote to my worst procrastination problems. I got done in one afternoon things I had been procrastinating on for weeks and months—things I've previously written about in these pages. Ironically, I had been procrastinating about calling because I get addicted to people, places, and things so quickly; and I do not want to become dependent on the Action Line for every action I take. I had to pluck up the courage to call.

I also have a phone phobia—a fear of being rejected—and that's probably been a big part of my procrastination over the years in not calling into any kind of phone meeting. I did call into the Action Line once before. Both times I was welcomed, and it was a wonderful experience. I highly recommend it. I will go back.

I also went to the tail end of the Monday noon Eastern Time phone meeting on procrastination and Step 1. I shared, which I have to make myself do, because I am shy over the phone when I'm not leading a meeting. I took down all the phone numbers, which I don't normally do. Now I have to use them. I even got myself a sponsor with a promise to start working on writing Step 1 after I've finished this article. As I write, it's New Year's Day, a great time to admit that I am powerless over my clutter and my life has become unmanageable because I procrastinate. Again.   ◢

Holiday 2021
Alison B., NJ

I've done it again…left it until the very last minute to write this article, and now I'm really angry at myself. I enjoy writing for CLA*rity*, so why do I treat myself this way? It seems I work better under pressure, and it's just an inner feeling that I can't explain fully. Now suddenly I feel like I am alive and fully functioning on all cylinders—like my fuse has been lit.

Often when I am by myself, I have a nasty rebellious streak–I call it my inner two-year-old. It's as if I fold my arms and stamp my feet and say to myself, "I'm not gonna do it, no-no-NO!"

Lack of quality sleep can also play a huge part in making me put off things I actually want to do. I've heard it said that lack of sleep leads to low self-esteem. Wow, if that's true, it explains a lot!

The adult in me has to treat my two-year-old kid kindly—if I make her comfortable, treat her with love and respect, feed her nutritious foods, allow her some play time, make sure she gets her full complement of quality sleep, and gets some daily exercise and fresh air, she's probably going to behave a whole lot better. And some form of meditation or relaxation really helps, too. Most of these things are in the green leaflet ("Declutter Your Mind[6]"), one of my favorites.

One problem for me is trying to be kind to a two-year-old when a big part of me is that little child. As I'm writing, it's after the deadline. I went to bed at 2 a.m. What was I doing? Watching sitcoms that I've seen two or three times before. I find them comforting. I was procrastinating on going to bed because I knew I had to write this article. Why did I make it worse for myself? It was like I wanted to punish myself for not getting it done on time.

Procrastination, for me, seems to be one of those problems from which I get only a daily reprieve at best. I am truly a chronic procrastinator. I call myself the Procrastination Queen. Having been in CLA for 19 years, other 12-Step groups going back 35 years, and having made sure I go to a home meeting every single week, recovery has sneaked up on me, but my natural inclination is to put everything off for as long as possible. It's a good thing my bills are automated!

Being on time has always been an issue. I remember everyone in my family of origin being late for pretty much everything, so it's obviously ingrained in me. I have improved greatly, though. I read in the literature where we need to leave ourselves plenty of time, but there is something about my relationship to time that I don't quite understand. Part of my problem is obsessive thinking. My thinking goes round and round on the same subject, and I just get lost in time.

The best I've been able to do in my preparations to get out the door or prepare myself for a video conference meeting in a timely fashion is to use a timer for each set of activities and then give myself a deadline that's ten minutes earlier than I really intend to leave or have my tablet open. Does it work? Yes, but only when I have serious intentions about sticking to the deadline. And I have to be deliberate with everything. I like to give myself three hours to get ready if I'm going anywhere. Personally, I like to take my time.

It is easy for me to take Step 1 here: "I am powerless over my procrastinating and my life has become unmanageable." The difficult part is remembering Step 2, that my Higher Power will restore me to sanity, and then Step 3, when I turn over my will and my life to the care of my Higher Power—or to put it in my terms, let go of my stubborn rebelliousness.

Some days I write a list, and then I can be much more successful in getting things accomplished. But not always. I have a sneaking suspicion I have to build play time into my schedule to make me less likely to rebel, so now I have it in my head that I have to sing for one hour every day. This is not for everyone. I happen to be a singer, and it makes me feel better. ◬

Meetings and Sessions

The CLA Tools of Recovery[16] state: "We attend meetings to learn how the program works and to share our experience, strength, and hope with each other..." This section includes informative material about meetings and also articles from the "Group Stories" column of CLA*rity*.

Group Stories

How is the Group Helping Me?
Teaneck, New Jersey

Summer 2017
Ruth G., NJ

The group in Teaneck, New Jersey, is going well for me. But, depending on how busy or how tired I am, it will go better or worse. Lately our group has been reading one of the leaflets provided by CLA. Each group member reads a

paragraph and shares on his or her own experience. I believe this gives me more information. Many times I experience the feeling that this evokes, which gives me insight into my own program and problems.

One of the aspects of the program that works for me is using the timer, but I set it for only a few minutes; then I go to another task.

We usually end the meeting a few minutes before 9 p.m. (it starts at 7:30 p.m.) and share what's going on. I'm grateful I found CLA.

≻⋅⧫⋅◯⋅⧫⋅≺

Alison B., NJ

We have a small but friendly group. We read from a format which everybody has access to, so that anybody can lead the meeting. We like to rotate leadership on a weekly basis, and we try to have a business meeting once a month. Every week we write down a list of commitments and report our successes and failures the following week. I need this because it makes me accountable, even though I don't always do the things on the list.

We do a lot of reading, including the 12 Steps and 12 Traditions. We also put our names on pieces of paper, along with our commitment lists and the date, fold up the papers, put them in a can, and pass the can around. Then we pick out each other's names to call during the week. This way, somebody can ask us how we're doing with our commitments.

The best part of the meeting for me is when we read a leaflet together. One person reads a paragraph and then shares on it; then the next person shares on it, and so on—all the way around the room. This can make for some very deep sharing. It may take us several weeks to go through one leaflet, but it's worth it. We also put the kettle on and make herbal tea. So if you're in our neck of the woods, come and join us—we'll make you feel at home!

>─┆─◆〉─•─◯─•─〈◆─┆─≺

Lauren R., NJ

I've been attending the meeting for a long time, maybe 16 years. Though I'm not "cured" and living clutter-free yet, I believe that attending reminds me to keep working on my recovery. Sometimes I get very inspired at the meetings and make good progress. I can go only with HP (Higher Power) and at my own pace.

I've seen clutterers come and go and come back again to the meetings. They have their own journeys, and it's nice to see them again.

I'm glad that our meeting makes time to write commitments for the coming week because it's something that I have a difficult time remembering to do regularly on my own. My list is often rather long, and I'm unlikely to do it all, but writing down what's in my cluttered mind gives me a chance to evaluate and prioritize. I'm bound to do at least some of it and feel good about that. Sometimes I write other lists during the week. I might experiment with a shorter list for a change to see if it's more helpful or if I feel a better sense of accomplishment.

I also like reading leaflets together, then sharing after each paragraph. It brings much more direction and focus than the way we used to share on general topics. ◬

Group Stories–Step Study Group

Holiday 2019

The following article was adapted from a presentation made by a Step study group at the CLA 2019 Convention in New York.
—Editor

Intention: To share with others the structure, foundation, and ways of interacting that we have used that allow us to come together in safety and cohesiveness to work the 12 Steps of CLA and to thrive in the solution and recovery.

Creating a Group

(Helpful tips in forming a CLA Step group)

- Find others.
- Members share what they need or would like to see in order to create a safe and productive group.
- Members may wish to write their own Mission Statement, which would include their purpose and non-purpose.
- Decide the following.
  - When will the meetings take place?
  - What is the duration of the meeting?
  - How will the meeting be run?
  - What are the rules of engagement, such as: Is cross talk allowed and is interrupting another person's share acceptable?
  - How will decisions be made?
- Reevaluate, discuss, and change if necessary.

An Actual Meeting

(How an actual meeting of our Step group goes)

- Opening is done by the moderator.

- Begin with a serenity prayer.
  - Establish attendees/absentees.
  - Determine the amount of time to be allotted for each person.
  - Establish a timekeeper.
- Each person shares.
  - The timekeeper asks how they would like their time and notifies the speaker.
  - If time is available in a person's share, the moderator asks if they would like feedback.
- Planning for the next session is facilitated by the current week's moderator.
  - Next week's moderator is established. (Rotation of service is essential.)
  - The focus for next session is talked about, voted on, and agreed upon. This includes materials and resources to be used.
- Other group business—if there is any, the moderator facilitates.
- The moderator sends out an email after agreement for the next session.

Critical Tools (Group principles we have found essential)

- Determine the Step and resources that the group will focus on, *and* there is always permission for individuals to focus on earlier Step work they may need to do.
- Follow Roberts Rules of Order, as best as is possible.
- The group conscience decides.

Our common welfare should come first—our Traditions in action!!!!
- Allow the group to evolve and adapt. Our group conscience is the tool.

Individual Principles
- Be honest. Be willing to speak up with thoughts and needs.
- Take personal responsibility for your feelings and needs.
- Commit to Steps and CLA recovery and the current group.
  - Be on time.
  - Notify the group in advance if you are unable to attend.
  - Commit to attending and be present during the meeting, really listening to others' shares.
- Leave egos at the door; no one person is in charge.
- Stick to the focus of the meeting.
- When giving feedback, share only from your experience, strength, and hope (ESH). We do not tell one another what to do.
- Offer loving, supportive energy.
- It is important to reach out to one another between meetings.
- Extend a helping hand, either during or after the session.
- Be willing to be vulnerable.
- Trust.

Benefit
- Be able to listen to how others see, interpret, and work a Step, which expands understanding and interpretation of the Step.
- Keeps one on track with Step work and helps build accountability.
- Others give one the ESH to take action in the Steps.
- One develops a resource for CLA recovery. By working and sharing Steps, especially 4th and 5th, members can reach out to others and receive support from others who know them.   ◭

My Experience, Strength, and Hope in Joining a CLA Step-Writing Group

Spring 2020
Mary R., PA

Last year, I had been on a "working the Steps" kick when I heard the phone moderator announce that evening at our CLA meeting that Step-writing groups were being organized. I bit. This was going to be a phone-only Step-writing meeting for one hour per week for those who suffered from, dare I say it, the disease of cluttering.

It took a while for us to get it going and get organized; but I mean, after all, we are clutterers, right?

We took turns being moderators, and I tried to keep that in order as well. But it goes like these things always seem to go: I think we started out with 12 members, "and then there were three" 11 months later. We were losing people almost every other week or so. As far as I know, the two remaining members are still meeting.

I made a spreadsheet with everyone's contact information and shared it with the group. And we gathered the Step-writing materials that were made available to us by our predecessors and then some more from other places. I also saved that to our shared spreadsheet. I was also on a "Big Book" (*Alcoholics Anonymous*[1]) kick, from the one that started it all: A.A.; so each week I pushed for us to follow and use the Big Book. For the most part, that was well received.

Here are some observations that I have made since going through this experience:

1. Unrecovered clutterers should not be left to their own resources to organize and then decide how they are going to run a Step-writing group. So much time was spent debating what we should use and how, etc. I'm still going to stick by my "kick," which is: the Steps have been written in a text book since 1939 and have been saving the hopeless varieties like myself, so why change that? However, if CLA had its own solid Step-writing method, that

would have been half our battle. If we just had had something—any...one...thing to use—to guide us, might we have been more successful?

2. Step-writing groups, or anyone working the Steps, should always be working with an experienced, recovered person. We did the best we could with what we had, but in the end, we didn't know what we were doing.

3. Time wasters—like when and where to meet, how to communicate, and what to use to work these Steps—were, in my humble opinion, our biggest stumbling blocks.

4 Communication—Group texts are the *worst*. Not everyone texts or can receive group texts. When one person leaves the group, you have to start a new group text. If I had any one thing to suggest to future Step-writing groups, it would be to email each other. I think it is easier to remove people from or add them to the email group.

To end on a positive note, we had some great moments and eye-opening things happen at each meeting. I learned so much from the others, no matter what materials they used to work the Step at hand.

My favorite use of our time was

when we'd read or even listen to something *on* the *line* and then write on it for 20 minutes and come back sharing on that writing or reading. This was always productive for me. I always say that I'm going to do homework, but I *never* do! So, instead of feeling guilt over this, we just built "homework" time into our meeting like other phone meetings do.

Finally, I got to meet fellow clutterers on this journey, which is always a good thing. That reminds me that I'm not alone and that they feel and do many of the same things that I do, which shares that burden. This gives me hope.

I hope this helps some future Step-writing groups that are starting to form right now! This process is, at times, painful; but I am a strong believer that a psychological and spiritual change is possible only by working these 12 Steps with a sponsor/guide or group and daily contact with God.   △

Group Stories

Fall 2020

Most CLA face-to-face groups have been unable to meet in person since mid-March due to COVID-19 distancing restrictions. While some groups are on hiatus until lockdowns and the dangers of close physical proximity have ended, others have devised different ways to meet.

Many of these groups are currently meeting via telephone or video conferencing. Some of them have limited attendance to members who have attended the groups previously, while a few others have opened them to anyone wishing to attend.

One member stated that—although a group meeting face to face benefits from larger numbers, with more input and a more electric feeling—too many folks meeting via video conferencing make it unwieldy and more difficult to deal with.

The facility hosting a meeting in Oregon is once again open, so the group has taken a novel approach. A few members are meeting face to face. Others are nervous about doing so with the virus still rampant and are meeting with the rest at the same time via video conferencing.

One member agreed that, for her, video conferencing is preferable to a phone conference call because the nonverbal feedback from other members is lost in a phone call—and that nonverbal feedback helps her a lot.

A few groups are meeting in the parking lot of the meeting location, wearing masks and keeping social distance.

One group has been holding their meeting on a group text,

using emoji's to denote emotion and adhering to strict meeting protocols. While it has been working well, they have been growing; and it becomes unwieldy when there are more than eight people, so they plan to move it to a telephone conference call.

In the end, it seems that, even though CLA members in face-to-face groups prefer a physical meeting, they have found ways to meet and keep their cohesion even in these difficult times.   ◮

CLA 12-Step Co-Sponsoring Study Group

Holiday 2020
Dave B., MO

In mid-June 2020, I joined a CLA men's 12-Step study group, which meets over the phone once a week. Also called a co-sponsoring group, it has been a great way for me to work the 12 Steps of CLA and to find clutter buddies for bookending.

The group I joined was open. Some volunteers jumped in early to send out the meeting format and the study questions; others created and sent attendee phone lists. After our group grew to around 14 members, we voted to split into an open and closed group. Nine of us decided to join the closed group; the open group remains today for any man in CLA

to join. I joined the closed group to allow more time for personal sharing; another joined for "safety, consistency, commitment, and a chance to grow relationships."

Both groups began using a common CLA 12-Step study group meeting format and a group's co-sponsor Step questions, a worksheet with open and closed questions for each Step. Co-sponsoring in both meeting types indicates we help each other work the Steps and conquer our struggles with clutter.

For each meeting in our closed group, a moderator opens the phone call before the start time. At 7:15 p.m. Central Time, or when a quorum exists, he calls the meeting to order using the group-approved format to run these 1 hour 15-minute meetings. He starts each meeting by reading the Serenity Prayer, the Steps, and the Traditions. He then asks for someone to time the shares. Timekeeping is done to keep us focused and accountable and allows all attendees to be heard.

Next starts the sharing. Each attendee gives a one-minute check-in on how his week went; then we each give our answers to the week's Step questions.

Each attendee is given up to four minutes for answers, depending on the number of people in attendance. The suggestion is three minutes to answer the questions, leaving one minute for gentle feedback from other members.

In our weekly business meetings, we choose the next question(s) to answer and the next moderator; we then discuss/vote on format changes, member suggestions, and any concerns. Outside the weekly business meetings, we voted to have a group text where we optionally share encouragement and decluttering victories at any time, day or night. We have also had two informal video social hours that several attended. They each went very well.

We have quickly come to know, respect, and value each other in ways I have never seen before in any 12-Step meeting. I believe our intimacy appeared because we became vulnerable early on and shared our other 12-Step Fellowships, our problems, and our fears. I believe we each began believing more deeply in CLA and in the power of working the Steps. I know I did.

Many thanks to Ben, who helped our group get started; he remains with the open group. Thanks also to our group's Herb and Deric for providing input for this article.

Before and During The Pandemic—Tucson Face-to-Face Meeting

Spring 2021
Mickey M., AZ

Deborah G. had joined CLA in the spring of 2011 and told people in another 12-Step Fellowship about how beneficial CLA was to her life. Hearing this, the others said they also had a problem with clutter and that they should start our own local group. So Deborah G., Susan C., Cyndi K., and Mary H. started the local group. This face-to-face CLA group is still meeting in rooms provided by Streams in the Desert Lutheran Church on Sundays from 4 p.m. to 5 p.m.

The size of our group has varied from month to month and year to year. At one time, we had as many as 15 to 20 members. We held business meetings to establish protocols to conduct our affairs. We set up a notebook with a printed 'script' to follow. The position of facilitator of the meeting was, and still is, rotated week to week. The other service positions are treasurer, WSO delegate, and literature person. Those were deemed to be held for a year; however, in practice, it takes a while before someone else is elected or volunteers.

Before the pandemic, we had a core group of about eight members who regularly attended. Now, in the middle of this event, we have three to four, and sometimes five, attendees.

We also had recurring problems with a person who didn't want to follow the "CLA Meeting Code of Conduct." This would irritate and antagonize practically all of us. We were challenged to practice kindness, compassion, and tolerance of her as a person. We read the code of conduct at meetings and discussed its meaning. When she continued behavior that was against the code of conduct, we held more than one business meeting to discuss what to do. It was decided that the moderator would speak to her and let her know she needed to keep her comments to herself. Although our very tactful moderator did so, she continued to violate the code of conduct. We had another business meeting and decided to ask her to refrain from coming for a month and to reflect upon the code of conduct. She would come every once in a while after that. Since the pandemic, we have not seen her. We wish her well, and we are committed to and very grateful for the "CLA Meeting Code of Conduct."

The church closed its meeting halls in April, 2020, and we received permission to meet outside on the patio of the grounds. The church also kindly loaned us folding chairs. November 1, 2020, the church reopened its rooms, only to close them again on December 1. They made an exception for our group and one other.

It is embarrassing, but crosstalk has crept into our conduct during the meeting. With such a small group, it's difficult to maintain our silent attention. For example, last week, a member was relating the same story with no apparent variation. I interrupted to ask if there was progress or what else had happened since the Sunday before. Nothing had changed. One of the most important things about our meeting is to remind the members that when they are relating their stories, to keep in mind what this story has to do with their recovery. ⬭

My Co-Sponsoring Group

Fall 2021
Karen L., ME

Over a year ago, I was matched with three other women also interested in starting a CLA co-sponsor group. I had hoped to find a sponsor to take me through the 12 Steps, as I had experienced in another program, but one-to-one sponsors were scarce. While we got our weekly meeting going, we were mentored by a seasoned CLA member, who had herself been through the Steps as part of a co-sponsor group. Thank goodness we had that guidance because

I could not imagine how four people could work the 12 Steps together by meeting for approximately 50 minutes per week. Our mentor was clear that it was entirely up to our group to shape the work we would be doing together, but she did offer support, feedback, and many resources and ideas.

As we four began meeting weekly, we chose to use phone conferencing rather than video conferencing. We committed to each other to do our best for everyone to be present every week. Three of us had prior experience in other 12-Step Fellowships. All of us shared with tremendous honesty right from the beginning. It was clear that we were all very motivated to recover in CLA.

Initially, we had thought we might work through one Step per month and have the process complete in one year. It has not worked out that way, but we have worked at a pace that seemed right for us, making group conscience decisions together as we proceeded.

We take turns facilitating our meetings, keeping time, and leading the prayers. Our meetings always start and end with prayers—to invite God in and to reinforce the spiritual nature of this work. Once we close the meeting, we discuss any business—such as

whether we will meet the next week if it falls on a holiday, when to move on to the next Step, and the resources we plan to use to prepare for the next time we meet. We rely on *Alcoholics Anonymous*[1] (the Big Book), A.A.'s *Twelve Steps and Twelve Traditions*[14], and CLA literature as a base on which to work.

Once our meeting opens, each person has the same allotted number of minutes in which to share. We can then choose to use our entire block of time for speaking, or share for a few minutes and then invite the others to comment or give feedback. We are silent as each in turn shares their thoughts or reads their writings, based on the "homework" decided upon at the end of our last meeting. We cut back on wasting precious time by generally taking our turns alphabetically. Whenever one of us is too hard on herself, we are sure to receive a reminder to be gentle with ourselves, putting the situation back into perspective.

Between our regular meetings, we go about our daily lives. Quite often we text or email resources to the others, such as prayers, notices of events such as declutterthons, or inspiring writings from various sources. We ask for and/or receive support for decluttering projects or other life events.

It is very clear to me that, while

our particular situations and the
specific character defects we struggle with are unique to each of us,
we have a great deal in common.
We understand and offer compassion to each other in a way that
only others in CLA can. I believe
that our co-sponsor group op-
erates as a healthy family would.
We make our decisions together,
always respectfully and with all
voices heard. There has never been
a word of criticism of one another,
and we can always count on loving
support from one another.   ◯

Other Articles on Meetings

Divine Decluttering Line

Spring 2018

Ruthe S., PA

Note: All times listed are Eastern Time.

I would like to share about one of CLA's secret weapons—the shared activity sessions and, specifically, the Divine Decluttering line. This session has been instrumental in helping me to start decluttering on a regular basis.

At the end of the summer, I attended a declutterthon, which is basically several hours of shared activity sessions put together. I noticed that I was more efficient at getting things done and had less fear and shame with other people there. Plus, people shared about themselves and about inspirational things, which I found to be very supportive. Shortly after that, I learned that there was a shared activity session called Divine Decluttering that had started in July 2016 under a different name. I am so glad that I found it. That session has been one of the things in CLA that has helped me the most.

I have now learned the history of the Divine Decluttering line. It started as De-Junk July, morphed into Action August, transformed into September Solutions, evolved into Organize October, grew into Nurture November, and found its permanent name in Divine Decluttering December. Because of the spiritual solution found in the first half-hour meditation, the name Divine Decluttering was voted in by group conscience.

Divine Decluttering begins at 10:30 a.m. Eastern Time and, until 11:00 a.m., there is a meditation and spiritual sharing. From 11:00 a.m. to noon, the format turns into a shared activity session, in which people say what they are going to do and later report back on how it went. Many times people are sharing and giving feedback throughout the session. We tend to talk about things with a lot of humor, which is helpful when dealing with clutter. I don't think I have ever laughed so hard as the day we got into a discussion about "How many clutterers does it take to change a light bulb?" (Answer to follow at the end of the article.)

Four days a week, there is a topic meeting at noon. The topics are: procrastination on Mondays, Step/Tradition on Tuesdays, self-nurturing on Wednesdays, and decluttering the kitchen on Saturdays. Some people continue to work on the line until late afternoon. There are also two recovery meetings about planning your week, 9:30 p.m. on Sundays and 8:00 a.m. on Mondays.

There are other shared activity sessions at different times of the day and evening, and they and the phone numbers are listed on our website, www.Clutterers Anonymous.org. The schedule for Divine Decluttering is listed above and can also be found, along with the phone number, on our website. If you are having trouble getting started with your decluttering, I would recommend that you give one of these sessions a try.

And as for the light bulb question, there were several answers, but I think this one sums it up best: "one, but she has to look for it—and if she can't find it, she has to go out and buy one, and if she needs to go out, she has to locate her wallet or purse and her keys, and…." Well, you get the idea. ⬣

Divine Decluttering Line— It's So Much Better Than TV!

Summer 2018
Alison B., NJ

In my last article on procrastination, I said that I could watch TV from the time that I got out of bed 'til the time I went to sleep, stopping only for brief breaks. That was true even on the days I had appointments; and I had been, daily, automatically switching on the TV more often than not. So I decided I had to break the cycle by forcing myself to try out the Divine Decluttering line. It's at 10:30 a.m. Eastern Time, slap-bang in the middle of my favorite morning show. However, it finally occurred to me that I could record it and play it back later as a reward for having done decluttering or some other annoying chores. To me, all chores are annoying. I really want a maid to come in and do it all for me, but that's not going to happen unless I marry a rich man… anyway, I digress…

To get on the Divine Decluttering line, call (712) 770-4010, and enter the access code 852600. There is a leader who facilitates a number of readings: Step 11 (the long form), a section of the leaflet "Finding Your Life Purpose[7]," a couple of paragraphs from page 86 of *Alcoholics Anonymous*[1] (the Big Book), and Daily Reflections[4] from A.A. or a CLA reading. Then there is silence while we have a meditation, which lasts for about eight minutes. During this time, we can just sit quietly or write while we reflect on the readings, which are mainly spiritual. When meditation time is over, we conclude with a prayer from page 87 of the Big Book, and then we go around the virtual room and share our spiritual revelations.

I am not good at this. I need more time on this line before I become comfortable sharing my spirituality. I think, if the truth be known, that I am angry at HP on a personal level for not letting me be where I want to be in my life. People are sharing positive things here, and I want to be able to contribute to that. I'm sure I will when the time is right. I do have an infinite respect for what I call the Universal Power—the one that affects every part of the universe and beyond—but my faith gets tested a lot because things just don't come easily to me.

Anyway, at the top of the hour, the leader says the Serenity Prayer. There is a time to leave phone numbers and welcome newcomers. Now it is time for us to go around the virtual room once again. This time we are getting into action. We each state something we have just done while listening and then a few things we want to get done over the next half hour. As time goes by, victories of yesterday and goals of today are added to the mix. Then the leader might ask if newcomers have any questions or want to leave their phone numbers. Just so you know, you can work on this line all day, if you want to!

Several days a week, including Saturdays, there is a topic meeting at 12:00 pm Eastern Time. Look at the website clutterersanonymous. org for the topics. Sometimes an article from CLArity is read. Then they announce a topic from it, go around the virtual room, and share.

This can be really intense. I actually got to read my procrastination article from the last issue and was extremely gratified when people shared on it. I gave them a topic of avoidance by doing something other than the thing they've been procrastinating on…which is another article!   ◬

Clutterers Anonymous Events

Various organizations in CLA hold periodic events. Clutter-Free Days are one-day events held by intergroups or local alliances of meetings. CLA usually holds weekend conventions annually, which are attended by members from around the US and other countries. Occasionally, the phone groups hold declutterthons.

Clutter-Free Days

Fall 2017

Ruthe S., PA and Betsey K., NJ

CLA-East's 22nd Clutter-Free Day was held on Saturday, April 29, 2017, at St. Luke's Episcopal Church in Metuchen, New Jersey. Approximately 80 people attended. The program included five workshops, a face-to-face meeting, a meditation session, and a keynote speaker.

The workshop titles were, "Step 1: My Life is Unmanageable, and So Am I;" "12 Steps in 60 Minutes;" "My Stuff/Your Stuff;"

"Releasing Shame: A Toxic and Cold Emotion;" and "11th Step: Warming the Spirit."

Many participants expressed that they liked connecting with others from the Fellowship and hearing their stories. Some attendees from the phone meetings liked that they were able to put faces to names.

The day overall was a success according to the reviews. Some of the comments were, "I am here for the first time and found peace that I need to change...," "feeling joyful and empowered," "very happy with and grateful for this experience," "...so inspirational," "lovely day of sharing," "wonderful day," "I always love Clutter-Free Day," and "...a good positive experience."

People enjoyed all of the workshops. Two that were especially popular were one about the 12 Steps and one about identifying your clutter. Some people expressed gratitude for the 12-Step meeting and the meditation. Others appreciated the food.

One of the criticisms was that we should make sure everyone is amplified and can be heard, and another was that they would have liked there to be more beverages. Someone also complained that the coffee was terrible.

Overall, Clutter-Free Day was very successful. The workshops and speakers were very well received, and people learned a lot that would further their recovery. The major sentiment can be summed up by what one participant stated on the evaluation form, "Thank you for having this day!"   ◓

Fall 2018

Terri J., OH

A pilgrimage is a journey or search for spiritual significance and healing. Typically, a pilgrimage is a journey to a location of importance for one's faith. My pilgrimage from Ohio to Clutter-Free Day each spring is important for my spiritual healing from the disease of cluttering. Many pilgrimages are to places where miracles have been documented and locations that have special spiritual power. I consider trips to CLA-East Clutter-Free Days pilgrimages full of miracles and 12-Step outreach filled with supercharged spiritual energy and recovery.

This year's Clutter-Fee Day was my third pilgrimage to find a spiritual solution to cluttering. Having my physical body in a place with 80 fellow clutterers dedicated to finding a spiritual solution was especially empowering this year because our focus was healing through the 12 Steps. Experience, strength, and hope and progress in recovering through the 12 Steps of CLA were shared by different members who shared their growth and recovery with one or two of the 12 Steps for about 30 minutes. We heard other members' recovery through all 12 Steps in a day. What was powerful for me was realizing there is not an exact science but an open progressive program that leaves room for creative spiritual solutions.

Individual tidbits were not important for my recovery this day. Hearing the determination, honesty, humanness, and spiritual connections with Higher Power were important for my recovery on May 20, 2018.

Preparations in planning meetings created a smooth-running day with insights structured on recovering from our spiritual, emotional, and physical dis-ease of cluttering through the 12 Steps. I enjoyed seeing the items discussed and plans followed through to a creative, smooth-running day with divine order.

The 12-Step focus of CLA Clutter-Free Day strengthened thoughts of getting our 12-Step clutterers' writing workbook begun. Different face-to-face meetings and phone meetings have Step questions that have led CLA members to recovering through the Steps, making sponsorship easier for the sponsor and sponsee. This is being addressed in the Literature Committee with the new sponsorship document. The next step seems to be collecting Step questions from our different CLA groups and getting a Step guide begun.

All in all, it was a wonderful Clutter- Free Day. ◢

Fall 2019
Rosemary F., NY

For years I had heard about the annual Clutter-Free Day hosted by CLA-East, held alternately in Brooklyn, New York, or Metuchen, New Jersey.

It had always seemed silly to me to drive from my Suffolk County, Long Island, home to either Brooklyn or New Jersey for just one day! Yet after being on the Divine Decluttering line for three years and speaking to clutterers from all over the world—coupled with attending the 2017 San Jose, California, CLA convention—Saint Luke's in Metuchen, New Jersey, didn't seem that far away!

I arrived the day before, on a Friday, at a hotel in the town of Edison, a short distance from Metuchen.

My drive was a bit eventful in that I'm a nervous driver, and this road trip was outside my comfort zone. I hit traffic, but everyone on the road—fellow drivers and toll keepers alike—was so pleasant. Already, I thought, I am manifesting good energy.

And the energy of Clutter-Free Day was just that—good. The next day, the keynote speaker, as well as the panel discussion and shares of other recovering clutterers, was both validating and inspiring. However, what left the most lasting impression on me was the presentation on the one-minute meditation.

After a fabulous lunch, we gathered in a back room of the church, and the facilitator, Ted S., introduced us to the one-minute meditation. As he instructed, I centered myself. I attempted to empty my mind, concentrating on a void, and within that void, I saw white. I focused on that white, going deeper into the void with no thought but the void...and just as I was further emptying my mind, the minute was up.

Ted explained that once a day consistently for one week was better than doing longer meditations inconsistently. He also suggested doing it at the same time, for example, in the morning.

I always struggled with a 15- or 20-minute meditation daily because 15 or 20 minutes seemed like a big commitment with my cluttered brain of "things I have to do." But a minute in the morning seemed doable. Who doesn't have a minute? And it works! Just about at the end of that minute, I always find myself slowing down, breathing regularly and freely. I also use it throughout the day when I feel "agitated or doubtful"…it seems to lead me to the next right thing.

My clutter-free weekend also proved to be great fun!

I'm a free conference call junkie. All my CLA meetings are on the telephone, so my clutter buddies live in various parts of the country. Within five minutes of my hotel arrival, I was greeted by two buddies. I had met them previously at the 2017 convention, and although I had not seen them since then, I speak to both of them weekly via our Step study group or private calls.

Because of the nature of our personal sharing, bonding, and growth, CLA buddies can prove to be forever friends. And there is nothing like connecting to a buddy face to face for some harmless mischief, mayhem, laughter, and fun.

Something CLA quickly brought to the surface for me is that life can be about fun. We are so much more than our clutter. When I lighten up and accept all of me for exactly who I am, clutter and all, I can be there for others and for myself as well. So, "if you're not having fun, you're not doing it right." (That's in our leaflet, "Declutter Your Mind[6].")

The all-day Clutter-Free Day provided more "people" surprises. I met for the first time, face to face, so many others whom I had previously talked with on our phone meetings. It's like going to a big family reunion, only our bond is bigger than blood. It's our hearts, souls, and personal realities we speak on those telephone lines.

Some might say that it's the biggest take away from Clutter-Free Day. We finally get to meet face to face, connecting a body to our shared stories. The circle of camaraderie is complete. Thank you, CLA-East, for a fabulous Clutter-Free Day 2019. ◬

Summer 2020

Alison B., NJ, and Ruthe S., PA

When we started planning for Clutter-Free Day 2020, we thought it was going to be a face-to-face event, as usual, but the outside world had other ideas. We actually cancelled it, but then we realized that there were other options. The idea came up that we could do it virtually. We considered a video conference, but it seemed too complicated. We took a vote and decided to do it by phone, which turned out to be the best idea.

Then the planning began in earnest. Speakers were gathered. A schedule was planned. We were in uncharted territory, but we soldiered on. One of the larger issues was that some people who go to face-to-face meetings are unfamiliar with conference lines, so it was awkward trying to convey instructions on how to access them.

To our delight, the Clutter-Free Day went splendidly. It began at noon with a keynote speaker and a session on "Getting Started." This was followed by "Step 4" and an "Inventory of Physical Clutter." Next was "Emotional and Mental First Aid, the CLA Way," and then there were "The Three Ps: Procrastination, Perfectionism, and Paralysis." The last two sessions were face-to-face groups speaking about the meaning of the word "Clarity," and "Working the 12 Steps as Co-Sponsors."

Attendees stated that the event was very powerful and profusely thanked the planning committee for pulling it all together. We were thrilled to be able to produce Clutter-Free Day this year. Because it was on the phone, we were able to accommodate many more people. At one point there were 184 people on the line. We are looking forward to seeing your smiling faces next year.

Fall 2021
Mary P., NY

CLA-East, the long-running intergroup, presented its signature event, Clutter-Free Day, on May 15. It was the 26th time the day was held, a number confirmed by Betsey K. of New Jersey, the only person who's attended all 26.

This year, as was done in 2020, the event was held on a conference-call phone line because of the ongoing pandemic. Although many members missed the fellowship of the face-to-face version, the phone format allowed many members to participate—there were close to 200 people on the line at some times. The presentations were recorded, so that many more CLA members will be able to listen to them later in the year.

The day began with a touching tribute to a long-time and very active member, Frederick W. of New York City, who had died some months earlier. Mafa, also from New York City, presented details of Frederick's prodigious service, including being a CLA convention and Clutter-Free Day speaker and doing a variety of types of service in a Manhattan face-to-face group. Others on the call shared reminiscences of Frederick as well.

Californian Paul K. gave the keynote address, inspired by the theme of the day: "Time is a precious gift, so we use it wisely." He spoke of time as a gift and how that realization can be a type of spiritual awakening.

Vicky V., another West Coast member, expanded on the topic "CLA Literature Choreographs My Progress." Six other speakers spoke on various aspects of time in relation to clutter. Kristin from Pennsylvania gave a workshop called "Powerless over Clutter." Maryanne from Massachusetts titled her talk "Losing Myself, Not Just Time."

Doris D. from New York City explained how "Time is My Most Valuable Resource."

Karen S. and Mary P., both from New York, presented contrasting views of how the pandemic affected their clutter and how they used their time.

There was time for sharing at the end of each presentation, and attendees participated enthusiastically.

Clutter-Free Day 2021 was produced by a small group of volunteers led by Alison B. of New Jersey, the chairperson of CLA-East. Recordings from the event will be available later in the year, so watch the website CLAEast.org or ClutterersAnonymous.org/wso-delegates/ for an announcement.   ⚠

Conventions

Holiday 2017

Seventy-six clutterers came together for fellowship and enlightenment at the 2017 CLA Convention on August 26 and 27 in San José, California. In spite of a glitch with no microphone on Saturday, attendees expressed having a wonderful time.

The convention consisted of a keynote speech by Susie S. of California, four workshop sessions covering all 12 Steps, and other workshops on self-nurturing, the CLA Tools of Recovery[16], "What Would My Life Be Like if I Didn't Have Clutter?," and "Exit Strategies: How to Deal with Loss."

There was also a skit on the Traditions, a phone meeting (that allowed non-attendees to call in), and a "Problems and Solutions" session (where clutterers shared their problems and others gave solutions.)

Attendees were asked to complete an evaluation form. One attendee called the convention "inspirational" and another liked "hearing the true realities; connecting." Another attendee remarked, "It gave me hope that I can do this with others. Reaching out is so important." Several folks complimented the emcee, Paul K., with one stating: "Paul was amazing."

Sessions were generally given positive marks, and comments were: "Real wonderful practical/personal life stories, insight and recovery, big helpful hints, honesty," "very inspiring. Loved application of 12 Steps, never been clearer," and "great Step work." One respondent especially liked "the variety of topics."

Two sessions specifically noted were the keynote speech by Susie S. and the workshop on Steps 4–10 by Laura T. One attendee liked "Susie and Laura T. talking about how they [personally] work the program with Steps." Another remarked: "Just loved keynote with Susie S.; so inspiring, wonderful application of 12 Steps; can't wait to apply this to my clutter situation. Steps 4-10 outstanding insight." Another said: "I was very grateful for the keynote speaker, Susie. I haven't been interested in the phone meetings, but it was good to hear how they can really help people."

Other comments were: "We bonded during "Problems and Solutions," and "The phone meeting went really smoothly."

There were many glowing comments about the fellowship that many experienced: "I wanted to be around other clutterers with strong recovery, which I accomplished," "[I liked] meeting many extraordi-nary people with [the] same challenges," "hearing the true realities; connecting," "Amazing connections! New clutter buddies, new tools, new friends," and "Meeting lots of people who are transforming their lives and their space."

Suggested changes included:
• more before and after photos
• more information on the website
• more small groups
• more timekeeping during shares
• how to start a face-to-face meeting
• a session about WSO and the committees specifically

And lastly, a couple of respondents remarked that we need more trusted servants to help plan the convention and to get the word out to local groups. ◬

Holiday 2018

The 2018 CLA convention was held on August 11 and 12 in Chicago, Illinois. The theme was "Less Is More." At the last minute, our slated keynote speaker, Joe A. of Texas, was unable to attend, so Chuck R. of Illinois stepped up and gave a great speech.

Workshop sessions and presenters included: "Higher Power for Non-Believers" (Margaret H.), "How the 12 Steps Helped Me Recover from Clutter" (Chuck

R.), "Practicing the Principles of Decluttering," (Mary P.), "Lights, Camera, Declutter!" (Wendy L.), "Lost Dreams" (Carol N.), "12 Steps in 60 Minutes" (Ted S.), "Sponsorship Workshop" (Erin B., Moderator), "Physical Clutter 4th Step Workshop" (Jane D.), "Digging Deep" (Pam B.), and "Using the Tools of Recovery[16]," (Kathy H.).

There were also a "Problems and Solutions Session," a phone meeting, Laughter Yoga led by Sherry A. and Frank A., and a skit on the 12 Traditions.

Many folks enjoyed the evening entertainment, with one remarking "I loved the talent show."

Our convention was a special weekend where we focused on CLA, clutter issues, and fellowship with other clutterers from all over. One attendee called it "CLA immersion." Other comments were: "Variety. Wonderful cooperation. Sincerity and genuineness," "fun being in a friendly and joyous crowd," "the openness and the honesty," "most valuable part of my year," and "Loved the focus on recovery versus problems…left the convention feeling very hopeful."

One of the most fulfilling aspects of conventions is having an opportunity to interact with other clutterers. This was reflected in the evaluations; in response to the question "What did you like

or find most useful?" one clutterer stated, "time spent with other clutterers," while others remarked, "meeting people face to face" and "sharing and interacting with participants."

"What an extraordinary weekend! So many 'ah ha' moments and shared heart experiences. I am so grateful to have been here to participate. Several times during the weekend, I thought 'That was worth the cost of admission!' I learned practical strategies, including the synchronicity of the universe; the gentle allowing of change and increased 'eye space'; the amazing inventory methods by two members; the encouragement of CLA meeting attendance and service benefits; in addition to fun! Less Is More!! Except for love!"

"Wow! The convention is a CLA Rehab Intensive. So many great ideas. Funny—sharing that make[s] you laugh as well as cry. Diving deep in the 12 Steps, Tools. The location was lovely, modern, and serene, with kind, supportive staff, great facilities, good food, and in a great Chicago location."

More than one person liked the variety of workshops and activities. The workshops were very favorably reviewed, with one commenter writing, for more than one workshop, "I couldn't take notes fast enough." Other comments were: "tools to let go of some of my things" and "I like some of the speakers' slant[s] on Step 4 being an inventory of NOW, not a history." Still another felt that "I am finally beginning to understand the Steps and Traditions because of these wonderful, dedicated speakers and all their handouts and hard work."

However, some respondents would like to see some changes, including: more interactive workshops, placing the program online ahead of time, a support meeting in the evening, a breakfast 12-Step session, more time for Q & A after sessions, and a workshop around examples of success in decluttering.

All in all, it was a wonderful weekend. As one attendee put it, "There was such a positive atmosphere at the convention; the focus was on recovery, and people shared their experience, strength, and hope. We laughed, cried, shared, played, and got to know each other on a deeper, personal level."

The Convention Committee is currently searching locations for the next convention. ⬧

Fall 2018

Those of us on the CLA*rity* Team love conventions. They are an opportunity to learn about our disease and connect with other clutterers. The 2019 CLA Convention was held on July 20 and 21 at Manhattan College in Riverdale, Bronx, New York, with the theme of "Road to Recovery: Celebrating 30 Years of CLA." More than 80 CLA members participated, and it seems that a good time was had by all.

Sessions included "Getting Started in Recovery," "Abundance Awareness," "The Magic of Article Writing," a panel on Service, "Attachments," "Documenting Your Recovery," "Clutterers, The Family Afterward," "Problems and Solutions," "Working The Steps: A Road to Recovery," "Discovering Your Legacy," "Clutter and Humor," slogans, "Road to Recovery," and "Mental or Nonphysical Clutter."

The evaluations were generally positive, and we are including comments below.

One member said, "It was great being at the convention and connecting with my fellows in CLA. All the sessions were informative, thought provoking, and filled with recovery. I came away with many new ideas to enhance my recovery as a clutterer. I now feel motivated to take action to start a physical meeting near me!"

One participant loved the before and after pictures shown in a couple of sessions, but another remarked "too many photos."

Some preferred interactive sessions, with one attendee remarking, "I liked...'Problems and Solutions.' I found that very helpful and fully engaged with others." Another said, "The writing and small-group discussion was the best because it forced me to be more involved than just listening or speaking," while still another liked the Step Group workshop. "Good to hear how another Step group was run...will use some of this information to better structure our own Step group."

The talent show at the banquet was a hit, with remarks such as, "Loved the talent show for viewing clutterers as more than our clutter," and "just awesome."

"Ted's meditation and spiritual reflections was golden."

One loved "all the workshops" and "making the connections between emotional and physical clutter!" Another said, "diversified activities: workshops, panel workshop, small groups—a good mix."

One attendee remarked, "So well organized. Love content of presenters, but even more important than that was the authenticity." Another stated, "This was a perfect balance on workshops and talks."

"Every speaker was articulate, skilled; unusual topics and focus. I expected tips but learned a lot about myself. Liked the connec-

tions between physical clutter and mind clutter and electronic clutter."

As usual, many attendees stated one of the things they liked most about the convention was the fellowship, such as one who remarked, "Meeting like-minded people, knowing I am not alone." Another said, "I liked the friendliness (and helpfulness) of the people," while yet another stated that, "interpersonal action and ability to connect" was what they liked most. Someone else stated, "it was hyper wonderful meeting people with similar struggles and mind-sets."

Other remarks were: "...getting validation that we are normals, as Ruthe from Pennsylvania said, 'we just have a cluttering problem,'" "realizing that I am not alone in dealing with the clutter problem," and "inspirational mentors and models."

One attendee liked the "many opportunities to share problems and solutions over meals and breaks," while another stated that "The CDs will be critical to the healthy growth of our face-to-face meeting in Center City One Philly," and one appreciated that she was "able to buy literature" and "learn more about WSO [and] CLA-East."

Attendees had many suggestions for future conventions. They

included: "A workshop to explore talents and interests by asking what sparked life in our youth…and how to incorporate back into our lives," and "more integration of 12 Steps in all presentations." Also, one remarked, "I would like to see more Step workshops, where someone talks for a few minutes and then facilitates time for writing."

One participant would like to see a lunch at future conventions feature tables for those with special interests, such as men, decluttering with physical problems, and newcomers.

Topics proposed for future conventions included: disagreeing with decision making, depression and hoarding, paralysis and procrastination, severe anxiety with releasing, self-compassion for the individual suffering, and resentment.

When asked about their overall impressions, one member stated, "It was a weekend that was wonderfully put together to offer many aspects of recovery. The variety was well thought out. Each presenter was obviously well prepared and excited about their topic."

And one summed up the convention, saying, "It was like an emotional and relationship feast."

Holiday 2020

This was our first virtual convention, due to the pandemic.—Editor

When asked, "Would you be interested in coming to the next convention?" most respondents said, "Yes." One said, "This has been an invaluable experience. So motivating and inspiring. So grateful for everyone's energy to provide all the healing information. This was my first CLA convention, and I am very interested in attending the next one. Wow Wow Wow!!!!!!"

However, one person will attend again only if it's a webinar.

When asked, "What did you like most or find most useful about the convention?" replies included: "the selection of speakers," "practical examples of challenges and recovery tools," "I liked every presenter, and I took copious notes that I will be devouring for quite some time," and "Lots of good, helpful information; nice seeing the people behind telephone meetings."

One attendee "very much enjoyed the variety of topics and speakers and was inspired into action after each day of the convention. It was great to see people whose voices I hear so often on the phone lines"; "Getting encouragement and new ideas;" "connection;" "*Excellent* topics, presenters, pacing and length;" "Learning about the 12 Steps;" and "I'm a newcomer, so it was just helpful to hear different speakers talk about their experience."

Some also mentioned particular sessions, such as: "Kathy H.'s talk on co-sponsor groups [part of a Tools presentation] and Susie from California's talk," "Ted's and Kenny P.'s shares and recovery," and "hearing the information about the Steps."

One liked "How to actually declutter with a system such as what Dave B. described in his workshop. At the same time, knowing that decluttering is spiritual like Ted mentioned in his workshop."

Another attendee liked "The sense of hope. Learning it's not about the stuff. Inspiration from all those who were of service and put together and pulled off a wonderful convention!"

Another felt that "All the speakers were informative and brought their experience, strength, and hope to each of their sessions. I found many helpful and encouraging words and ideas that will help me declutter."

But there were those who would like to see changes next time, such as: "More how to's and the proper way to do the very basics;" "some entertainment and panels;" "a virtual option as well as an in-person option;" "more time and inter-

action with the 100-plus attendees;" "more audience questions;" "pdfs with each day's schedule and speaker with contact info;" "experience, strength, and hope of those who are living at the maintenance level after successfully getting rid of their hoards;" and "having Martha do the 4th Step of the pink leaflet."

One attendee wanted "more specific information about how this is a 12-Step spiritual approach to overcoming clutter (as a symptom) rather than just another method to get organized or using willpower to change behaviors."

And another asked for "face to face, obviously! Let's hope our present dilemma is arrested by the next convention. I enjoyed all the sessions I was able to attend."

The words of one attendee were very complimentary: "I attended in person in New York last year and loved meeting fellows in person. I was so happy we had a [video] convention this year! Thank you all for a fantastic job! It was a meaningful and well-organized event!! I hope in the future when we have in-person conventions, we could consider still offering a [virtual] option too! *Thank you all very much!*"   ⏛

Holiday 2021

The CLA 2021 Convention was

held Friday and Saturday, October 1 and 2, via video conferencing because of restrictions due to the pandemic.

The response was generally favorable, with one person saying "Pen was busy, writing down experience, strength, and hope of speakers from five nations."

The convention started on Friday evening with a prerecorded message from Mary P. of New York. One attendee remarked, "Mary's welcome=engaging." The scheduled keynote speaker was Joe A. of Texas; but he was unable to participate, so Kathy H. of California filled in. One person remarked of her speech, "Kathy=calmness/serenity; set tone for the weekend."

After her speech, attendees were directed into breakout rooms for CLA recovery meetings. (These breakout rooms were also used during Saturday's lunch break.) Some comments were: "I loved the breakout rooms, since it allowed me to meet my fellows." Another liked: "asking for consideration of my personal questions in the breakout rooms when no one was sharing."

There were six sessions held on Saturday, with an hour break in the middle. One attendee commented, "I liked the variety of the speakers, and I enjoyed hearing about the history of CLA," while another liked "the sincerity of the speakers and their willingness to bare their souls to help others to recover." Other comments were: "so much more valuable than any expert on organizing or decluttering," "Being a new member clutterer, I found the tips about dealing with clutter and the reason for cluttering and types of cluttering (food) very interesting," and "Referring to specific traditions and steps and slogans[18] of the program was great."

Still other attendees liked: "hearing people who have lots of experience, strength, and hope, explain how they work the program," "hearing the recovery stories, seeing some familiar faces, and some new ones!" and "the far-flung speakers, everyone's being so well-versed in the principles and literature of the program." One attendee thought, "The topic of what the speakers do when they get overwhelmed was the most useful."

One attendee really liked Alison's qualification, while another remarked that Chuck's presentation on the 12 Steps was "one of the best/most personal that I've ever heard!" One remark about the last presentation was that, "Gail S. in Australia shared a lot of great experience, strength, and hope... before and after pictures, too!" One said, about Susie's presentation on the Tools, "it helped to remind me that I can use them to get things done."

Some attendees liked the 12-Step Group Panel, with one remarking: "learning about co-sponsoring and 12-Step groups, want to do one!!" Another said, "Cee was great in the panel," with another calling Herb outstanding. One said Terri was "inclusive/personal."

There were some comments about the technological aspects of the convention. One attendee liked that the schedule was posted in the chat feature, while another remarked on the "vast improvement to the technological aspects." Another said, "It is awesome to be on Zoom with hundreds of people across the country and the world." One mentioned, "It was not easy to get in, it took a long time and I had already registered," although another appreciated that Marge informed the audience about tech hiccups.

Overall, the response was positive, with one person remarking, "There is hope! So many excellent Tools," although another remarked that, "There was a lot of repetition about using the Tools, but not so much how people got started or how useful the Tools were or why."

Many commented that they liked hearing from a wide range of membership, with another liking, "the sense of global connection and how much the Fellowship is growing." One newcomer said, "This was my first CLA meeting, so it was all good."

One said, "I found it inspiring to find people overcoming their clutter. If they can do it, then so can I," with another saying, "Broadened my understanding of the CLA Program as it is evolving," and others saying, "so many things—I have 8 pages of notes," and "I thought everything was really well balanced."

One attendee said, "This convention was very well done! Thank you for all the time and effort all of you put into this presentation. ◢

CLArity Box

The CLArity Box column in CLArity includes various topics. It consists of questions by clutterers and answers to those questions.

Spring 2017

Where can 7th Tradition donations be sent? *Wondering in Wisconsin*

Dear Wondering,

Thank you for asking; 7th Tradition donations are important. They are what support the Fellowship.

Except for those to the CLA-East Intergroup, all 7th Tradition donations are sent to the CLA World Service Organization (WSO). There are committees and funds that accept money through WSO, including the CLArity Newsletter, the Convention Committee, and the Convention

Scholarship Fund. Donations can be made at ClutterersAnonymous. org by clicking on the "Members" menu, then "7th Tradition Donations," and following the prompts. Donations may be sent via postal mail to: CLA WSO, PO Box 91413, Los Angeles, CA 90009, except for those to CLArity. Those may be sent to: 184 South Livingston Avenue, Suite 9-203, Livingston, NJ 07039.

Donations to CLA-East can be sent only via postal mail. The address is the same as that for CLArity, shown above.

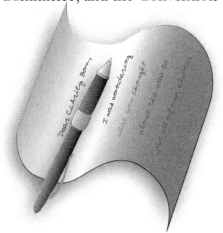

Summer 2017

My friend is helping me to declutter, but she is insisting that I get rid of something that is not actually clutter. How do I explain to her that my theater programs are part of a collection that is important to me?
Theater Lover in Tennessee

Dear Theater Lover,

I see that your programs are important to you. As clutterers, we all have things we love. I am assuming that your friend thinks they are clutter because they are mixed in with your other papers.

Perhaps you would consider gathering the programs and then putting them in one place so you could easily refer to them. This could be a scrapbook or a special container. Then you could look at the collection you love any time you want.

You could even have your friend help you so that she could see the collection that you care so much about and could help you store it in a way that feels good. This might help her to understand that, rather than being clutter, it is a sense of joy for you.   ◯

Fall 2017

My daughter asked me to buy a set of books for her birthday, but I have no space left on my bookshelves. I don't want to disappoint her; what should I do?   *Frantic in Florida*

Dear Frantic,

We understand your dilemma; we've all been through this. The CLA Tool of Earmarking states, "...When we add a new item, we release an old one..."

You could peruse your bookshelves. You're bound to have a few books there that you read a long time ago and no longer want. You could donate them to your local library or take them to a thrift shop. That may give you a sense of satisfaction in knowing that you'll be passing them on to someone else who could use them.   ◯

Holiday 2017

I have been decluttering for at least 15 minutes each day, but it doesn't look like I have done anything, and I am discouraged. What should I do?

Discouraged in Delaware

Dear Discouraged,

You've been decluttering for 15 minutes a day—great job. Remember, it's progress, not perfection. We have some suggestions that may help you.

They are:

- Attend meetings and share your progress each week. In fact, there are two activity sessions on the CLA phone lines which touch upon the subject. The Victories and Goals session takes place from 9:45 to 10 a.m., Eastern Time, at (515) 604-9000; the access code is 670013. There is another session titled "Release Victories Shares," from 7:30 to 7:45 p.m. each day, Eastern Time. The number is (712) 432-3900, and the access code is 727176.
- Try bookending with a CLA buddy.
- Keep a daily record of the work you did.

- Remind yourself of what you have done, regardless of what the area looks like at the present time. Remember, you spent 15 minutes decluttering!

Decluttering is a process, not an event, and it takes time. Remembering how far you have come, rather than looking at how far you have to go, may give you motivation to get started again. Slow and steady wins the race. ◬

Spring 2018

Help! I'm drowning in mail. It just keeps coming in, and I add it to the piles. I do separate the bills and time sensitive items, but they accumulate as well. Now the piles are so big that I don't know where to start.
                    Drowning in Delaware

Dear Drowning,

Mail can definitely be a problem for clutterers. A first action that may help is to open your mail the same day you receive it. Then throw away anything that is junk or unneeded, even envelopes and fillers. That way, a large portion of your problem is solved immediately because, if you are anything like us, much of your mail likely falls into these categories.

Some clutterers find it helpful to set up mail processing areas in their homes. This generally includes a trash can, a recycle bin, and two paper-sized trays for time-sensitive mail and things to be filed. You can use any type of container to hold these items. You don't even have to buy anything fancy; you can use whatever you have around the house.

The key to this system is to take a scheduled amount of time weekly to file and to handle action items; then mail doesn't become out of control, which leads to your pile problem.

You could take a small amount of time each day to process your back mail in the same way. By taking daily action on this, you will eventually rid yourself of the piles.

We are confident that, by taking one step at a time, day by day, you will see improvement. ◬

Summer 2018

Help! My clothes are taking over. What should I do?
                    Bewildered in Boston

Dear Bewildered,

We love clothes, too. In fact, it's easy for us to have more than we can handle. Some of the problems that clutterers can have are: not doing laundry often enough, not putting clothes away after they are laundered, compulsive shopping, and not releasing clothes that are not being worn.

One thing that could help is to have a schedule to do your laundry.

This could be a certain day of the week or when you have enough for a load of dark or light clothing or whatever conditions you choose. In addition, it is important to complete the laundry cycle, so you may want to plan when you will put the clean clothes away.

It is helpful to go through your clothes before you shop. How much can you really wear? Do they fit? Do you need, use, and love them? Are they out of date? Are they in bad condition? It's better to shop when you know what you need. A common issue for clutterers is in not releasing clothing. A good rule of thumb is to release one item for every item you bring in.

Just remember to be gentle with yourself, and remember that decluttering can take time. ◭

Fall 2018

What do I do if I want to share a non-CLA resource with my group or if someone else brings one up in a meeting?
Wondering in West Virginia

Dear Wondering,

As you probably know, in accordance with our Traditions, non-CLA information should not be discussed during a CLA meeting. It's okay to bring up a resource if you don't mention the name or give details. Of course, it's

perfectly fine to discuss whatever you want outside of the meeting.

If someone else brings up something that is not part of CLA during the meeting, you can gently remind them that we do not discuss outside issues during the meeting and that they are welcome to share about it after the meeting.

Remember that most people don't do this on purpose—either because they are newcomers or because it just slipped out—so please remember to be kind and respectful. ◭

Holiday 2018

What is the difference between Clutter-Free Days and conventions?
Curious in Connecticut

Dear Curious,

In a nutshell, the biggest difference is that Clutter-Free Days (CFDs) are held for one day and conventions are held for two. CFDs are planned by local groups for local groups, whereas conventions are planned and run by CLA members from the entire Fellowship and tend to attract members from all over the United States— and even other countries.

Workshop topics tend to be similar, but because conventions are held over two days, there is an opportunity to have more varied types of presentations, which could include panels and the ever-popular phone meeting with the international Fellowship.

Conventions usually have a banquet and entertainment, whereas CFDs generally do not. Since folks come from longer distances and stay overnight, there are more social gatherings at a convention. A convention is more immersive.

Conventions often feel like a celebration of CLA, with people gathering together from all over. And often people interact who seldom get to see each other, and it's also an opportunity to make new friends.

Both CFDs and conventions are ways to share our experience, strength, and hope with one another. Whichever one you attend, you are sure to have a great time and learn a lot.

Summer 2019

Recently, a family member of a clutterer came to our meeting seeking information. This led the group to wonder how to handle nonclutterers who attend the meeting.

Wanting to Share the Message the 12-Step Way

Dear Wanting,

In order for a nonclutterer to attend, the meeting has to be an open meeting. Closed meetings mean that only clutterers may attend, while anyone is welcome at open meetings—although only clutterers should share.

There are several categories of nonclutterers. First are family members and friends looking to help a clutterer. They are welcome to listen, and you may give them information after the meeting and encourage them to bring their loved one with them.

Next would be students looking to write papers on 12-Step meetings. They are welcome to attend, but you should explain to them that they are not allowed to break anonymity by speaking of or writing about anything that would identify an individual.

Last would be professionals. While they are welcome to attend to learn about clutterers or CLA, please remember that they should not use the meeting or the after meeting to solicit clients—which means also that they should not take members' contact information from the phone list or give out their own.

Fall 2019

How can I handle the anxiety that causes me to procrastinate or choose a short-term diversion, rather than decluttering?

Anxious Arthur

Dear Arthur,

We are not sure if your anxiety stems from the clutter or other issues, but either way, the answer is the same.

You're in luck. There are CLA Tools that may help. There are also several approaches CLA members have tried and found to be helpful.

Two of the Tools that might help are Bookending and Buddies. Bookending is when you call, text, or email and let someone know the task you want to complete and when you expect to have it done. Later, call them back and let them know what happened.

Buddies can be used for Bookending, but they can also support you in your decluttering plans; and, sometimes, to help you declutter on the phone or in person.

A great help to many people are our CLA Shared Activity Sessions. These are sessions when a group of people get together on a phone conference call to declutter together. For scheduled times and phone numbers, go to ClutterersAnonymous.org> Meetings>Activity Sessions.

Other things that we recommend are:

- In your decluttering, concentrate on a small space for a small amount of time at once. Some people find it helps to use a timer for this task. These things make decluttering less overwhelming.
- And, of course, no one says you

have to start with the hard part. Sometimes, when you're very anxious about something, it's better to start with something easier. Once you've accomplished that, you may have more confidence to take on the harder things. When members have more experience in recovery, sometimes they find it works better to start with the hardest item to get it out of the way first.   ◬

Holiday 2019

How do I get the willingness to ask for help?

Helpless Hannah

Dear Hannah,

Many clutterers have trouble asking for help because of feelings of shame and fear. Many of us are often embarrassed about our clutter and afraid of people's reactions. This can apply to nonphysical clutter as well, such as making decisions, being late, or missing deadlines.

Good news! You have come to the right place. CLA offers several Tools that can help.

Meetings are where you can hear others share about the same problems and realize that you're not alone.

A Sponsor will take you through the Steps, which can give you insight into your issues and help you to make changes in your behavior. This can help to lessen your shame and fear over time.

A great way to get support is to find a Buddy for mutual support. You can bounce ideas off your buddy and share your decluttering goals. You can also Bookend, which is when you call or text someone before and after attempting a task.

One of the nice things about CLA is that we also have declutterthons and shared activity sessions on the Telephone, where you can declutter and talk with others about how you are doing.

All of these can help build Trust, which is an important concept in CLA. Trust is part of Step 3, turning it over to and knowing that your Higher Power will take care of you. Sometimes it can take some time and effort to get to this point, but perseverance in working the program will pay off.

And then you'll be able to say, as it says in CLA's "Declutter Your Mind[6]" leaflet, "I trust that when I need a fact or an item, it will be available to me." ⏷

Spring 2020

How do I deal with feeling too overwhelmed to tackle my enormous piles? 　　*At My Wits' End*

Dear Wits' End,

It is not unusual for people to feel overwhelmed when they are dealing with their clutter.

It helps to break things down into small sections, taking only a small portion off the top of the pile. When that is finished, then begin another section.

There are several Tools in CLA that can help with this. If the task seems too overwhelming to start, you can call someone before beginning, sharing your goals and a time you will call them again. Then, when you call back, share how it went. This is called Bookending.

Another Tool can be Meetings. At meetings, you are bound to hear something that relates to your difficulties.

Another Tool can be to find a Buddy. A Buddy is someone you can talk to about your clutter and your plans for dealing with it. They can share with you also, so you can mutually support each other. When you help others, you usually end up helping yourself (Step 12).

Also, if you haven't already done so, it would be helpful to at least begin to work the Steps, preferably with a Sponsor or a Step group. Basically, the first three Steps remind us that we are powerless over clutter when left to our own devices. The Steps talk about turning things over to a Higher Power—and your Higher Power can be God or anything that brings you strength. Some people use the group as their Higher Power. Working the Steps is the most important part of CLA recovery.

It's important when you're overwhelmed to get as much support as possible. Also, CLA has a slogan[18] that may help: "progress, not perfection."   ◬

Holiday 2020

Making decisions: does it ever get easier?   *On the Fence*

Dear On the Fence:

Many clutterers have trouble making a decision because they are afraid it won't be the right one. But, with few exceptions, it is more useful to make a decision and take an action than for the action to be the perfect one—and there may actually be no perfect answer.

One of CLA's recovery slogans[18] says "Clutter is about decisions waiting to be made."

Decisions are difficult for some clutterers. One of the big decisions about clutter is whether to keep it or not. "We fear throwing things out because we might need it, fix it, or wear it again."—from the CLA leaflet "Recovery from Cluttering: The 12 Steps of Clutterers Anonymous[12]."

Through working the Steps and the program, we begin to understand ourselves—what is important to us and what we will actually accomplish, rather than what we'd like to do.

Let's use paper as an example because many of us struggle with this. There are guidelines on disposing of some important papers, like taxes—that decision has already been made for you. As you progress in the program, you may realize that you will never read all those old articles, newspapers, and magazines, so it may become easier to dispose of them. Also, old school and job papers change often with new discoveries and guidelines and are probably available online, so it won't be necessary to keep the paper. Of course, there are some important papers that need to be kept, such as insurance policies and deeds.

Sometimes we have found that after we throw something out, we never think about or miss it again. And if you need it, you can always get it again, as it states in the CLA Tool of Trust.

If you are having trouble making decisions, it may help to talk it over with a buddy or a sponsor and share it in your meeting.

And remember, most decisions don't have to be perfect. Most of the time, they can be fixed.   ◬

Summer 2021

I hear people in meetings talk about a Clutter-Free Zone. What is that?
          Baffled Newcomer

Dear Baffled,

When we begin tackling a job of decluttering, it can be overwhelming. Some people choose an area that will be free of clutter each night when they go to sleep—a clutter-free zone. This does not mean you don't use this area, it means you ensure that it is clear when you are ready to retire at night.

You could start with a small area, such as a corner of a table, and then expand it as your decluttering efforts progress.

Maintaining a clutter-free zone can give you a feeling of accomplishment. It can also help you to learn to put away what you take out, which is often a contributor to clutter. Most importantly, it shows you that you can, indeed, declutter and gives you the confidence to continue. ◬

As it's been said in CLA, clutter is an outward manifestation of an inner emotional problem. Without working on our inner problems, we are not able to deal with the problem of clutter for any length of time. CLA is a spiritual program with a spiritual solution.

To begin this spiritual journey, we admit we are powerless over clutter and that our lives have become unmanageable—which is Step 1. Step 1 is surrendering the idea that we can declutter by ourselves, which we have all tried without success. Your sponsor may be suggesting you start with this Step to understand that CLA is a "we" program and that we don't do it alone.

In addition to working with our sponsor, we use the telephone to keep in touch with other CLA members as we declutter, as well as attending CLA meetings. More information about this can be found in the CLA Tools of Recovery[16]. ◬

Holiday 2021

I am having a problem getting started with my clutter, and my Sponsor keeps talking about working Step 1. How will that help me?
          A Perplexed Newcomer

Dear Perplexed,

Letter from the Chair

Articles in this section appeared in the "Letter from the Chair" column and were written by chairpersons of the CLA World Service Organization. They include both information about CLA and sharing on personal recovery.

Summer 2017
James C., NY

I would like to offer my sister and brother clutterers three reflections upon finishing my year as Chairperson this past March 31. First, for CLA's survival, let's get out of our "comfort fortresses." Second, make appreciation win over negativity. Third, say not, "I

don't need this," but rather, "Do HP and other clutterers need this of me?"

For CLA's survival, let's get out of our comfort fortresses. Yes, I say comfort fortresses rather than comfort zones because many of us (and I certainly include myself) can be very skilled at protecting ourselves and concentrating so much on our own recovery that we fail to see the benefits of service to other clutterers and to CLA. We fail to see that if everyone else acts just like us, concentrating only on our own recovery, CLA or WSO will no longer exist. So, for CLA's survival, let's get out of our comfort fortresses.

Second, make appreciation win over negativity. When some of our brother and sister clutterers do decide to take the risk of being in leadership and service, many of us, being quite intelligent and naturally rather judgmental, can readily notice flaws of and mistakes by these leaders. But we must not allow our negative feelings about these flaws and mistakes to conquer the appreciation that their service allows our Fellowship as a whole to survive, grow, and receive new energy and spirit. Any contributions our own negativity make towards feelings of discouragement in our servant-leaders spell disaster for our Fellowship. Try to have appreciation win over negativity.

Third, say not, "I don't need this," but rather "Do HP and other clutterers need this of me?" We know that the only way out of the unmanageability of our cluttering is to submit to HP and HP's view of our lives, rather than our own views. Well, then, let's ask HP in thought and prayer what HP thinks of our service and leadership, as opposed to simply our own feelings and reactions. May we also consider whether our sister and brother clutterers feel they need our service and not just ponder our own needs and feelings. Say not, "I don't need this," but rather "Do HP and other clutterers need this of me?"

I feel that my year of service as Chairperson for 2016–17 has been a challenging and great experience. I am so grateful to the other officers of the WSO Board and Executive Committee for "hanging in there" with me. May all of us together move forward and grow in our recovery. Thank you again.   ⬥

Love and Service

Fall 2017
Dalia, Israel

When I was nominated and asked to consider becoming CLA WSO chairperson, I was shocked because I felt there were so many other members much more qualified. However, I felt something that wouldn't let go during the ensuing month before the elections: a flood of gratitude that just would not let me say "no." I received, and have been receiving, so much from CLA—my home, serenity, sense of worth, purpose, and so much more. I couldn't say no where a need existed in CLA and where others thought I might have been able to do it. And in my prayers about this during the month before the elections, I kept hearing "you should at least try." So I did. I thank WSO members who voted for me for allowing me to do that and just express my gratitude—because that's all it is.

The way I see my role is as a facilitator of the group conscience of the various meetings that I need to chair—the Executive Committee, the WSO general meeting, and the Board—and CLA as a whole, to the best of my abilities. I see any service meeting or committee that I am part of as a 12-Step recovery meeting. It's a place where we get together to work our 12th Step in all its parts: to practice the fact that we have a spiritual awakening as a result of the Steps, trying to carry the message to other clutterers, and practicing the principles of the Steps in all our affairs. And we do this by keeping to the 12 Traditions and A.A.'s 12 "Concepts of Service."

Here is my prayer for our term of service: "Our creator, we come before you now as the new leading team to serve the Fellowship of Clutterers Anonymous. We thank you for our recovery and for the opportunity to serve you and our fellow clutterers in CLA. Please help us express our gratitude in our roles and various activities in CLA. Please bless this committee—and the other committees and meetings that we'll participate in—as we serve in CLA. Please divorce us from any self-will, self-seeking, and self-centeredness; and keep us focused on our unity in promoting our primary purpose of carrying the message of spiritual awakening through the 12 Steps and the Fellowship to other clutterers. We submit to you as our one ultimate authority—our loving God as expressed through our group conscience—and remember that, as leaders, we are but trusted servants; we do not govern. Amen."

Please pray for us and consider working your Step 12 in a "we" setting in one of the many committees and WSO meetings. Information can be found on our website—at www.Clutterers Anonymous.org>Members>Service Committees—where you can find a calendar with all the meetings and contact information.

In grateful service ⬢

Spring 2019
Joe A., TX

My name is Joe A. from Houston, and I am a grateful recovering clutterer. As I begin my fifth year in Clutterers Anonymous, I am about to complete a year of service as Chairperson of our CLA World Service Organization. What an exciting time it is in CLA, as we start our 30-year anniversary celebration!

Two California women who wanted to bring order into their lives started CLA on February 26, 1989. They founded CLA to simplify their lives so that they could free their time to use their God-given talents and help others to accomplish the same thing. The first meeting was held in Simi Valley, California, May 1989. Today, CLA spreads the hope-filled message of recovery in 76 face-to-face meetings in 20 states and in at least four countries. And using technology, we reach folks all over the world with 19 phone-bridge meetings, 12 activity sessions, and a Skype meeting.

My cluttering is enhanced by my character defects of procrastination, avoidance, and thinking that I have all the time in the world. This program is slowly teaching me to stop bringing more stuff in, take daily action, and live in the present moment. My addiction is cunning, baffling, and powerful. I admit my powerlessness over clutter and daily take Steps 1, 2, and 3: I can't, God can, and I think I will let Him.

I am so grateful for this powerful, powerful 12-Step spiritual program of recovery that we call CLA. My dis-ease, or addiction to compulsive cluttering, has controlled a large part of my life. Today, as a result of working the 12 Steps, using the 12 Tools, and following the 12 Traditions of our program of recovery, I have started to transform my life into what my Higher Power, whom I choose to call God, intended for me all along. My addiction is truly three fold—physical, emotional, and spiritual. I am learning, one day at a time, how to take daily action in order to continue my recovery.

I know that I will never graduate from this program, and that is OK with me—and today I can say that I am a grateful recovering clutterer. I have been given so much by folks sharing their experience, strength, and hope with me;

and I owe a debt to CLA that I can never repay.

I truly believe that I have a responsibility, which I see as a privilege, to give back to the Fellowship in the form of service, for all that I have been freely given. Service is truly freedom from bondage of self. ◆

Spring 2021
Karen S., NY

Hello to all the Fellowship of Clutterers Anonymous. I know many of your voices and words of recovery from our phone lines and the 2019 convention in New York. And I know that some of you saw and heard me on our wonderful live-streamed virtual convention on October 17–18, 2020. I hope to meet you all someday.

I came to CLA shortly after my sister passed away suddenly. I had been a prisoner of my clutter for many, many years and then found myself with all my sister's clutter as well. We were living in this same house together. She was also a clutterer. I then knew that I had to get involved in CLA. The powerlessness was extremely evident to me, with my clutter doubling overnight.

I was seeing a counselor, on an ongoing basis, for a different disease and also attending 12-Step meetings for that challenge.

I was encouraged to check out CLA once again. I had not found enough meetings until I found the CLA phone meetings. Then I could connect to a meeting or more daily. It began my recovery with my cluttering disease. Hope finally returned to me. I grabbed on tightly to the Fellowship. And for me, to have many close to my age also added an extra feeling of understanding and connection. I began to stop lying on the couch with the TV—but instead looked forward to getting on the phone lines each day.

I quickly remembered that giving back through service had truly helped my recoveries in other 12-Step programs and connected me to friends and feeling a part of the Fellowship. So I began to volunteer to read, be a timekeeper, and share as often as I could at meetings. This came easily to me. And I knew I could also easily moderate, having done so very often in my other programs. All this has given me a deep grounding in CLA and a wonderful foundation to be able to recover from cluttering.

Then I began attending the CLA World Service Organization (WSO) general meetings to see what they were about. I heard a need at many meetings for delegates to represent the meeting at WSO. Since I found no problem attending WSO once a month, I stepped up to be a delegate. Then I would pass on information from the WSO meeting to my own represented meeting, as well as others I would be on that were minus a delegate volunteer.

From there, elections in WSO came up for new position openings. Since there is a rotation of positions every so often, some people must step down to allow others to step up and volunteer. Rotation of leadership is in our bylaws and is necessary in monthly moderating situations with our recovery meetings as well. This meant an opening for chairperson of WSO.

It had been suggested to me to consider running for this position. It took me many months to agree. I learned that everyone on WSO committees was knowledgeable and willing to pass on that knowledge.

Although I have lots to learn, I am positive that I can be supported by those who know. That, and the belief that I was "capable" by many people in CLA, helped me to step up. Although I was a flight attendant for 43 years and know logically the skills that it affords me, I needed others to validate my capabilities. So here I am!

I just hope that this will encourage more of you to step forward to give back to our Fellowship through service on any level. In that way, CLA can continue to flourish and remain there for us and others who suffer from the effects of our disease of cluttering.

Happy to let you know some about me. Hope to meet you as we recover together! ◬

___

Summer 2021
Karen S., NY

Hello, Fellow Clutterers! This is my second article for our CLArity newsletter since being elected as WSO Chairperson in October 2020. For this article, I thought to write about the progress in my recovery that has come about for me since joining CLA two-and-a-half years ago.

I belong to three other 12-Step Fellowships. I have been involved with 12-Step recovery for 31 years now, although I consider myself a beginner the most in my CLA recovery. In CLA, I immediately "poked my head" out of ten years of isolation, depression, and basically giving up on myself and my life...to see "The sunlight of the spirit" once again. I knew I had found help out of this cluttering disease, which I was literally "buried under."

My sister had passed away in her sleep without warning. We were living together in this house I now live in alone. We grew up in this house and acquired it after my Mom passed away from cancer.

We had both divorced and sold our houses. She was a clutterer also, so I found myself now doubly buried in clutter, with no one but myself to find a way out from under it all!

It took me one-and-a-half years to go through it and donate my sister's possessions from inside the house. I donated about seven large pick ups to charities over that time. Then I emptied a shed in the back yard which my sister had taken over as her storage unit. It was filled to the ceiling and packed tightly. That was four more charity pick ups and also took months.

Next, I emptied my own storage unit of 12 years. I had been paying $250 per month all those years and had gone into it maybe four times! Now that is a true insanity, as spoken of in Step 2! I sent out many more charity pick ups of those items. It showed me how very little that had been stowed in there was needed to be kept for all that time. I did ask for help in moving these things from the facility and to my home. A friend was happy to do that with me.

I have made headway in some of my overwhelming financial clutter. I have reduced my car insurance cost by $500 per year. I also dropped my cable service and saved $80 per month. These had needed to be addressed for some time. But the biggest thing

I have addressed financially is to have started with a tax resolution company for filing both my federal and state taxes for the past eight years. The fear of this has been with me for all those years! This is a big step forward out of darkness for me. Also, I left behind my constant late fees for forgetting to pay bills on time by switching to online banking. This has brought my credit score up greatly.

Spiritually, I have been recovering for two years now in a CLA Co-Sponsoring Step Group with my Step sisters. However long it will take, I have come to understand that my cluttering disease comes from a spiritual malady. It is working through the Steps and, in turn, learning to "live" the Steps in my life, that can promise me ongoing recovery from this cunning and baffling disease. So I immediately signed up to join a group when it was offered at the 2019 convention in New York. The rewards of that decision are ongoing for my recovery.

I have been in my house for 95% of the days of this last year to stay protected against COVID-19. It has been easy to achieve due to my CLA friends and CLA daily meetings and giving service to the Fellowship. God has blessed me with CLA, and I am forever grateful for that gift. 'Til next time. ◭

Why I Am a Resentful Person

Fall 2021
Karen S., NY

I believe looking into my resentments in Step 4 is to see why I choose to hold on to ill feelings, disappointments in others, anger towards them, and just choosing to stay injured and poisoned over and over within my mind, heart, person, soul, and being. No one can do that to me but me myself. So why do I choose to victimize myself? Why do I choose the self-imprisonment of being a resentful person?

I think maybe I believe it softens my part in the happening or, in some cases, anger seems easier to deal with than sadness or disappointment at myself or life on life's terms. Maybe I believe, deep within, that I am a better, nicer, more loving person than the person I resent. Therefore, it gives me a false right to judge them over and over about their chosen actions or beliefs. In that case, I choose to play God and stand in judgment.

When I feel hurt or harmed by another, I want to instinctively hurt them back. By choosing to hold resentment towards them, I continue to hurt and harm only myself over and over again.

Maybe it comes down to my continued efforts at controlling things in my life that I have no control over. I truly believe that all that is not "love" will never be able to happen without consequences in the end. So evil in the form of "revenge" in any form will breed only more evil in return. Therefore, thinking unkindly of others and doing so in the form of holding onto those thoughts as a resentment, can only block me from the "sunlight of the spirit," which to me is God, and God is love. I think I am getting revenge, when it is only revenge targeted at myself.

So I believe that I am a resentful person primarily because I am not yet spiritually fit. Learning to deal with others in my life as God would takes great surrender and change for me...and mostly a change in attitude, perception, understanding, acceptance—and especially humility and trust. I remain resentful to the degree that I choose to seek and do God's will in all affairs. And God's will is always with love and caring.

So for today, in my life's journey, I choose to learn to live without taking offense at or resenting others who come into my life. And my 12th Step work is the vehicle that God gives me to grow—and grow in this direction.

I can turn away from those who harm me and be thankful I can. I can pray for strength to learn of and change my shortcomings in God's time, connected always to His guidance. And I can "live the 12 Steps" daily—improving myself always. Because I choose to live in love and in that way be the happiest that I can be. I no longer care to resent others and instead learn to leave that behavior behind and work on my relationship with God and how to take care of myself and learn to surround myself with others who choose love and goodness as a goal. ◬

Officers' Corner

This column includes articles from officers and committee chairpersons of the Clutterers Anonymous World Service Organization (WSO) and CLA intergroups. Some of the articles deal with the officers' service positions, some with their personal recovery from cluttering, and some with both.

Holiday 2018
Terri J., OH

The reciprocity of energy has been an awareness in my life while raising my children. I was powerless over my entire life, and my life had become unmanageable. I had a belief in a Higher Power and knew that he would restore me to sanity and help me. The human help he provided came in a support system with reciprocity. Friends would exchange child care, pickup, and listening when needed. I, in turn, offered the same. We borrowed each other's cars, met each other's parents, attended our children's sporting events. Looking back at those days, I wonder how I survived without a spouse, working a few full-time jobs, and healing from a life that was not my vision of how life was supposed to be. I was able to heal with a strong support system, with a give and take and a flowing reciprocity.

I have realized that CLA has been a healing 12-Step support system that has helped me to heal from the effects of physical, spiritual, emotional, relationship, and time clutter. Again, I see the reciprocity of energy as a healing link. In Step 2, we came to believe that a power greater than ourselves could restore us to sanity. The energy in a meeting is a power greater than myself. Clutter, in whatever form, is depressing. Clutter can drain me and leave me immobilized. Personal relationships with other clutterers, the fellowship in meetings, meditation, and personal outreach all help me in so many

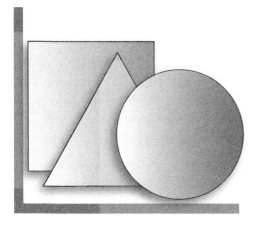

different ways to raise my energy.

One of the least favorite aspects of my dis-ease is overwhelm and the stuck feeling that indecision can lead me into. I have a strong support system in my Step writing group, the Divine Decluttering meetings and sessions, and service work. The giving and receiving keeps me out of the inertia that likes to creep into my life and thoughts. If I use the energy and healing aspects of our program, giving and receiving, I keep my heart open for the natural flow of love between my Higher Power, my CLA buddies, and myself.

I have been blessed to be a part of many different aspects of the "business" parts of our Fellowship. The first service that got me out of isolation was at a nightly phone meeting reading the Steps. The only reason I read the Steps was because a friend was leading a meeting and planned ahead so that we would not have the awkward gap in time when no one steps forward to read a designated reading.

My next steps into service are a blur. I guess I began sharing and reading sporadically. I knew a daytime meeting that fit my schedule was having trouble getting leaders, and I stepped up on the spur of the moment because I wanted a Step meeting to keep the feeling of love and gratitude and the circle of fellowship energy.

I have also been blessed to attend many committee meetings: convention planning, Clutter-Free Day planning meetings, etc. I would encourage my fellows to find our newest web page, "Fellowship Announcements." On this page, we list committee meetings, changes in face-to-face meetings, and changes and needs for service in our Fellowship.

I would encourage you to come to some of our committee meetings by checking the calendar for dates, times, and phone numbers. You may also call our toll-free number, and your questions will be forwarded to the appropriate committee. An even easier way to contact committees is to look on the web page drop-down menu of committees' email addresses.

Below are some of the ways to get your Fellowship energy to flow in reciprocity. The Convention Committee is in planning mode for the next convention. Researching hotels, colleges, and retreat centers close to airports is the current mission. The Convention Committee needs members with recording experience to economically record conventions. The Literature, Internet Technology, and Finance Committees are looking for chairpersons and members.

There has been interest in starting a West Coast intergroup and having a West Coast Clutter-Free

Day. The Literature Committee will be looking at different Step study guides to compile a submission for a Clutterers Anonymous Fellowship-approved Step Writing Guide to help us heal.

Keeping the flow of give and take and keeping my energy unstuck has been an important awareness. The reciprocity of energy is embodied in Step 12: "Having had a spiritual awakening as the result of these Steps, we tried to carry this message to others and to practice these principles in all our affairs." ⌂

Spring 2020
Miriam G., FL

Literature Committee Chairperson: How did I get here? Fairly easily, actually. I showed up!

I started in a different 12-Step Fellowship that taught me detachment from other people's problems that affect me. The program taught me to focus on myself and double-check the true meaning of blame.

As I was working on this in the other program, I eventually used the word "clutter" in my share and Higher Power delivered!

A fellow took my phone number, immediately called, and described CLA and how to find meetings. To this day, I remain grateful toward this person who reached out to me! Clutter is truly my symptom and prevents me from living my life to my fullest.

I jumped into the activity sessions on the Divine Decluttering line, simply because those meetings fit my schedule. Once I adjusted to the meditation portion of these meetings, I was able to tone down my anxious thoughts and pay attention to those around me and how CLA works. As I became familiar with voices and names (as I primarily attend phone meetings), I realized the dedication of members who were showing up daily at every meeting I was in. I heard calls for service. In the beginning, I thought that, with so many before me, someone would pick them up.

I stood up for service, with fear and courage, when the Monday morning meeting—one I enjoy to help jumpstart my week—needed moderators. When I perform service, my mind feels less cluttered because the "pity party for one" disappears.

Then the easiest call of service was announced. The sponsorship document was ready for review by CLA members for their approval and could be found on the Fellowship page. In essence, my opinion was asked, and that I can deliver. I found an edit and attended the Literature Committee (aka LitCom). This turned out to be an area in which I can feel safe to awaken and facilitate my dormant skills.

The LitCom group had been working on the sponsorship document for two years, and my arrival seemed appreciated, especially because I offered to write the minutes for the meeting.

Eventually the group pointed out that the Literature Committee was devoid of a chairperson; would I do it? Most of the members had done it before and now held other committee positions. With fear and courage and faith in the Promises of the program, I said "Yes, I'll try it." I was voted in. A few weeks later, they informed me that I have voting rights at the WSO meetings; and my attendance would be appreciated.

No one forces me to go; everyone in the Literature Committee wears many hats in the many WSO positions and can offer the LitCom update in my place. Again, with their mentorship, I still want to step up to the plate and show up.

All these experiences help affirm my learning of the Traditions, starting with Tradition One, which is "Our common welfare should come first; personal recovery depends upon CLA unity." Therefore, I can become responsible to reach out to other clutterers who still suffer. ⬙

Fall 2020

Jenny R., OH

After I had been in CLA for about six months, I knew I wanted to do more service. The Steps and service are the foundation in my 12-Step programs. I had worked the Steps on clutter with a clutter buddy, so moving on to service was the next layer of my growth in CLA.

An opportunity to become part of a three-person committee forming the WSO corresponding secretary position was offered to me. Many kudos to Kathy H. from California—who used to do all of our positions! She still mails out the CLArity books and CD sets. Plus, she works in several other areas of service. She is a treasure.

The three of us have grown into a team over the last year and a half. The corresponding secretary position now has one person who posts and records all literature orders on a spreadsheet—including hard copy booklets, leaflets, CLArity books, hard copy CLArity newsletters, and CD sets. This member is always coming up with new ways to help track orders and simplify the process for all of us. She is also recording all of our digital sales.

The individual who takes care of single-customer orders also does our committee reports and keeps up with inventory. The majority of our literature comes as individual orders, so this gal is always busy. I do bulk orders and international ones. By having several members familiar with this process, it isn't all on one person—plus, if one is sick or dealing with serious outside issues, the others keep literature flowing.

I volunteer to be the main contact for questions on any order to save confusion from multiple responses. I also go back over the orders and check to see if anything is missing. Since I have some health issues, when my body needs rest but my mind is active, I can be of service doing those activities while also doing positive self-care.

I have not always been on my best behavior when dealing with those inquiries. So learning to stay calm when explaining issues to members and to the members of our committee has become another wonderful growth opportunity in patience, tolerance, and making amends!

If I hadn't taken advantage of this opportunity, I would have missed getting to know more wonderful individuals in the Fellowship at a deeper level, along with getting to know more about myself.◭

Recovery is More than Just a Change in Behavior

Summer 2021
Marge S., NC

As I reflect on my early years, I know I had hoarding tendencies …I always had to keep everything. Most of my things were in a jumble in my dresser. Occasionally my mom would dump everything onto the bed and tell me to "clean up or you can't go to bed." The most distressing part was that someone else saw all my stuff and touched it…I felt so violated. Later in life as an adult, our house was robbed. My room looked like a tornado had hit. I pretended to the police that the intruder had done it, but the truth was the mess was all mine!

In 2011, I had been in recovery in another 12-Step program for 25 years; but after a lifetime of cluttering and thinking I was a "slob," I hit bottom and researched hoarding on the internet. I had spent years hiding my "stuff" and never really faced the truth, even to myself. On one website, I heard about CLA, and I felt the word "clutterer" was gentler than "hoarder," and I could admit I might be one—so I sent for the leaflets. When they came, I looked at all the colorful leaflets thinking, "Aren't those nice?" but then just stuck them in a drawer…and that was that; years went by.

Having downsized in 2015, I moved everything to storage and then, in 2016, to my spare bedroom—but kept the door closed. I retired and thought I'd finally go through things. But I didn't. The room was full of 100 boxes stacked to the ceiling. I felt sick every time I passed the door. Then I hit bottom again. Finally in September 2017, I felt ready to start. I opened one box at random, and on top was the envelope I had received from CLA six years earlier. What a gift from my Higher Power. That was three-and-a-half years ago!

Like a person dying of thirst, I plunged into the phone meetings and called in every single day. I started on the Divine Decluttering line and instantly knew I was in the right place!

After a year of meetings, declutterthons, reading, and praying, I cleared my spare bedroom enough so that boxes filled only the closet. I believed that, since I had already worked the Steps, I didn't need to do them again. I thought I had gotten a handle on the problem. But I've heard that an addict never tapers off; they always taper on. That's what happened to me…the problem started seeping its way back in.

So I hit bottom again in CLA… my recurring clutter finally convinced me that there was

something deeper that contributed to the piles, the overscheduling, the procrastination, etc. That's when I really accepted that the solution would require more than just changing my behavior. My physical clutter was just a symptom, and I truly was powerless over clutter…that even in CLA, my life had become unmanageable once again.

It is now spring 2021, and I have been in a very supportive co-sponsorship group for about one-and-a-half years that has pushed me deeper into facing the causes and conditions of this insidious issue that has haunted me all my life.

Two years ago, I was mentored into service and, at WSO meetings, discovered there was so much to do! My career led me to managing the website and then becoming the assistant treasurer.

In October 2020, I headed the Technical Support Team for the virtual convention. In December, I joined the literature fulfillment team. I have also worked on some projects requiring specialized knowledge and skills that fell outside the scope of my volunteer positions.

At times the work has been too much, and I get the feeling of overwhelm—and then I just want to say, "forget it" and run away; but then I remember what I was told early on…service is its own reward. As long as I keep thinking that way, I'll be just fine. ⬯

Social Taboos, Clutter, and Doing Service

Fall 2021
Lisa G., FL

When meeting someone new, proper etiquette is not to discuss religion or politics, as these are deeply personal values that penetrate the core of our being. Many times (not always), we take these values from our family of origin. But could clutter be discussed when meeting someone new? Egads, I shout a resounding, "no!" Could emotional or physical clutter, like religion and politics, be passed down? I ashamedly believed I was the only one in my family who clutters. But when I spoke with my mom recently, I learned she is also a clutterer. What's the difference between us? She has storage facilities…in a few different states. Meanwhile, it feels like I'm living in a storage facility. I have disarray all around. I still have unpacked moving boxes (yet I'm here almost four years). I have no rhyme or reason of what I put down or where I put it. It's all in a temporarily temporary location. Last year, I had the revelation that I can't find a home for my belongings…because I can't find a (true)

home for myself. I learned the "home sweet home" that I can't find spans not only physical, but emotional and spiritual landscapes as well.

The preamble before each CLA meeting states, "The only requirement for membership is the desire to stop cluttering." I have barely touched my things to be decluttered, but the desire is still there. In my childhood, I was never told to clean my room, put my things away, or anything along those lines. Growing up, I saw alcoholism and dysfunction—though I couldn't quite name these as a child. As I saw the dysfunction unfold, I made a promise to not be like my unstable relatives at all. I am grateful I have never taken up alcohol, drugs, or smoking.

But here I am, over half a century old, and suddenly I woke up one day to realize I am more like those relatives than I care to admit. The addiction just presents itself in a different manner. How I got here could be analyzed and picked apart, but why bother? It's pointless to be so critical—of myself and of my family. I see that shouldn't be my focus. Recovery so often teaches me many things, such as my clutter does not define me. When thinking of those long-dead family members whose memory can still trigger me, I am learning to say or think, "bless them, change me." Any recovery phrase that comes to mind should help, and there are many. Rinse and repeat.

How else can I work on my recovery? By doing service.

When the pandemic peaked, mailings were being delayed… sometimes up to eight weeks. I recall how desperate and emotional I felt while looking for help, without knowing where to go. In isolation, literature can be a lifeline, especially when local meetings aren't happening.

I dipped my toes in the water and asked to take over the mailings, but it took a while to get to me. This was in my Higher Power's time, not mine. Around the same time, I promised a friend I'd clear out one bookcase shelf filled with random items that had no home. It took me three weeks. When I finally cleared it out—boom!—that was exactly when the supply of envelopes came, so they could have a home. Then the literature arrived. I have a place for that, too, despite my small apartment. Once a week I do the mailings. Some weeks have more orders than others. I see these mailings as a good excuse to take a walk to the post office for a bit of exercise.

But I can't do this service on my own. There are other volunteers behind the scenes, too.

These dedicated angels really make the magic happen by extracting information from online orders and then putting the data into an easy-to-read spreadsheet with everything spelled out for me. I have the easiest job, and I feel it's my calling. Along with each of those mailings, I send prayers that the recipients should find peace…and a decluttered home.   ◆

Service

Step 12 says, "…we carry this message to others…" Service is embodied in Step 12. There are many ways to do service at all levels of the Fellowship. The CLA Tool of Service says "The CLA program gives us the opportunity to enhance our progress by taking on service responsibilities, from holding office to doing cleanup."

About Service

CLA Service

Fall 2017

Le Ann W., TX

The following article is the opinion of the author and does not necessarily reflect the opinion of others in the Fellowship.—Editor

Service in 12-Step recovery is like the old adage, "a place for everything and everything in its place."

It is my belief that the proper place for service is the second half of Step 12—and, for a group to

function best, service needs to be kept in its proper place.

The questions often come up: "What about service in CLA?" "Where does service fit into my program of recovery?" "What is CLA service?" and "When can I begin to give service?"

The 12 Steps were designed to be taken in order. Service doesn't show up right away. It is number 12 of 12. Even then, service is not mentioned by name. Service is just one of the principles referred to in "Having had a spiritual awakening as the result of these Steps, we tried to carry this message to others, and to practice these principles in all our affairs."

A newcomer ought not be asked or expected to do service. The first half of Step 12 indicates that there is a prerequisite to giving service. If we work the program as suggested by its founders, we do not officially begin service until we have turned our lives over to God, taken a thorough personal inventory, and made our amends. These things have resulted in a spiritual awakening, and we have made prayer and meditation a constant exercise.

The rest of the 12th Step is what "finally translates the 12 Steps into action upon all our affairs." (A.A. *Twelve Steps and Twelve Traditions,*[14] p. 109). It was written this way intentionally.

Giving service is an important part of recovery; however, service work alone will not bring recovery. According to Bill W., there is a pitfall that can occur with giving service:

> *We temporarily cease to grow because we feel satisfied that there is no need for all Twelve Steps for us. We are doing fine on a few of them. Maybe we are doing fine on only two of them, the First Step and that part of the Twelfth where we "carry the message." In A.A. slang, this is known as "two-stepping."*

In short, passing the message to the clutterer who still suffers doesn't actually take place if neither person knows the message. We can't give away what we don't have. The message has to be learned and earned. The message comes from working the first 11 Steps.

The 12th Step is both an ending and a beginning. As we complete our intense and focused efforts to clean up our past lives, we begin to use principles to guide us in our current and future lives. The 12th Step not only calls us to service, it calls us to live out our lives each day, in all our affairs, with a servant's heart.

In its proper place, service is one of the legacies of the program. ◭

Spotlight on Service

Holiday 2018
Dody W., PA

Those of us who attend phone meetings and/or CLA World Service Organization meetings have gotten fairly used to frequent requests for members to please step up for service.

I've been thinking a lot more about that recently. In some ways, it doesn't make much sense that people would hold back. Over the past several years, I have "met" many members via phone meetings and activity sessions. I've also met many at Clutter-Free Days and conventions, and these folks are some of the very nicest, warmest, most genuine people I have ever met.

So I'm thinking, "We are super

nice people—why don't more of us jump in to help?"

Then I ran across a study involving hoarders, and the results helped me to look at our problem in a new way.

The study revealed that more than 75% of hoarders may have a mood and/or anxiety disorder. More than 50% of us may have a diagnosis of Major Depressive Disorder. One out of four hoarders may have either Generalized Anxiety Disorder or Social Phobia, while 8.8% of us may have Avoidant Personality Disorder.

Suddenly, I was able to view this problem with so much more compassion!

I began to be amazed that enough people stepped up for service for our organization to run, and that it continues to be here for the new person who is suffering and reaches out.

Does it sound as if I am making excuses for those who suffer with these diagnoses to not step up? No, I'm not. I personally know many in our Fellowship who serve and yet also carry a potentially debilitating mental health diagnosis. A couple have told me that they never saw themselves being able to do the things that they eventually did, but they would not go back. They thought that serving had helped them personally, as well as in their programs. It got them

out of isolation. Some share their struggles openly at meetings, while others confide in a few, and still others not at all. This is a personal matter.

I don't have a magic answer for our service problem. I am convinced now, more than ever, that we need to make every effort that our phone lines are as safe as possible and that each person is treated with the utmost dignity and respect. We ought never take for granted those who are giving service.

My favorite method to invite someone on board to a committee or to facilitate a meeting is by personal invitation. That is how I first came to serve. I gained more than I ever gave. I remain grateful!

Service Opportunities in CLA

Spring 2019
Service Opportunities in CLA

The 12-Step way of life embodies service. We can experience a great deal of satisfaction when giving back to the Fellowship, whether in a small way or large.

There are many opportunities for service in CLA. Some of them are listed below. For more information on any service opportunities, use one of the contact methods listed on the inside front cover.

• Groups need officers, and face-to-face groups sometimes need members to help set up, clean up, or bring refreshments.

- Intergroups need officers and representatives, as well as folks to do other tasks. The Telephone Intergroup could use volunteers to be newcomer greeters and also some willing to serve as moderator trainers. CLA-East currently has need for all officer positions to be filled, as well as planners for the next Clutter-Free Day.
- New officers for the CLA World Service Organization (WSO) will be needed for the next term, beginning April 1, 2019. (Refer to ClutterersAnonymous.org or the Holiday 2018 issue of CLArity for a list of WSO officer positions.)
- Many meetings have not elected delegates to WSO. Delegates need attend only one two-hour meeting once a month (except November), and it is also possible to have alternating delegates. Delegates should report to their meetings what they have learned at the WSO meeting and also seek group conscience on upcoming WSO votes.

Other service opportunities abound.
- WSO could use help in updating meeting changes, for both the printed and online CLA Meeting Directories.
- CLA could use the help of a member to index our literature. This would mean reading each piece of literature and adding page and publication references for each subject, as applicable.
- WSO would like to fill the archivist position, which is currently vacant. The archivist would maintain an online archive that would include copies of WSO agendas, motions and motion logs, minutes, and financial reports.
- As of this writing, the Finance Committee needs a new chairperson and members. This committee prepares the annual budget and considers other financial matters. It usually meets quarterly.
- The Bylaws Committee also needs a new chairperson and would welcome more members. Now that the bylaws have been completed and approved, this committee will meet only a few times a year to review the bylaws and address any issues that arise.
- The Literature Committee is soliciting questions from members to be included in a Step writing guide.
- CLArity is always seeking articles from CLA members. Do you have good English skills? CLArity could use a few more editors. This would entail a few hours' work once every three months. Another service opportunity is to help with indexing

CLA*rity* by reading an issue and adding relevant references to the existing online index.

- It takes a lot of work to plan a CLA convention. There are many ways to give a helping hand. The Convention Committee would welcome any new members, including a new chairperson. The Program Committee needs members to help plan the convention program. The committee would welcome someone to act as a volunteer coordinator and members who are willing to help during the convention. Members who are willing to get the word out about the convention are definitely needed. Do you have experience in recording conferences? The committee especially needs someone to help in this aspect. There are many other small tasks which could be useful; please contact the Convention Committee if you are interested in helping. ⚠

Spotlight on Service

Fall 2019
Terri J., OH

Our ninth leaflet asks us to look at what's enhancing our recovery and what's hindering our recovery. Let's use this thought process to look at the gaps we have in our present-day CLA service structure.

It was shared by a sponsor at the 2018 convention that he and his sponsees agree at the beginning of their working together that they will do service and be there for the still-suffering clutterer. He believes that if he's going to invest his time in their recovery, he wants assurance that they will be willing to give back to keep the energy flowing. I think one reason we have gaps in service in our Fellowship is because we also have gaps in sponsorship.

The first time I came out of isolation in CLA to give service was because a buddy asked me to read the Steps at a meeting she was moderating. It is easy to sit quietly in the background and let others do the work. I am much more inclined to give back to avoid letting down a friend. When I do give back, my recovery and energy are not stagnant.

Our new sponsorship document will aid us in looking at our sponsorship process. It includes suggestions on how to get started with sponsors, co-sponsors, sponsees, or Step-writing groups. The personal bonds and relationships we form can help CLA grow by encouraging each other to step out of isolation.

We will look at some of the ways you can give back.

Both CLA intergroups are struggling to fill officer and committee positions. Both groups are successful with their special workshop activities. CLA-East's strength is their Clutter-Free Day (CFD) every spring. The Telephone Intergroup's strength lies in its holiday declutterthons. Both are working to aid our recovery, raise our energy, and help us stay out of isolation by connecting us to other members.

The Telephone Intergroup has talked about a system for updating formats online, keeping track of moderators and delegates, training moderators and newcomer greeters, and also creating a message telephone for members to listen into recordings of meeting times.

Some committees are not functioning, leaving gaps in our structure. The IT committee, when functioning, designed our webpage. We do have a paid webmaster who makes changes. For many years, we had an extraordinary individual make changes and coordinate our website updates. In following our tradition of rotating service, WSO is looking for an individual capable of making changes or submitting our ticket changes to our webmaster.

Our Finance Committee has been struggling also. CLA lacks long-range projections and visions for future growth, such as many Fellowships have. What would CLA's future wish list look like?

Some ideas involve an e-book to purchase online, digital downloads of literature, podcasts and a members only section, or a physical location with special workers.

Our Literature Committee is a functioning committee that needs support with its work projects. They have completed "Sponsorship in CLA," which took a few years in writing. Some of the ideas presented for future projects are a Step writing guide, a Twelve and Twelve, indexing our current CLA literature, looking at the electronic versions and digital downloads of our current literature, and looking at creating CLA promises.

The CLArity Committee is also one of our functioning committees with the blessing of longtime members. These members need your support in submitting articles, learning the editing process, learning the layout process of our page layout program, and indexing recent issues of CLArity.

The Convention Committee was blessed to have more workers this year. It was difficult not having a face-to-face contact for site research. The vision for the next convention would be to have a face-to-face contact for the physical location of our convention site.

Anyone interested in giving back to any of the CLA service committees can email info@ClutterersAnonymous.org, come to the monthly WSO meeting, or call our toll-free number.

By the way, if you're not on our mailing list, go to the ClutterersAnonymous.org Contact Us page, and press on the email button. ⬖

Spotlight on Service

Fall 2021 and Holiday 2021
Ruthe S., PA

Service: The CLA[Clutterers Anonymous] program gives us the opportunity to enhance our own progress by taking on various service responsibilities, from holding office to doing clean up. As we serve, we risk moving out of isolation, to grow, and to practice the principles of our program within the Fellowship. Service is giving back to the Fellowship.—from "The CLA Tools of Recovery[16]"

Service is so important that it is listed as our first Tool. This is because it is essential for us to help in some way in order to get better. "You can only keep it if you give it away" is a slogan often said in 12-Step programs.

CLA's primary purpose is to help the clutterer who still suffers. That is the way 12-Step programs work. And when you are helping others, you are helping yourself. You are also getting out of isolation. Service can be as little as reading the Steps at a meeting to as much as chairing a committee. There is opportunity for service available in every possible form. And if you realize that a service is needed, perhaps you can create a way for that to happen. CLA is always looking for new ideas.

So how can you help? There are four types of service—personal, meeting, intergroup, and world service. Personal service includes being a buddy or bookending with someone. This is a way of helping yourself while you help others. Also, making and receiving phone calls and texts is another way. These types of service help us to stay out of isolation and benefit both members.

Of course, sponsoring is another form of personal service. That involves taking someone through the 12 Steps, which are the foundation of our recovery in CLA. We traditionally have not had a lot of sponsors, so we have started Step groups. This leads to another form of service. If you have been in a Step group yourself, you can help to start a group by being there the first few times. Then you can explain the ropes, so to speak, to the members.

If you are looking to get your feet wet with service, meeting service is the way to go because there are many shorter-term opportunities. The easiest meeting service would be reading the Steps,

Traditions, or other literature at meetings or being a timer. Also, sharing is a form of service.

Another short-term position would be leading a meeting or being a substitute moderator. The wonderful thing is that all of the formats (at least for the telephone meetings) are on our website. You don't have to know how to do anything but read. We also have meetings at all different times of the day. There is bound to be one that fits into your schedule. If you are nervous about leading, you are welcome to try it one time to see how it goes. Qualifying at a meeting is another way to give one-time service. Wherever you are in your recovery, you are likely a few steps ahead of the newcomer.

Another shorter-term type of service you can do is to moderate a session at a declutterthon. This usually involves taking check-ins and reading literature while people are decluttering. On the Divine Decluttering line, there are also action sessions where it is more informal. There is some form of this daily.

In addition to action, the Divine Decluttering line has many different types of activities. It has exercise; meditation; meetings; reading of *Ten Years of CLArity*[13]; and, of course, the previously mentioned action sessions. You can lead a meeting once per month, moderate one half hour of reading *Ten Years of CLArity*[13] one day per week, or moderate one of the other activities. There are many shorter service opportunities available on this line.

For those of you looking for a little more action, there are several events that happen each year that always require help. These committees get more active as the event gets nearer. The Convention Committee is one of those. We have been presenting conventions most years since 2014. By all accounts, they are wonderful experiences. People get to meet the faces that go with the voices they hear on the phone meetings or declutterthons. Attendees learn more about how clutter affects them and new ways of recovering. And, most of all, everyone has a lot of fun.

The other event that happens every year is the East Coast Clutter-Free Day (CFD). It is basically a mini convention that is held for one weekend day in the spring in New Jersey. Basically, the same things I've written about the convention apply here as well. Sometimes, other regions also put on a CFD. If you are ambitious, you can start one in your area.

These events bring a wealth of recovery and understanding to the people who put them together and the attendees. The best part is they are shorter-term commitments. In addition, they usually produce CDs from the various speakers and workshops that people can purchase long after the event is over.

Some examples of longer-term commitments would be helping on business committees. CLA has several groups that meet to work on various issues that affect the Fellowship. There is one for virtually every type of personality and skill. And the beauty is that you are working with others, so all of the burden doesn't fall on one person. Our committees are: Bylaws, CLA*rity*, Convention (spoken about earlier in this article), Finance, IT, Literature, and Registration. You can get involved as much or as little as you like. Check our website to learn more about them.

The service commitment that would take the most time would be serving as an officer in the World Service Organization (WSO). WSO is our governing body. WSO officers include: chairperson, vice-chairperson, treasurer, assistant treasurer, recording secretary, web mail correspondent, voice mail correspondent, corresponding secretary, and archivist. In addition, meetings send delegates to WSO in order to bring back information from the monthly meeting, so there is another way to volunteer. There

are also service opportunities in CLA-East, including helping with the CFD and the service committee. CLA-East comprises all face-to-face CLA meetings in the United States east of the Mississippi River. The service committee works with the 8 p.m. Eastern Time telephone meetings.

Traditionally, clutterers have a difficult time stepping up for service. We have physical and nonphysical clutter. We often have a difficult time prioritizing and scheduling. We feel overwhelmed and depleted. We have so much to do, how can we add one more thing into our schedule? I'm here to tell you that service helps because it gets us out of our head and into action. It can actually help you get things done. It also helps self-esteem. Whenever I am down, I notice that if I lead a meeting, I feel better. And I often hear something that helps me as well while I'm there.

Just try it. I'm sure you will see how much your recovery improves. And you are giving back to the Fellowship that is helping you.

Intergroups

Good News from CLA-East

Holiday 2019
Mary P., NY

You may have read (in the last issue of CLA*rity*) or heard that the CLA-East intergroup was struggling to keep functioning. There was a danger that the group might fold and that its signature event, Clutter-Free Day, might be discontinued. Now there are some positive signs of revitalization to report.

An intergroup is a group of two or more meetings with common interests or in a given region; CLA-East, in effect, represents meetings in the eastern half of the U.S. Its functions may include: answering inquiries about CLA and locating meetings; fielding 12th-Step calls; maintaining a website; providing guidance on starting new meetings and growing established groups; and organizing Clutter-Free Days or other conferences or workshops.

CLA-East was established in October of 2001 and has sponsored 24 Clutter-Free Days, with two held in each of the first six years and one per year since. Its monthly meetings are conducted on conference calls.

The intergroup has had great difficulty getting members to step up and to hold office. Members doing service have been doing it for years, and rotation of service was impossible.

At the July CLA convention, a fervent pitch for participation was made, and 15 people signed up to offer service. A meeting to resurrect CLA-East was held in early September, and the turnout was encouraging. Alison B., NJ, who has done considerable service in the past, was elected chair of the intergroup. Others volunteered for other roles, but more help is still needed.

The revitalized group plans to meet monthly, on the second Saturday, at 2:30 p.m. Eastern Time on (605) 468-8016—access code 132160. The phone line for information is (866) 800-3881. The website is claeast.org.   ◬

Do You Wonder What CLA-East Does?

Spring 2020
Alison B., NJ

CLA-East is an intergroup of face-to-face meetings that meets on the phone and functions according to CLA's bylaws, the 12 Traditions, and the principles illustrated in A.A.'s "12 Concepts for World Service."

The intergroup has chosen to work on the following items from the bylaws: providing guidance on starting new meetings; fielding 12th-Step calls (extending a hand to someone in distress); providing information and encouragement to new and existing groups; answering inquiries about CLA; doing local public relations; disseminating meeting lists; organizing Clutter-Free Days or other conferences or workshops; sending news to the CLA*rity* newsletter; maintaining a website; and selling CLA materials (e.g. literature, CDs, etc.) at Clutter-Free days.

We are just getting off the ground again and are continuing to reorganize and accept members willing to give service. Those who have served before will give guidance and assistance. If you cannot go to meetings, there are other ways you can be involved—and we will let you know when we have figured them out—we still have a lot to work on!

Anyone can be a member, but voting representatives must be elected by their face-to-face groups. We would like to encourage every group east of the Mississippi to have an elected representative at our meeting. We want to send information out to all 33 groups, but we need help to do this.

We especially need a chairperson for the Clutter-Free Day Planning Committee, which started meeting in December 2019, for the event to be held on April 18 in Metuchen, NJ. The new chairperson will get assistance and written instructions. Please think about it. If you can lead meetings and write emails, you can learn to do it, and it is a great project for anyone who needs something to make their life better. You will be doing a fabulous service.

CLA-East meets on the phone on the second Saturday of most months at 2:30 p.m. Eastern Time There will be a separate meeting for the Clutter-Free Day planning. If you wish to be included in either meeting, please call 866-800-3881, and leave a message, including your email address and phone number.

CLA-East

Fall 2020
Alison B., NJ

The CLA-East Intergroup is, in theory, a gathering of representatives of all face-to-face groups east of the Mississippi. At the moment, not too many of these groups are meeting, so I'm very proud to say we had nine people at our last monthly meeting. This shows dedication and looking forward to better times.

Some groups are video conferencing or meeting on the phone privately, which is great. A lot of individuals have finally started using the main phone lines, especially since our virtual Clutter-Free Day (CFD). Up until then, many face-to-face people had barely used the phone lines, if at all.

CLA-East takes phone messages from individuals or groups reaching out for help, and we call back. We answer emails. We have a website at claeast.org, although it needs a makeover. We are working to update meeting lists, and we are now liaising with WSO in an effort to get on the same page. The face-to-face meeting page is sadly outdated. We have decided to take the phone meeting information off our website and instead have a link to WSO's website, Clutterers Anonymous.org. We will be looking into some more possibilities for updating the website in the coming months.

The outreach committee wants to help face-to-face groups set up dedicated conference lines for their groups, if so desired, while groups are on hiatus and encourage each group to have a contact and a representative to the intergroup. The committee is currently not meeting. It needs encouragement and a willing chairperson. Ask your group if you can be a representative to CLA-East—we would love to have you. If you don't have a group to represent, you can still give service.

CLA-East also sends updates to the CLA*rity* newsletter. And, of course, we plan our annual face-to-face Clutter-Free Day, which took place this year on the phone, on Saturday, April 18, and was a terrific success.

We are now working on getting the recordings from CFD edited into sessions. We think people will enjoy them better that way. It has taken us a while to get ourselves together because we have had some intense discussions. There will be a disclaimer about Traditions at the beginning of each recording. They will be put on the websites in file form rather than be sold as CDs, although we will have the capacity for both.

The CLA-East meetings are held on the second Saturday of each month at 2:30 p.m. Eastern Time. If you would like to come to the meeting, please call 866-800-3881 to leave a message with your email address, and you will receive an agenda about two days before the meeting.   ⌂

Clarity Clear-Away Action Monthly Event(s)

Spring 2021
Mariah W., NY

Grab a cup of coffee or your favorite beverage du jour and let me bend your ear a bit about the origin story of the Clarity Clear Away Action Session, which is the third

Saturday of every month on the main meeting phone line—(515) 604-9021, access code 102163#.

Allow me to briefly digress about origin stories in general before getting to the point of the CLA origin story for this event. I grew up *adoring* cartoons. I adored comic books, cartoons, manga, and all forms of animation. Yes, I love superheroes too. Anyone who loves superheroes and comic books knows they all have origin stories. So that's my digression on origin stories, which may or may not provide context for the origin story for the monthly Clarity Clear Away Action Session event(s). C'est la vie if it does not.

I mention origin stories because the origin of the Clarity Clear Away Action Session began as I was a newcomer to Clutterers Anonymous (CLA). At that time, I was asked to moderate a two-hour action session on another CLA line every Saturday from noon to 2 p.m. I said okay. We would have different suggested projects/themes each month, such as: kitchen, living room, your car, etc. I had a disruptor early on who swore at me. I was mentored off the line on how to handle such matters, and moving forward I did so. My two-hour moderating frequently ran many hours beyond the designated two, since there were no other moderators after me; and

other CLA members loved to be in action on, say, cleaning out their refrigerator or whatever project of action they chose.

Eventually I moved on to some other CLA service work for a while, then circled back to organize/coordinate what has become a monthly seven-and-a-half-hour focused action session.

We know from the literature that "Action is the Magic Word," so with the informal help of a team of seasoned CLA members, the monthly event (after collaborative tinkering) was dubbed the Clarity Clear Away Action Session. Again, via informal CLA communication, themes or topics—which may be seasonally appropriate—are suggested for those who care to join the action for recovery and to make progress on decluttering projects. For example, December 2020's suggested themes on topics were: emptying, pacing, and the completion cycle. January 2021's were "First Things First," the 1st Tradition, the 1st Step, and clutter-free zones.

A different moderator volunteers to facilitate each hour of the action session and may read from CLA or A.A. literature on the suggested themes/topics or from a topic of their choice. There is an average of 40-60 CLA members who attend and participate in the monthly Clarity Clear Away Action

Session.

The final moderator of the event encourages/invites all attendees to remain on the line for the nightly Release Victories session, followed by the Home Our Sacred Space Saturday night meeting. ◬

World Service Organization (WSO)

What Is WSO?

Spring 2018

The Clutterers Anonymous World Service Organization (WSO) was formed to support the CLA Fellowship. It is comprised of delegates from CLA groups and other interested CLA members. While any member may attend and speak at the meetings, only delegates, officers, and WSO committee chairpersons may vote. All groups are encouraged to elect delegates to represent them at the meetings.

What does WSO do for the Fellowship?

- Literature: The Literature Committee writes and amends CLA Fellowship-approved literature. Once a piece is written, it is sent to the entire Fellowship for input, revised, and then sent to WSO for approval. Upon approval, the committee formats the piece for printing, and the corresponding secretary fulfills literature orders.

- WSO maintains the CLA website, ClutterersAnonymous.org. The website includes information about CLA, its literature, committees, and other aspects of the Fellowship, like events, CLA*rity*, etc. It also includes a list of all CLA meetings and information on ordering literature, giving 7th Tradition donations, paying for CLA conventions, etc.

- WSO maintains a toll-free phone number, (866) 402-6685, where interested parties can leave voice mails. One of our voice mail correspondents promptly returns calls made to the number.

- WSO maintains the post office box used for CLA's mailing address: PO Box 91413, Los Angeles, California 90009. The corresponding secretary picks up mail from the box and follows through with any necessary action.

- WSO may advise local groups, as requested, especially in matters dealing with the public and questions about CLA Traditions.

- WSO facilitates communication between CLA groups and elements of the Fellowship.

- WSO's public information officer communicates with the media and other professionals.

Each group, through group conscience, can elect a delegate to WSO. WSO meetings are held via telephone conference call the fourth Saturday of most months at 1 p.m. Eastern Time (10 a.m. Pacific Time). The number is (712) 775-7100, and the access code is 727026.

Officer elections this year will be held on March 24, 2018. All positions are for a one-year term, with the exception of the treasurer, which is a two-year term and is not up for election this year.

About WSO

Holiday 2019

How did you learn about CLA and find its meetings? Was it through our website? Did you order and receive CLA literature? Did you have a question or problem and either emailed or called WSO? Did your group have questions it couldn't answer, especially in dealing with the public or the media? All of these tasks and more are handled through WSO and its elected officers and committees.

All officers of WSO, except for treasurer, are up for election next year.

Many of the current office holders are in their second one-year term, which means that they normally cannot be elected for an additional term. Filling these positions is very important for the smooth functioning of WSO. The functions of WSO are maintaining CLA's website, answering emails and phone calls, writing and printing literature, fulfilling literature orders, maintaining a directory of meetings, helping groups that are encountering problems, and communicating with the public and media about CLA and cluttering, and more.

Nominations will be taken at the WSO meeting on February 22, with elections being held on March 28. All WSO meetings are held at 1 p.m. Eastern Time. To attend, call (605) 313-4445 and, when prompted, enter the access code of 512645. Any member can attend WSO meetings, but only delegates, officers, and committee chairpersons vote. Your meeting can elect a delegate if it hasn't yet done so.

The positions up for election are chairperson, vice-chairperson, assistant treasurer, recording secretary, corresponding secretary, webmail correspondent, voice mail correspondent, public information officer, and archivist. All these positions consist of one-year terms, from April 1, 2020, through March 31, 2021. The term of treasurer is a two-year term, which runs through March 31, 2021, for the current office holder.

For officer guidelines, as well as a description of requirements and duties, go to Clutterers Anonymous.org>Members>WSO Officers.

CLA History

CLA was started in February 1989 by two California women who wanted to bring order into their lives.

CLA's 30th Anniversary

Summer 2019

In honor of the 30th anniversary of Clutterers Anonymous, the CLA*rity* Team would like to reflect on where we were in the past and how we got to the point we are at today.

In early 1989, Varda M. and Nicole H. met while attending a conference on cluttering. Neither of them was interested in the commercial aspect of the conference but wished there was a 12-Step Fellowship which addressed the issue. They started Clutterers Anonymous on February 26, 1989—although the first meeting, in Simi Valley, California, was not held until May of that year.

CLA grew slowly in the beginning. In May of 1995, there were 15 meetings, all but one of them located in California. By early 2000, the count of meetings had grown to 22. All of these were face-to-face meetings. As of this writing, there are now more than 70.

In 2003 or 2004, Peter L. of New Jersey started the first CLA telephone meeting. Phone meetings provide an opportunity for those who have no meeting located geographically close and for those whose physical limitations make it difficult to attend face-to-face meetings. They also make it possible for many who attend a face-to-face meeting to go to more than one meeting per week.

The phone meetings have grown. There are now 20 phone meetings as of this writing, including one held in Italian. There is also a Skype meeting. A few years after the first phone meeting, participation on the phone lines increased to activity sessions, the Action Line, and the Commitment Line.

The CLA World Service Organization (WSO) was started in late 1991, in response to letters written to the Simi Valley group from outside California. It was founded by Larry E. of California, along with Varda and Nicole.

In the beginning, WSO meetings were held in Los Angeles, California. However, many of the officers and delegates were concerned that having face-to-face meetings virtually excluded participation by members outside Southern California. Jan G. of California made wider participation in these meetings possible by setting up the first WSO conference phone line. The first WSO meeting to be held on the telephone was in August 2005. WSO meetings used the same number and access code through January 2019.

There are currently two CLA intergroups—CLA-East and the Telephone Intergroup. There had been an intergroup in Southern California, but it is not currently active.

CLA not only has more meetings than it did a couple of decades ago, but there are several resources that did not exist then. Our literature consists of nine recovery leaflets, the "Introducing Clutterers Anonymous to Professionals[10]" leaflet, the booklet "Is CLA for You? A Newcomer's Guide to Recovery[9]," the "CLA Meeting Starter Kit[3]," the CLArity newsletter, and the book *Ten Years of CLArity[13]*. The Convention Committee has hosted conventions in most years since 2014 and sells CDs from some conventions. CLA-East holds yearly Clutter-Free Days, and several Clutter-Free Days (by that and other names) have also been held in California.

Clutterers Anonymous has had an online presence since a bulletin board was established in 1996. The first CLA web site was established in the late 1990s and was very minimal. It has been redesigned three or four times since then and is now the beautiful site we see when we visit Clutterers Anonymous.org.

Much has happened in CLA's first 30 years. Let us wish for a strong, vibrant Clutterers Anonymous to see us through the upcoming decades.

Holidays

This article discusses how clutter affects the holidays, and how the holidays affect clutter.

Holiday Decluttering

Spring 2018
Martha H., MD

I've been downsizing my medium-sized home—I'm one year into a five-year plan. This December, I decided to declutter my Christmas decorations. I should begin by saying that I love Christmas! I always have, as far back as I can remember, and that's a long time. I also love Christmas decorations and have collected them for all of my adult life.

My group, the Rising Sun, MD, Thursday night group, encouraged me in my endeavor. Each week, we bookend a decluttering task, and I bookended sorting through all the bins and boxes of Christmas "stuff." (I use that term because I'm a lady.) My group suggested that I donate my surplus to the local shelter for battered women. I called the shelter and they said they'd be thrilled to have anything I wanted to donate. The residents there need a little cheering up.

The first job was assembling everything in one place. I hired a local college kid to bring up every single container full of decorations and supplies from the basement. There must have been 15 in all. My foyer was full, and the mess spilled over into my Gathering Room.

My plan was simple—decorate the house modestly and donate the rest. My two granddaughters pitched in to help. They put up the tree and decorated it and also decorated a big cedar in my front yard. The younger granddaughter was in charge of the little Santa figures. I used one wreath, instead of four. All the extra stockings went away, too, except for my husband's. It's too soon after his death to give it away.

Knowing that the decorations were going to the women's shelter made decluttering decisions easy. I found myself giving away items that I had previously treasured. I had a mental picture of the shelter being brightened by garlands and ornaments and wreaths. Meanwhile, my group was cheering me on.

When the decorating was finished, the leftovers went into big boxes. My granddaughter and I delivered them to the shelter yesterday. We hope that those decorations bring a little cheer to those women at a very difficult time in their lives.

I couldn't have managed this decluttering project without the encouragement and support of my group. I was made accountable by our weekly bookending. (That's one of my favorite Tools!) They helped keep me focused and on task. Their obvious charitable natures inspired me.

My foyer is empty now and my house is ready for the holidays. So am I, thanks to CLA and my group. ◬

Artwork, Poetry, and Puzzles

Members share their experience, strength, and hope through artwork and poetry.

Artwork

Issue
Author

Rose

Poetry

Poem

Holiday 2018
Adelaide M., IL

How can I express how I really feel
When the pain of this affliction is
    just too real?
Alone I struggled not to drown at
    sea.
Alone I struggled to be clutter
    free.
With the gift of desperation, I
    picked up the phone.
And suddenly I was no longer
    alone.
There were people who listened;
I could feel their love.
We struggled together when push
    came to shove.
I learned to trust God throughout
    the day
Because
My Higher Power led me to CLA.
◬

Meet Me

Summer 2019
Wendy L., IL

Meet me here,
Meet me there,
Meet me almost anywhere.

On the phone or in the rooms.
You'll meet our members,
We'll see you soon.

Start with our website,
If you're Internet literate.

Order our literature,
And become proficient,
About cluttering and hoarding,
And what you can do about it.

We know how awful cluttering can
    be.
We've all been there,
Searching for our serenity.

So don't hesitate,
Your Higher Power awaits,
Find that serenity,
With our Tools of Recovery.

Step by Step,
The struggle is real.
Find a buddy and,
Together you'll heal.

CLA members become your
    friends,
Follow our Traditions,
And make amends.

For resentments will fade,
Over time.

You're safe in our rooms,
Your anonymity is mine.

Consider reading CLArity,
Our newsletter supreme,
And read our literature,
As clutter IS what it seems.

Perhaps try a phone activity
    session,
And declutter with company.
Our Declutterthons are held to
    help with this,
And happen several times a year.

Opportunities exist,
For you to volunteer,
And you are welcome to donate
It's a part of our 7th Tradition that
we hold dear.

We hope you like this little ditty,
It's what we're all about.
Clutterers Anonymous
Is yours without a doubt. ⬠

Pushed Down

Holiday 2019
Kristin W.

Under the waves of darkness
Where I can't come out to play.
The grownups have taught me
I can't draw.
Only a few people are truly cre-
ative.
They don't come along very often.
That still small voice inside of me
Says why not rhyme?
Why not mix colors?
Or draw outside the line?
I don't fit in the box,
Only it looks like I do.
But I feel crushed.

I keep hearing that tiny voice.
It says
What if my way works?
Try it.
I get older.
The box gets tighter.
The voice gets stronger.
I try.
I push back.
The box breaks.

The light enters
Through a tiny pinhole at first.
That still small voice
The darkness fades away.
Creativity Shines. ⬠

Autobiographic

Spring 2020
Lisa G., FL

When I was a child, I spoke with a
lisp, not a stutter.
Little did I know I'd grow up to
clutter.

With not many toys or clothes
owned as a child,
What little possessions I had, my
cluttering was mild.

When mom left dad, I was age
nine.
I knew nothing about decluttering
divine.

At age 14, I started to work.
Time management suddenly made
me berserk.

Sweet 16, acne and boys,
My clutter and my brain started
making more noise.

Consistent work, then college
commute, no dorms,
Essays and paychecks and cluttering storms.

Leaving home and getting room-
mates anew,
My sloppiness was contained, yet
somewhat askew.

Finally getting a place of my own,

A studio apartment now that I'm grown

But college lasted longer than four years,
New boyfriends and jobs and more and more fears.

Growing now past age 20 and 30,
Bathroom and kitchen and all rooms stayed dirty.

Forty hit me upside my head,
This old maid is finally set to wed.

Sloppiness followed me wherever I went.
Hurricane Lisa is what I was called by this gent.

My inner voice shouted, "It's a mistake."
A divorce soon loomed, this relationship at stake.

Moving back to my hometown with no purpose or aim,
Survival now is the name of the game.

My youth has passed me by with no plaques on the wall.
Procrastination has been my major downfall.

Depression, anxiety, yes isolation, too
A downward spiral, as time surely flew

Somehow fifty soon came along.
My will has weakened, but my clutter stays strong.

I moved south to avoid the harsh winter's wrath,
But my problems followed me like my shadow on a path.

But then recovery knocked on my door,
12 Steps and meetings and phone bridges galore.

I thank my Higher Power from the depths of my core,
And I don't feel alone, that much, any more.

I learned of a conference held once each year.

I couldn't refuse, I want to let go of this fear.

The conference is in my New York home town.

Well, now, how can I possibly turn that down?

Hearing familiar voices and putting a face to a name,

Seeing friends, too, I'm glad I came.

Hoping to let go of frustration and shame,

After all, releasing rumination is the name of the game.

Camaraderie, hugs, and many new friends,

I hope this weekend helps with my amends.

The scars of emotional, physical, and mental strife
Are valuable lessons interwoven in

this fabric of life.

The next decade seems not so near.
I face it with hopes of love over fear.

And as we wrap up with laughter, hugs, and tears,
I pray to release all my clutter through the years.

Poem— Unrest: A Comic Tragedy

Summer 2020
Lisa G., FL

Why is my apartment always so darn messy?
I want less cluttery and maybe more dressy

I fantasize about a décor, ideally a Southwestern style
Instead, I often see cat puke, litter, and maybe some bile

My rug may be vacuumed, my floors may be swept
But I woke up to reality and then nearly wept

My walls might have paintings or a lovely photo in a frame
But no, for now they are bare and cause for shame

My windows could have fancy drapes with stylish colors and some flair
Alas, I hang shower curtains to keep them from being bare

Each room is a challenge to keep organized and clean

But why would I make my home feeling serene?

I moved 22 times—and that's not a final number
I only want a permanent home to relax and to slumber

Each apartment should have a sign saying "I'm just passing through"
So why should I unpack my belongings just to start anew?

Where I am now is the future meeting the past
The layouts always change, but my clutter keeps me aghast

A foyer doesn't exist in my current abode
So a random chair by the door is where I unload

My living room has no furniture, save one reclining chair
Yet with all my other clutter, it hardly seems bare

I have bookshelves galore and room dividers to hide the mess
But when maintenance comes over, it's like I have to confess

I scramble... and suffer... and procrastinate... it's true
Then when they leave, I wipe my brow, and say, "Whew!"

Floors are strewn with papers, and notes, and who knows what else lurks
These are the visual signs of my sloppiness quirks

The kitchen is cute, hmph, another
  word for small
Never enough cabinets to hide it
  all
The cupboards are not bare,
  they're filled with canned goods
  and dishes
But when will Mr. Clean come
  visit to fulfill my wishes?

My stovetop is used day in and day
  out
Lots of ignored spills make me
  always pout

The fridge has food, I thank my
  Higher P ower for that
But is that green stuff a veggie....
  or a forgotten splat?

The bathroom has a vent and a
  large mirror with six lights
When I turn them on, I see reflections of frights

A toilet that needs scrubbing and a
  tub longing for new grout
When I see this eyesore, I want to
  scream and shout

The sleeping chamber might be
  cozy, with fluffy pillows galore
My bed's garments may—or may
  not—be on the floor

A dresser with fine linens is something I might possess
Instead a plastic bin is used, if I
  may confess

I could make this room into a
  place that I adore
But day by day, the sight disturbs

me to the core

My cats give me affection...and
  purrs...and lots of love
Yet that damn litterbox, out the
  door I could shove

My apartment is transient, I'm just
  passing through
Where I will clutter next, I haven't
  a clue

My jobs are a bore, and bring no
  joy to my life
Then I think of my clutter and it
  gives me more strife

I sometimes wish for a boyfriend
  or a date
But my life is on hold, everything
  must wait

I think time is a thief and there's
  never a moment to spare
Yet I waste hours on my smart-
  phone, sitting on my derrière

Sooner or later the clutter will go
  bye-bye
But until then, I pray and I sigh
Adios to the mess
Hello to having less
Once and for all, tears of joy I shall
  cry!

Procrastinator

Fall 2020
Lisa G., FL

a poetic acronym

Putting off what I don't want I do

Realizing every task is overdue

Oh, the reality of clutter is always
a drain

Crowded apartment, schedule, and
brain

Really, my paralysis never goes
away

Action is the magic word, so they
say

Still, I try and try and try I tell
myself

Though I should be willing, place
that trying on a shelf

Impossible—that shelf can take no
more clutter

No time to do anything, I tend to
mutter

Always feeling rushed and needing
to do more

Time is an illusion, but I always
wish I had more

Over and over the chores must be
repeated

Really all I want is to no longer
feel depleted   ◬

Puzzles

A CLA Sampler

Holiday 2022

We hope you enjoy this puzzle based on CLA concepts and terminology. (P.S. Most words are in the Index to the *CLA Literature Collection*. The Glossary at ClutterersAnonymous.org also includes some terms.)

See the following page for the answers to the puzzle.

Definitions

Across:

1. "We may call this person with our daily plan or ask for help…" —"CLA Tools of Recovery[16]"

5. A CLA slogan: "____ and let God."

8. "We simplify our lives, believing that when we need a fact__ an item, it will be available to us."—"CLA Tools of Recovery[16]"

9. It is said in CLA that "The _____ relate to the group as the Steps relate to the individual."

12. A feeling that things will be better. We can achieve this by working Step 2.

14. Most people do this nightly. It is a part of self-nurture.

15. Opposite of war. "We hope these suggestions will bring you…and inner _____ ."—From "Declutter Your Mind[6]"

16. A CLA slogan: "_____ does it."

Down:

2. "Personal recovery depends upon CLA _____ "—Tradition 1

3. To disengage. "The more we live our dreams, the sooner we_____ from our clutter."—From "Finding Your Life Purpose[7]."

4. "Anything we don't need, want, or use…"—From "Recovering from Clutter: The 12 Steps of Clutterers Anonymous[12]"

6. We use the CLA____ of Recovery[16] to achieve and maintain physical, mental, and spiritual sobriety.

7. A recovery meeting; usually meets weekly.

10. What we work to recover from cluttering.

11. "Some people come to CLA expecting housekeeping hints, ___s on sorting and filing…"—from the "Welcome[15]" leaflet

13. A CLA slogan[18]: "___ day at a time."

Puzzle Answer

[1]B	[2]U	[3]D	D	Y		[4]C			
	N	E		[5]L	E	[6]T	G	O	[7]G
	I	T		U		O		[8]O	R
[9]T	R	A	D	I	T	I	O	N	[10]S	O
	Y		C		T	L		T	U
[11]T		[12]H	[13]O	P	E	[14]S	L	E	E	P
I			N		R			P	
[15]P	E	A	C	E		[16]E	A	S	Y

Humor and Cartoons

Scientists have discovered that laughing is not only great for your emotional well-being; it also enhances the immune system. So CLA*rity* has included some humorous articles and cartoons.

Humor

Why It's Good to Be a Clutterer

Spring 2017

Wendy L., IL

Please note, this article has been written tongue-in-cheek and uses sarcasm as a means of creating humor. Most of the examples below should not be used as a substitute for working your CLA program.—Editor

1. By not deciding what to do with things and just adding them to piles, I create more free time for myself.

2. By not throwing things away, I am not adding to landfills.

3. My paper clutter can make kindling for a fireplace if there's no newspaper around.

4. If I save paper clutter that includes private information about myself, I won't have to shred it, and my shredder is really loud.

5. By not deleting most emails from my in-basket, my email host has proof their mail servers can handle heavy loads of email.

6. By putting some of my paper clutter in my storage ottoman and drawers around my home, I make full and efficient use of these valuable storage units.

7. Speaking of storage units, I rent one—thus helping to ensure a job for the facility's front desk attendant.

8. Also, the company that owns the storage unit facility also

benefits by receiving my rent as income—thus also pleasing stockholders (if they exist).

9. By not yet, if ever, living out my dreams to be a business owner, I am benefitting other business owners by not being their competition.

10. When I tell others that I'm a clutterer, they learn about the term "clutterer" and can often relate it to themselves or to a friend, family member, or coworker—and an "ah-ha" moment often ensues.

11. My clutter means I always have something to do, i.e., declutter it, lest I become bored.

12. I have something in common with other CLA members and get that good feeling of being part of a group.

13. When I declutter, I get the satisfaction of having accomplished something. Because if there's no clutter, there's nothing to declutter, and I would need to find something else to do. Ahhhh, it's so much easier to have clutter.

14. By not filling store plastic bags with my paper clutter and putting them in recycling bins, I am protecting those bags from potentially being filled with nonrecyclables and going into the garbage, thus extending their little plastic lives.

15. By not living out my dreams, I am not failing at them.

16. By repeatedly moving my physical clutter around, versus getting rid of it or storing it, I get much-needed extra low-impact walking and lifting exercise.

17. By avoiding or procrastinating doing decluttering, I get a lot of other tasks accomplished—i.e., doing the dishes—and that way I effectively avoid doing things I hate, like opening the mail. Bonus!

18. By not remembering where I put things—because I have ADD as well—I create the mystery and intrigue of trying to find my "lost" things.

19. By remaining a clutterer, I can continue to write cutting-edge Pulitzer Prize-caliber articles for CLArity.

20. And that provides our crack CLA editors additional opportunities to practice their editing magic.

Why Clutterers Make the Best Health Club Members

Spring 2018
Wendy L., IL

Health clubs tend to be fond of members who join but don't work out. Simply put, the gym gets their membership fees, but these members don't take up space in classes or on any of the equipment.

This has never been more true than at the beginning of the year, when people tend to be full of ambition and resolve and the determination to either actually use their memberships, or to join.

We may start out going to our clubs on a regular basis but slowly begin to come up with excuses for why we can't go. Lucky for us, being clutterers provides some good built-in, familiar excuses for not going, as seen below.

1) I can't find my favorite yoga mat, which is supposed to be in its designated spot in my closet. I begin to suspect thievery, spontaneous combustion, or perhaps my dog ate it, because I know I put it there, where it belongs, just yesterday. Anyway, now I'll have to skip my yoga class, so I might as well sleep in. Yay! Oops, I mean it's such a shame to miss class.

2) It's time to leave for yoga class, and it occurs to me that my yoga mat is still MIA. Okay, I should've looked for it earlier; but, like other clutterers, I didn't give myself enough time to prepare before I had to leave. Class won't be the same without this amazing mat, so I'll have to skip class. I hate it when this happens. Really.

3) It's a few weeks later and time to go to class, so I grab my new yoga mat then realize in horror that, as usual, I'm way behind on my laundry. This means that all my workout clothes are dirty. What I really need to do now is go shopping, as I obviously need more workout clothes. Plus, walking around the mall is good exercise. A win-win.

4) Another day, another class, but this time none of my clean workout clothes match, so really, I still have nothing to wear. Per number 3 above, I'll have to go shopping again.

5) As usual, I can't find my lock and thus can't lock up my stuff at the club. I could leave my purse in my car, but where would I put my car keys and clothes? I could hide them in a locker, but that's risky. Perhaps I should buy a bunch of locks and leave them in a basket by my front door. I suppose this would be clutter, but is it clutter if it's good for me?

6) Today the weather is really bad and if I can't find my boots, I would probably catch a cold now on the way to the gym. Grandma would be proud of me for not going out bootless in bad weather, and I feel blessed. I miss you, Grandma!

7) I make it to the gym, but I've missed my yoga class again for

any of reasons 1–6 above. Regrouping, I stare out at the vast array of exercise machines that I don't know how to use— machine clutter, really—and I feel intimidated because they look so complicated and un- comfortable. I have no idea where to start, so I head to that cute little club café to consider my next move. I already feel like I've accomplished something today by just getting to the club. I go to finish my carrot juice with kale but toss it when no one is looking—because it tastes so awful that surely it's a bad batch— and leave. Tomor- row is a new day.

8) I'll need to shower after I work out, and I want to use some of those little hotel shampoos and conditioners that I've been col- lecting. Though I can't remem- ber where I put them, I'm sure they're a lot nicer than what the clubs put in those wall dispens- ers in the showers. Anyway, I need to stay home to look for them, because it just isn't right not to use them.

9) The weather is awful, and I can't find that super warm coat in my cluttered front closet. No other coat will do, and working out is not worth my life.

10) I read and update my social media for a few minutes, which accidentally turns into 45

minutes, and now it's too late to go to the club.

So, in conclusion, if you ever have the chance to invest in health clubs for clutterers only, do it. ◙

Humor in Recovery

Holiday 2021
Sue M., FL

Recently on a recovery line with a perfect stranger, after sharing many funny stories, I was asked if I ever thought about being a comedian. This experience was a natural high for me and her and really struck a passion in me to write some of these stories down. I love to laugh and make others laugh, too. Scientifically, laughter is proven to release endorphins that act on the opiate receptors in the brain, which reduces pain and boosts pleasure resulting in a feel- ing of well-being. Laughter is con- tagious and something the world needs more of and is a powerful feeling I truly love to share.

As clutterers, life can become overwhelming and seriously de- pressing with isolating due to shame and guilt. On sharing some funny and crazy stories over phone conversations with clutterers, I was compelled to do this article for the CLArity newsletter.

Years ago, on my way to my boyfriend's place, I had stopped in my house, noticing rats were eating my books. Being a bit upset, I told my boyfriend about it, and his response was, "Are they getting any smarter?" It wasn't a laughing matter, but it did make me laugh and share this story.

Other shares were laughing at myself about the crazy things I would save and not knowing why. This included the leftover portion of blinds cut down to fit a shorter window, partial decks of cards, and a few other items. The time wasted on sorting and counting the cards was one thing, but having a hard time releasing them was another. I did give them to some kids along with other items I found while cleaning my carport. After sharing, another person added, "and you're still not dealing with a full deck!"

My favorite story to share was during a Stay-at-Home Declutterthon where a lady was sharing about a game she was playing. I was thinking it was a phone or computer game and, guilty of wasting time the week before, I thought she said she was playing "Weirdo Disco." I was way off base. She was picking up items around the house and asking, "where does this go?" I had to call her and tell her what I thought she said, and we laughed and shared it online with other clutterers. We were then calling the earmarking technique the "Weirdo Disco" game and thought it would be

good to have the Action Line playing disco between check-ins and calling it the "Weirdo Disco Line." Most of the clutterers liked the story, and I finally completed the promise to write about it. ◬

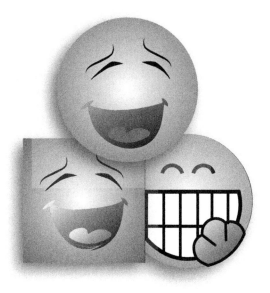

Cartoons

Cartoons are each placed on two pages.

Where I am AT

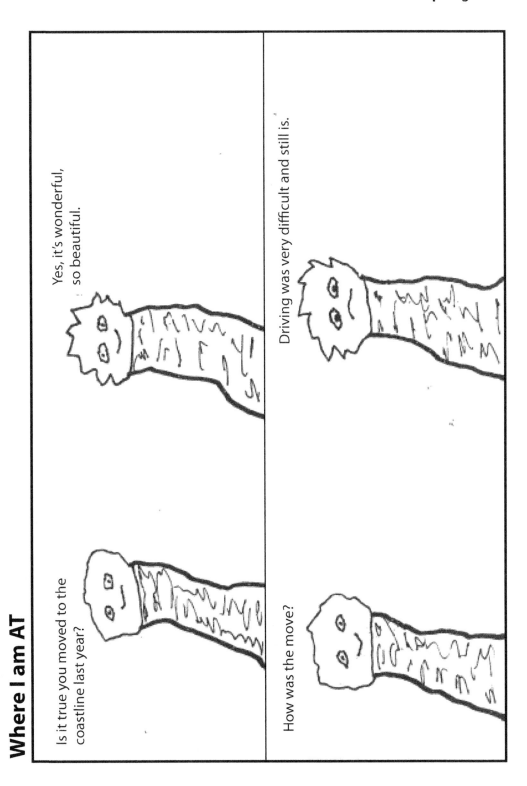

Summer 2017

Where I am AT

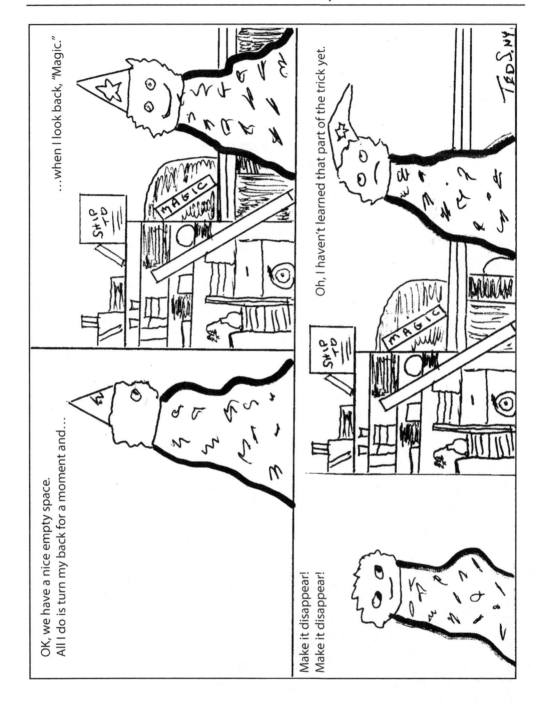

Where I am AT

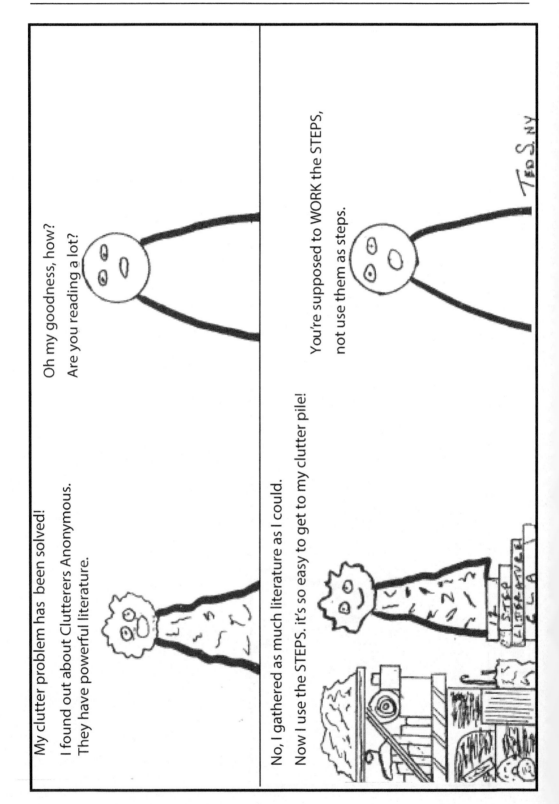

Where I am AT

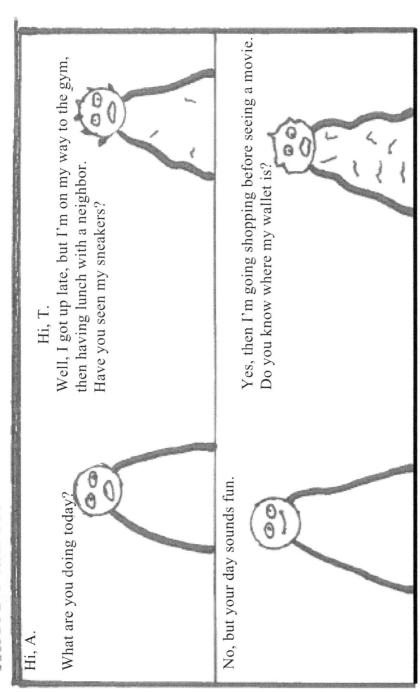

Hi, A.

What are you doing today?

Hi, T.

Well, I got up late, but I'm on my way to the gym, then having lunch with a neighbor.

Have you seen my sneakers?

No, but your day sounds fun.

Yes, then I'm going shopping before seeing a movie.

Do you know where my wallet is?

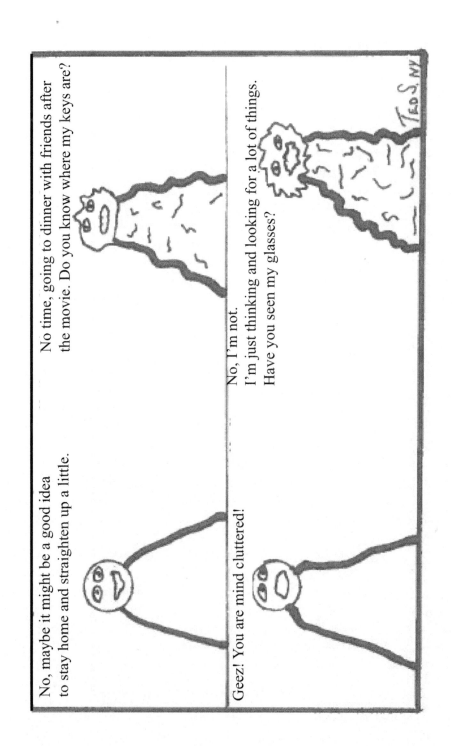

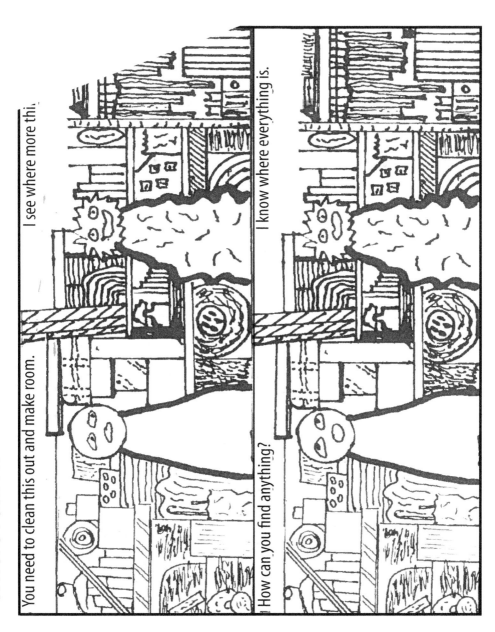

Where I am AT

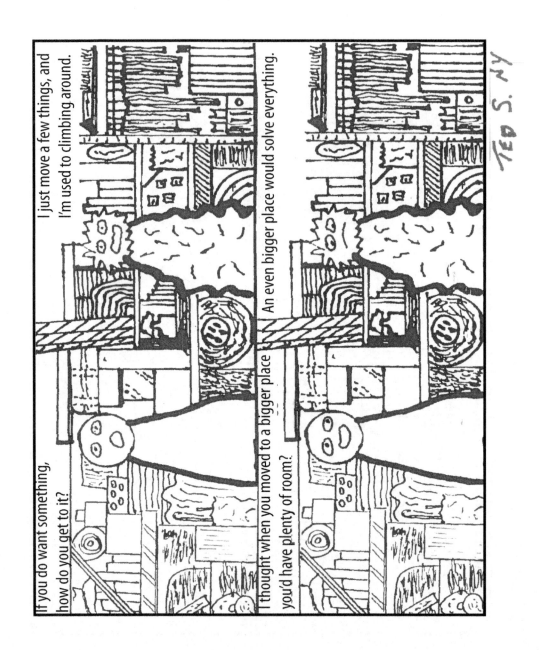

Where I am AT

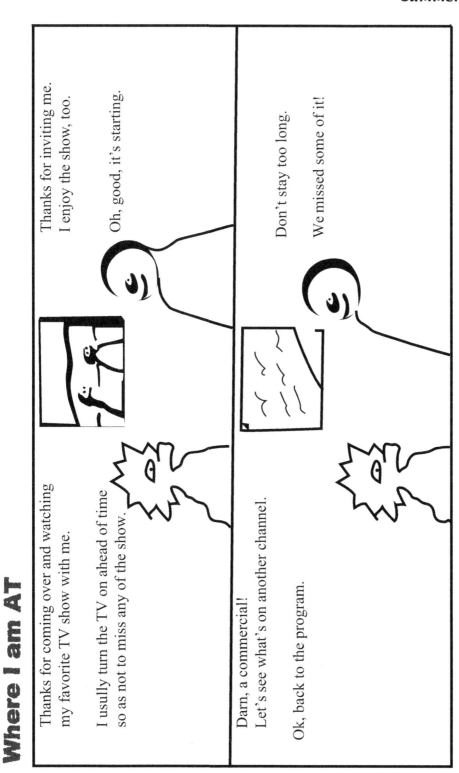

Thanks for coming over and watching my favorite TV show with me.

I usully turn the TV on ahead of time so as not to miss any of the show.

Thanks for inviting me. I enjoy the show, too.

Oh, good, it's starting.

Darn, a commercial!
Let's see what's on another channel.

Ok, back to the program.

Don't stay too long.

We missed some of it!

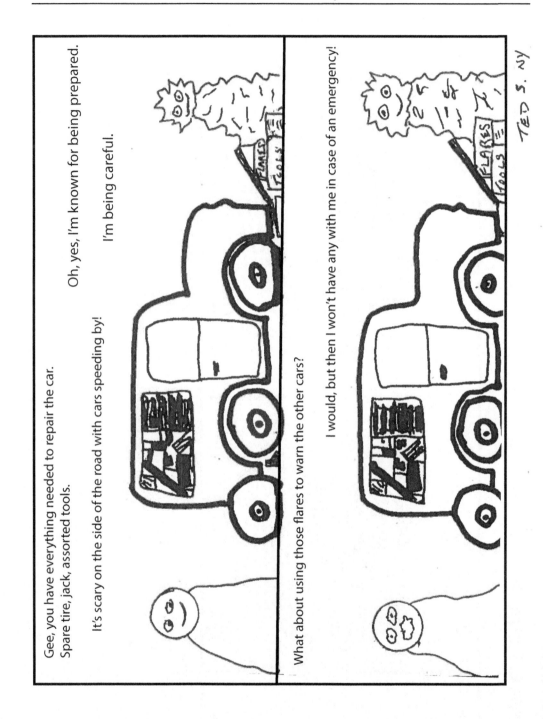

Where I am A.T.

January 1, 2018
It's a new year. I love a new beginning. I'm really excited to get started working on my clutter.

March 21, 2018
Oh good, spring is here, nice warm weather. Such a great time to clean.

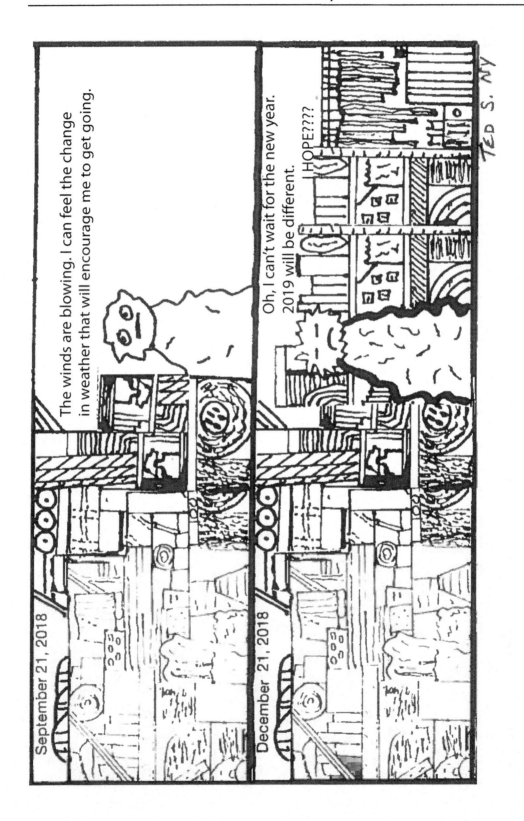

Inspired by a true event. Note that no clutter was harmed nor gotten rid of during this creative moment.

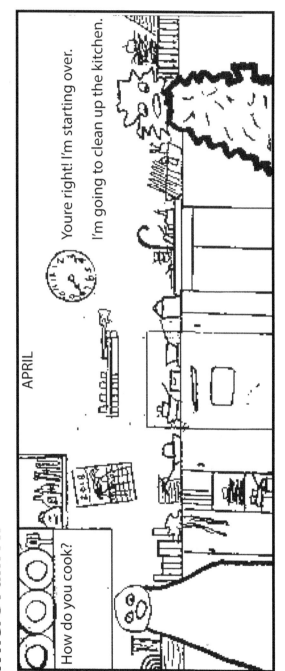

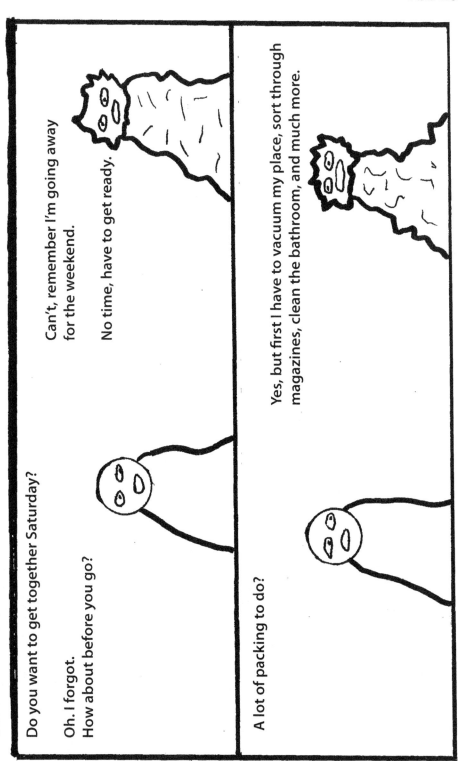

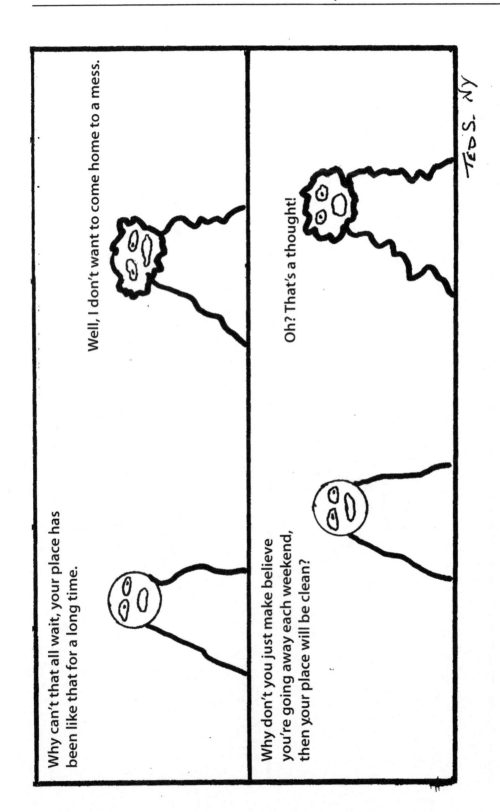

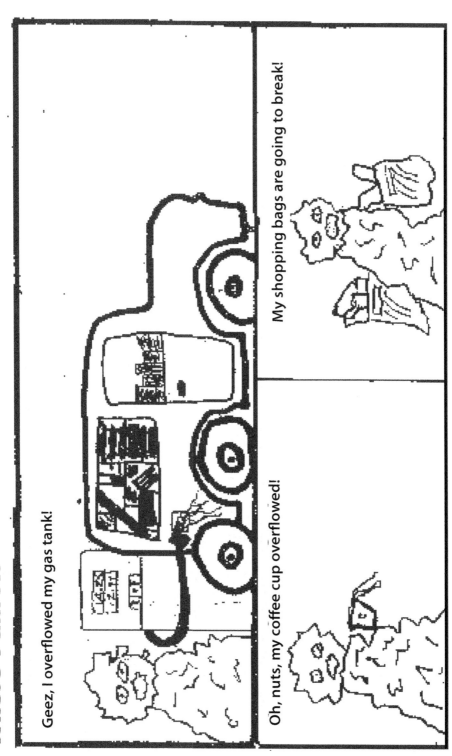

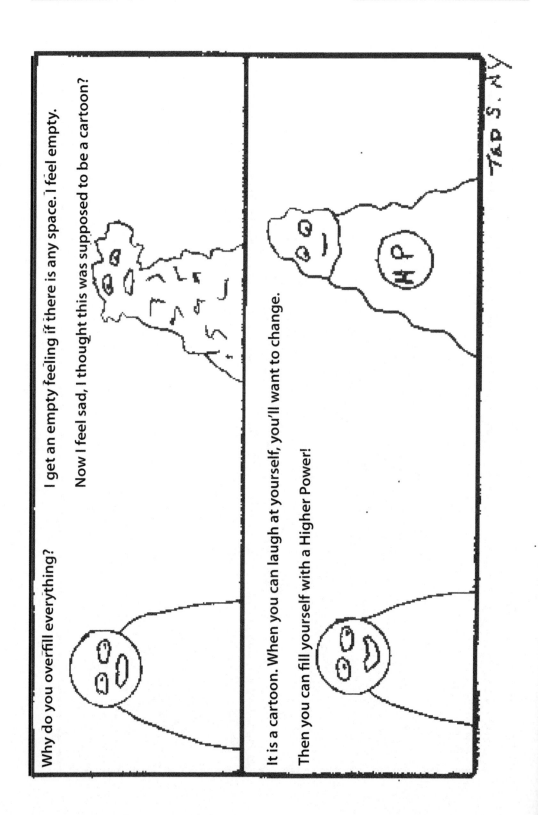

Where I am AT

I keep moving things around, and I'm quite good at finding available places for them to fit.

Wonder if this talent can be made into something?

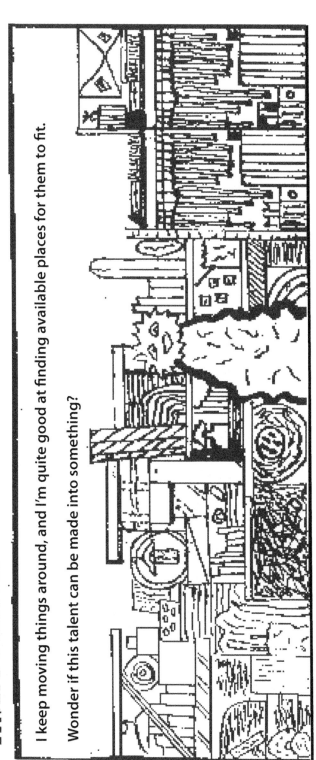

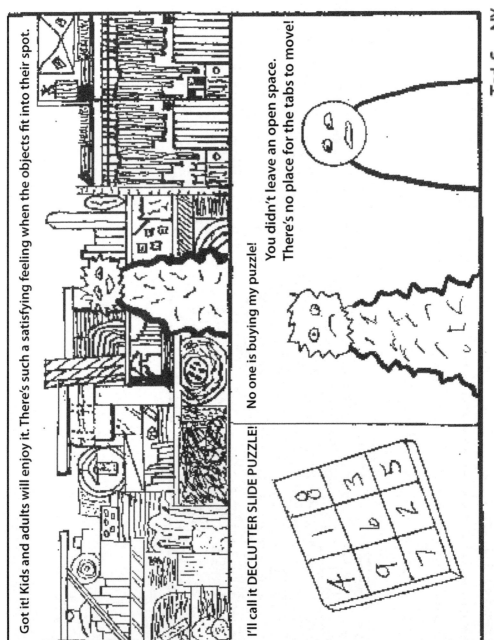

Got it! Kids and adults will enjoy it. There's such a satisfying feeling when the objects fit into their spot.

I'll call it DECLUTTER SLIDE PUZZLE!

No one is buying my puzzle!

You didn't leave an open space.
There's no place for the tabs to move!

Ted S., NY

Where I am AT

I'm fed up, this is completely unmanageable! Everything is just a big pile of clutter!!!

I'm going to clean up this weekend! Books on getting organized and lots of containers ought to do it.

Where I am AT

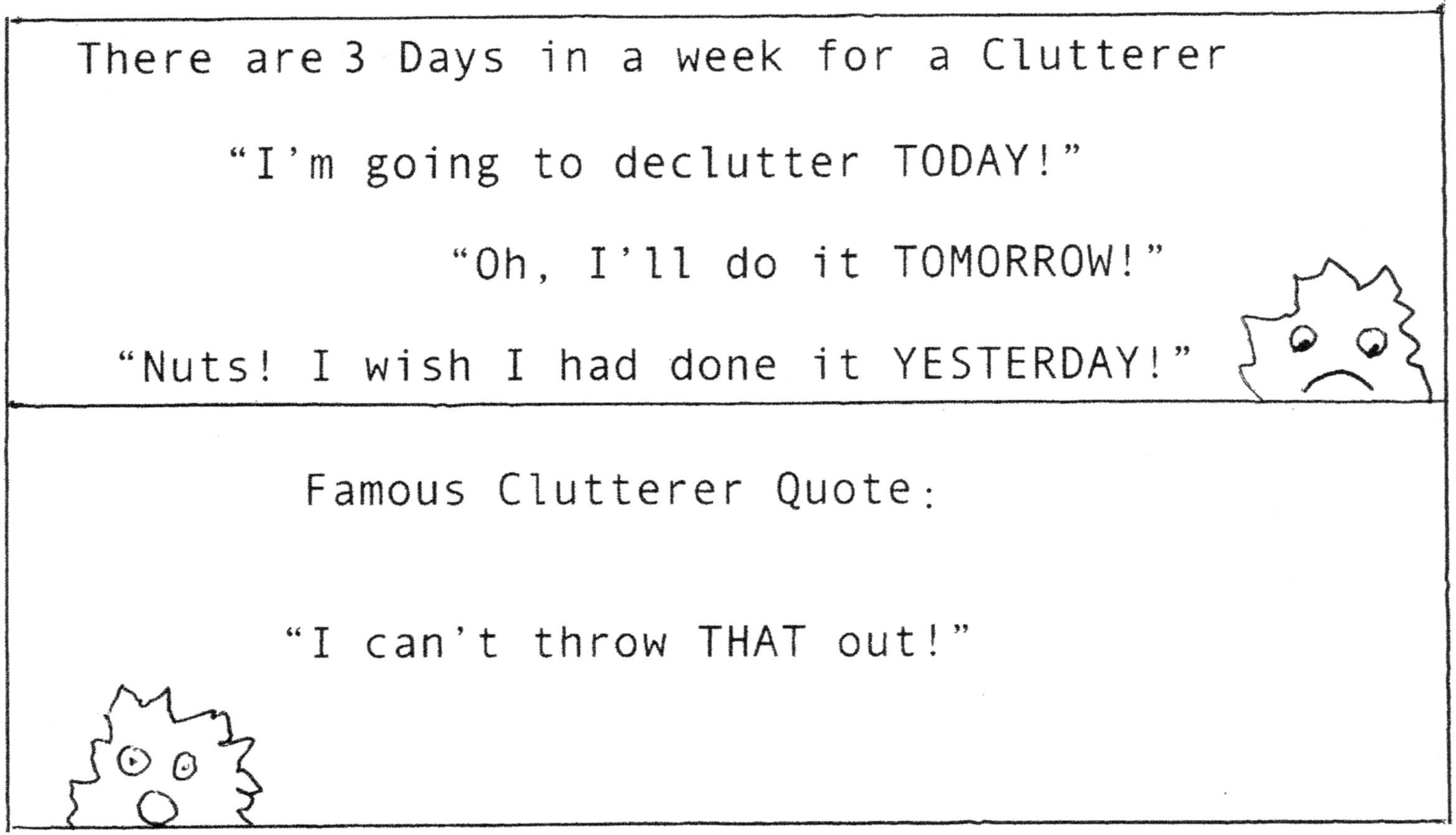

There are 3 Days in a week for a Clutterer

"I'm going to declutter TODAY!"

"Oh, I'll do it TOMORROW!"

"Nuts! I wish I had done it YESTERDAY!"

Famous Clutterer Quote:

"I can't throw THAT out!"

A Clutter question ?

"If I know something has been saved,

but can't find it,

is it the same as not having it?"

A Clutter Commitment

"I have some items to declutter.

They will be, as soon as I can find them."

TEOSNY

Where I am AT

Words from wives, husbands, landlords and friends.

"I can't take this anymore, when are you going to clean up YOUR mess?"

Words of the Clutterer's perpetual promise.

"Yes, my clutter is a mess. After getting organized, I promise to hereafter keep things neat."

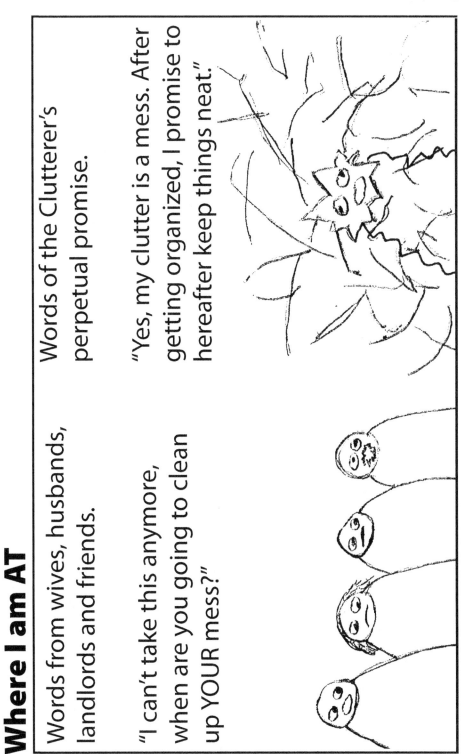

Where I am AT

I'm so stressed out about my clutter!

My sponsor says if I don't know what to do, to sit quietly.

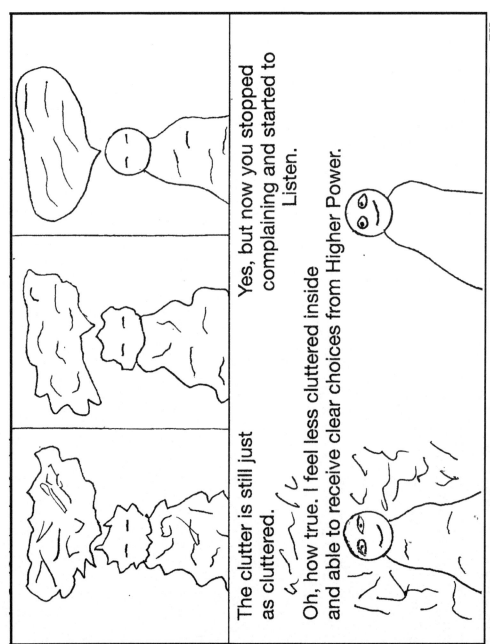

Where I Am AT

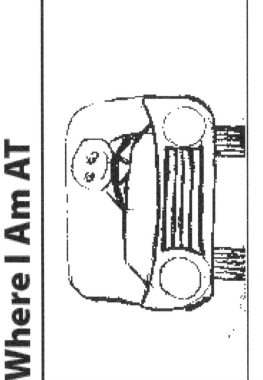

Ah, it feels so good to be driving with a full tank of gas. The car appears to run better. I feel pressure free, and everything seems to feel just right.

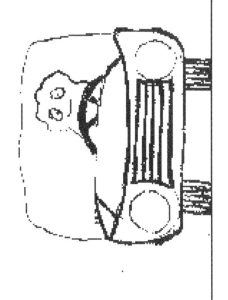

The gas gauge moved a little lower. Well, plenty of time to get gas. Something I learned long ago, cars have a gas pump symbol on the gas gauge. There is an arrow pointing to the side where the gas goes in the car. Important to know when driving a different vehicle.

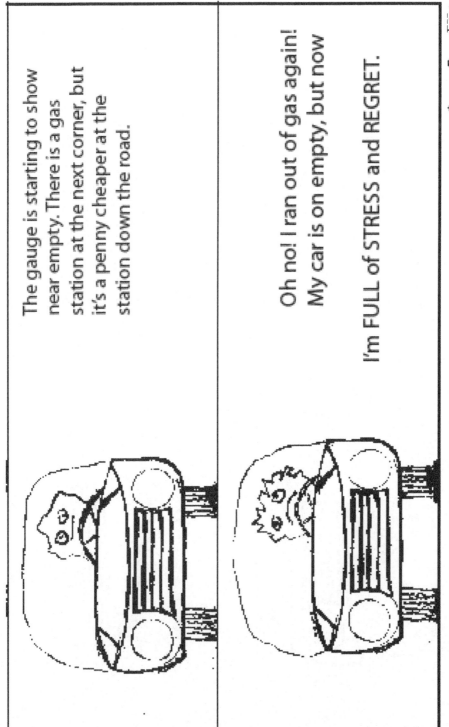

Where I am AT

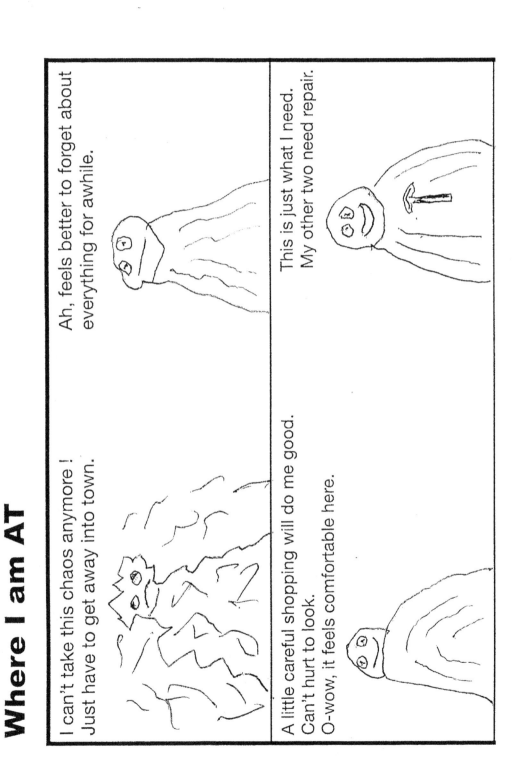

I can't take this chaos anymore!
Just have to get away into town.

Ah, feels better to forget about everything for awhile.

A little careful shopping will do me good.
Can't hurt to look.
O-wow, it feels comfortable here.

This is just what I need.
My other two need repair.

Nonclutterers

This section contains an article about friends: dealing with others, how clutter affects others, and how the family members' actions affect clutterers.

On Becoming My Parents' Parent

Summer 2019
Wendy L., IL

It started innocently enough with my Dad needing help getting the garbage bins outside and back for my parents' weekly garbage pickup. He was too great a fall risk to do this on his own, so my sister and I took over this responsibility. It meant one of us would go to my parents' house on Sunday to bring the full bins out, and the other would visit on Monday to bring the emptied ones back.

Then, seemingly overnight, the relationship with our parents changed from just helping, to that of caregiving. Both our parents had now been diagnosed with different forms of dementia, and both had already developed painful physical limitations. They were in denial about being sick and resistant to help.

As a clutterer, I was already working off what seemed like my own infinite to-do list. Some days, I could barely keep up with my own responsibilities, let alone help two more people with theirs. As a result, I found myself getting angry and resentful about helping them.

I started missing appointments and deadlines and losing paperwork. My physical clutter got worse, as did my stress level. Amidst all the physical and mental clutter, I missed paying a credit card late fee twice, and my credit report got dinged, causing my credit score to drop by 93 points.

I'd asked my parents about hiring a caregiver, and my Dad told me that's what his two daughters were for. I hated that he felt entitled to our assistance because, in speaking for myself, he'd been very hard on me as a kid, and not nurturing enough.

He laughed at me when I told him I was feeling overwhelmed, and getting way behind on my own responsibilities. "All you do is spend a half hour grocery shopping, so what are you talking about," he said. He had no idea how much time I was spending behind the scenes, calling his doctors, scheduling his appointments, etc.

We finally hired a part-time caregiver months ago, but my parents fired her after three days, saying there wasn't enough for her to do. Apparently, this is a common reaction for older adults with dementia. We've got a new caregiver starting next week, and my parents are more receptive now, so fingers crossed that she works out.

When the anger and resentment start building, I remind myself that I'll miss them desperately when they're gone. This has also been an opportunity of sorts to spend more time with them, as I had been visiting only about once a week. My Dad has gotten to be so frail that I find myself being protective of him when we're out. Sometimes I actually enjoy being a parent of sorts to my parents, maybe because I get to be the nurturing parent I'd always craved.

Fingers crossed this second caregiver works out. Meanwhile, I purchased some pretty office supplies to get my paper clutter organized, and I remind myself to be patient with both my parents and myself.

I recently joined an improv group, as humor has always been my go-to stress reliever. Maybe one day I'll be able to joke about this time in my life. Until then, I'm doing the best I can. ◒

Glossary

7th Tradition—*There are no dues or fees for membership; we are self-supporting through our own 7th Tradition contributions, neither soliciting nor accepting outside donations.*

Clutter-Free Day—Day-long, regional recovery event that consists of CLA speakers, workshops, and fellowship

Convention—Two-day recovery event that consists of CLA speakers, panels, workshops, recovery meetings, fellowship, and entertainment

Declutterthon—Event that takes place on a phone conference line where clutterers share their decluttering actions. There may also be speakers, goal setting, progress reporting, etc.

Delegate—Elected group member who (1) serves as a liaison between his or her home group and WSO by communicating information between both and (2) represents the group's conscience at WSO

Executive Committee—The Executive Committee consists of WSO officers, committee chairpersons, and intergroup chairpersons. The purpose of the Executive Committee is to address specific concerns critical to the functioning of CLA.

Group Conscience—The group conscience is the collective conscience of the group membership and thus represents substantial unanimity on an issue before definitive action is taken.

Intergroup—Grouping of meetings in a limited geographical area or a group of telephone or special-interest meetings

Representative—Elected group member who (1) serves as a liaison between his or her home group and an intergroup by communicating information between both and (2) represents the group's conscience at the intergroup

WSO—World Service Organization, Inc. WSO is the CLA service body responsible for producing and mailing out literature; maintaining the CLA website;

answering phone, email, and postal correspondence; support and communication among CLA groups; furthering communication among groups; and making decisions which affect the Fellowship as a whole. All CLA members may attend and participate in WSO General Meetings. Voting members include elected delegates from meetings, WSO officers, WSO committee chairpersons, and inter-group chairpersons.

Guidelines for Submission of Articles

Affirmations
(300-400 words)

Articles discussing a CLA Affirmation

CLA History
(200–400 words)

Articles relating to events in the history and development of CLA regarding any CLA individual or group, including face-to-face, phone conference meetings, and activity lines

CLA Toolbox
(400–600 words)

Articles about using CLA-approved Tools, such as Telephone, Buddies, Bookending, etc. (Contact CLA*rity* staff before writing, since we wish to cover all the Tools before we repeat any.)

Event Articles
(250–400 words)

Major news items in CLA, especially conventions, Clutter-Free Days, and declutterthons

General Articles
(400–600 words)

Articles about CLA or cluttering issues not covered in the other sections, especially how the writer's personal ESH—experience, strength, and hope

Getting Into Action/Motivation Articles
(400-500 words)

Articles about experiences and methods for motivation toward recovery and on beginning and maintaining the process of decluttering

Group Stories
(400-500 words)

Articles about productive, creative, and successful practices in local groups

My Favorite Saying
(100-200 words)

Articles discussing a CLA slogan, prayer, or the like

News Flash
(Up to 50 words per item)

Brief announcements of CLA news, including upcoming events

Qualification
(500–700 words)

What it was like before, what you did to recover, and what it is like now

Recovery Moments
(200–400 words)

Short articles and anecdotes of personal recovery stories

Spotlight on Service
(200–300 words)

Articles about service opportunities as applied to CLA and profiles of members doing service

Articles on Steps/Traditions
(400–500 words)

Articles sharing personal experience working any of the 12 Steps and 12 Traditions of CLA

Let us know if you wish to be listed as the article's author (with first name, last initial, and state or country of residence) or whether you wish to be anonymous or use a pseudonym..

We honor program Traditions. Due to our Traditions, and to avoid copyright infringement, we cannot print material collected from the news media—whether newspapers, magazines, television, film, or other sources; we do not publish or reprint material written by any person who is not a member of CLA.

We reserve the right to edit submissions, as well as titles—although we try to keep what the author said. Submissions near deadline may not allow time for communicating with the author. Include a contact number in case we need to speak with you. The submissions deadline for the spring issue is January 4; summer issue, April 4; fall issue, July 4; and holiday issue, October 4. No submissions to CLArity will be returned; do not send original manuscripts, art, photos, etc. We reserve the right to modify or change submission guidelines without notice to meet the needs of the publication.

If you are uneasy about writing an article, contact CLArity; we will interview you and help you with the article.

Contact CLArity for details: CLArity@Clutterers Anonymous. org, visit our website at ClutterersAnonymous.org or send postal mail to CLArity, 184 South Livingston Avenue, Suite 9-203, Livingston, New Jersey 07039.

.

Bibliography

1— *Alcoholics Anonymous,* 4th Edition, Alcoholics Anonymous World Services, Inc., 2001 (also known as "The Big Book")

2—"A Brief Guide," Clutterers Anonymous, 2011

7—"CLA Meeting Starter Kit," Clutterers Anonymous, 2016

8— *Daily Reflections*—Alcoholics Anonymous,

9— Decluttering Resentment: Steps 4–10,"Clutterers Anonymous, 2009

6—"Declutter Your Mind," Clutterers Anonymous, 2011

7—"Finding Your Life Purpose," Clutterers Anonymous, 2009

8—"Home: Our Sacred Place," Clutterers Anonymous, 2009

9—"Is CLA for You? A Newcomer's Guide to Recovery," Clutterers Anonymous, 2011

10—"Introducing CLA to Professionals," Clutterers Anonymous, 2008

11—"Measuring Progress on Out Journey in Recovery," Clutterers Anonymous, 2015

12—"Recovery from Cluttering: The 12 Steps of Clutterers Anonymous," Clutterers Anonymous, 2009

13— *Ten Years of CLArity,* Clutterers Anonymous, 2007–2016

19— *Twelve Steps and Twelve Traditions* (also known as the "Twelve and Twelve"), Alcoholics Anonymous, 1981

15—"Welcome," Clutterers Anonymous, 2009

See next page for more references.

Note:

Some items mentioned in the articles are not individual titles, but they occur in other publications as indicated below.

16—"CLA Tools of Recovery" can be found in the leaflet "A Brief Guide," the booklet, "Is CLA for You? A Newcomer's Guide to Recovery," and the "CLA Meeting Starter Kit."

17—"Recovery Affirmations" can be found in the booklet, "Is CLA for You? A Newcomer's Guide to Recovery," and the "CLA Meeting Starter Kit."

18—"Recovery Slogans" can be found in the booklet, "Is CLA for You? A Newcomer's Guide to Recovery," and the "CLA Meeting Starter Kit."

19— "What Is Clutter?" can be found in the leaflet, "Recovery from Cluttering: The 12 Steps of Clutterers Anonymous" and the "CLA Meeting Starter Kit."

20—"Am I a Clutterer?" can be found in the leaflet "Welcome," the booklet, "Is CLA for You? A Newcomer's Guide to Recovery," and the "CLA Meeting Starter Kit."

Index

Printed in Great Britain
by Amazon

37685447R00156